Walthamstow Wolves
London's forgotten speedway team

Keith Corns

London League Publications Ltd

Walthamstow Wolves
London's forgotten speedway team
© Keith Corns
Foreword © Reg Fearman

The moral right of Keith Corns to be identified as the author has been asserted.

Front & back cover design @ Stephen McCarthy.

All photographs are from the John Somerville Collection (JSC) unless otherwise credited to the photographer or provider of the photo. No copyright has been intentionally breached; please contact London League Publications Ltd if you believe there has been a breach of copyright.

Front cover photos: Reg Reeves and Charlie May riding for Walthamstow; Back cover: The four Walthamstow riders selected for the Britain team that rode against Overseas at Walthamstow in 1950: Jimmy Grant, Jim Boyd, Reg Reeves and Benny King; Walthamstow supporters club badge and Walthamstow stadium façade (photo: Peter Lush). The 'Wolf' illustration is from a 1934 Walthamstow programme

This book is copyright under the Berne Convention. All rights are reserved. It is sold subject to the condition that it shall not, by way of trade or otherwise, be lent, resold, hired out or otherwise circulated without the publisher's prior consent in any form of binding or cover other than that in which it is published and without a similar condition being imposed on the subsequent purchaser.

A CIP catalogue record for this book is available from the British Library.

Published in August 2023 by London League Publications Ltd, PO Box 65784, London NW2 9NS

Second printing November 2023

ISBN: 978-1-909885-32-5

Cover design by Stephen McCarthy Graphic Design
46, Clarence Road, London N15 5BB.

Editing and layout by Peter Lush

Printed and bound in Great Britain by CPI Group (UK) Ltd, Croydon CR0 4YY

Foreword

This account of the brief existence of Walthamstow speedway also gives a glimpse of life in north-east London from the 1930s up to the early 1950s.

The book recalls the difficulties faced by the speedway management in trying to establish and sustain the sport at Walthamstow on two separate occasions. Problems at Lea Bridge led to the first attempt to take the sport the short distance to Walthamstow. Unfortunately, the age-old problem of noise nuisance which has affected speedway and given promoters headaches at so many venues over the years cut short the team's pre-war operation.

I remember well the post-war return of speedway to Walthamstow, where my pal Benny King was a member of the team. At that time, I was riding for West Ham of the First Division and was in the Hammers team which met the Wolves of the Second Division home and away in the London Cup.

The Chandler family, who owned the Stadium, were very keen for the team to be elevated to the First Division where they would have joined so many other London tracks. On being denied the opportunity to enjoy the financial rewards of numerous local derbies they closed the speedway and the sport never returned to the venue. Ironically, Walthamstow might have got their wish to join the top division had West Ham, by then my former team, not been saved from closure by a change of promotion and the acquisition of World Champion Jack Young for 1952.

I went often as a spectator to Walthamstow and thoroughly enjoyed my visits. The Chandler family were leading figures in the greyhound racing and betting world, William Chandler having developed the stadium in the early 1930s. I knew his son Charles Chandler well later in life when he was chairman of the Greyhound Racing Association and I was involved with Poole speedway and greyhounds. The Chandlers updated the stadium from time-to-time and indeed it was a most welcoming arena for the public.

My track time at Walthamstow was limited, but I was a guest at the stadium for a greyhound meeting in about 2004. It is sad that yet another former speedway and greyhound venue was subsequently lost to redevelopment, particularly as it was such a fine stadium.

Reg Fearman
January 2023

Photo: Signed photo of Reg Fearman during his riding days.

Introduction

Walthamstow Wolves speedway team came into existence in August 1934, with a track laid in just two weeks. This enabled the Lea Bridge National League team to re-locate just over two miles north to complete the season after the licence was withdrawn at their Leyton track. Legal proceedings instigated by neighbouring residents, relating to noise from Walthamstow Stadium, resulted in conditions being imposed by the High Court which could not be fully met. This led to the Wolves moving on again, this time three and a half miles south to Hackney Wick, for the following season.

It would be 15 years before speedway returned to the Chingford Road venue in north-east London, this time as members of the Second Division of the National League. After three seasons at this level the club unsuccessfully sought elevation to the top division in an attempt to ensure financial viability. The team consequently withdrew from the sport, sadly never to return. The speedway bikes had been silenced for the second and final time at The Stow, as the stadium was known.

This is an account of how Walthamstow Wolves came to be born, the early trials and tribulations the club faced, the post-war resurrection and the ultimate demise in 1951. It includes meeting results, scorers and biographies of the riders and personalities associated with the team.

Keith Corns
April 2023

About the author

Keith Corns first took an interest in speedway through reading the sports pages of the national and local newspapers. He was keen to see the thrills of the track for himself. With no other family interest in the sport at the time, at the age of 11 he initially ventured alone each week to Cradley Heath and Wolverhampton, the two nearest tracks.

Within a few weeks of attending his first speedway meeting he began to take an interest in the history of the sport. The collection of speedway programmes, magazines and books was soon underway and continues to the present day. Over the years Keith has travelled extensively around the country visiting numerous venues and in addition to the two local tracks regularly attended meetings at Leicester, Stoke, Coventry, Oxford, Birmingham, Hull and Peterborough, particularly during the period when he was a rider's sponsor. A retired surveyor, who also served as a school governor for over 20 years, nearly all of them as chair of the board, he has a keen interest in social and economic history. He is also a contributor to the *Speedway Researcher* website, particularly focusing on the period from 1928 to 1964.

Contributors

Jim Henry: A fan of Edinburgh Monarchs since 1961, Jim became interested in speedway history in the 1980s. With Graham Fraser he founded *The Speedway Researcher* magazine. This spawned the website which carries, thanks to many helpful contributors, a large and ever-growing record of speedway meetings in the UK since 1928. Jim compiled information for Scottish venues and has written the history of *Glasgow's Speedways 1928 to 1940*, *Where Eagles Dared – The History of Speedway in Motherwell* and *Tigers at White City*. With Ian Moultray, Jim wrote *A History of Marine Gardens Speedway* and *Speedway in Scotland*. He moved on from track raking at Powderhall, Edinburgh to become Clerk of the Course at Powderhall, Shawfield, Armadale and Linlithgow between 1989 and 2014. A retired town planner Jim has been chair of his Local Community Council, is a volunteer at the National Mining Museum Scotland taking a special interest in Mining Memorials in Scotland. Jim is married to Anne and they have two sons and four grandchildren.

Matt Jackson: Matt was taken to Sheffield Speedway by his parents at the age of six and has held a keen interest in the sport since that day. He has watched the sport around the country and also tried his luck as a rider, appearing in a few second halves in the mid–1980s at Belle Vue, Sheffield and Scunthorpe. However, after realising that he did not have the required attributes to make the grade, he gracefully retired. Since then, Matt has remained on the safer side of the fence and has developed an interest in rider biographies as well as assisting with the maintenance of the *Speedway Researcher* website.

Acknowledgements

The author is grateful to Jim Henry and Matt Jackson for their help, advice and encouragement. Both work tirelessly to maintain and develop the *Speedway Researcher* website. Matt has provided most of the biographies for Chapter 15 and Jim has compiled content for Appendices 1, 2 and 4. We are indebted to the many people who have contributed over the years to the records contained on the website (www.speedwayresearcher.org.uk), from where the statistical information is drawn. Alan Bates took the lead in compiling Walthamstow details for 1949 to 1951 in the early days of *The Speedway Researcher* and we thank him for this work.

Sources include the author's collection of meeting programmes, speedway booklets and magazines, together with national and local newspapers, many via the British Newspaper Archives.

Magazine and booklet sources include: *Stenner's Speedway Annuals*, *The People Speedway Guide*, *Speedway Gazette*, *Speedway News*, *Speedway Echo*, *Speedway Reporter*, *Speedway World*, *The Broadsider*, *Sports Reporter*, *Midland Speedway Observer*, *On the Track*, *Track News Weekly Illustrated*, *Speedway Star*.

Newspaper sources include: *The Daily Mirror*, *The Daily Herald*, *Daily News* (London), *The Sketch*, *Weekly Despatch* (London), *The People*, *Walthamstow Post*, *Police News Illustrated*, *Norwood News*, *Sunday Mirror*, *Reynolds's Newspaper*, *West Ham & South Essex Mail*,

Harrow Observer, Leicester Evening Mail, Coventry Evening Telegraph, Sports Argus, Rugby Advertiser, Halifax Evening Courier, Birmingham Daily Gazette, Fleetwood Chronicle, Western Morning News, Staffordshire Sentinel, South Shields Football Gazette, Irish Independent and *Aldershot News*.

The author thanks those people who responded to requests via social media for memories of Walthamstow in the 1950s. Thanks also to Reg Fearman, who rode for West Ham against the Wolves, for sharing his recollections.

Many of the photographs have been supplied by John Somerville from his superb speedway photograph archive. Permission to use them is very much appreciated. Thanks also to Newsquest Group for permission to use photographs to which it is believed it owns the copyright.

London League Publications Ltd would like to thank Steve McCarthy for designing the cover, John Somerville for supplying most of the photos for the book and the staff of Ashford Colour Press Ltd for printing it. We would also like to thank Keith and the other contributors for their work on the book.

Advert from the *1951 Stenners' Speedway Annual*
(Courtesy Peter Lush)

Contents

1. The growth of Walthamstow — 1
2. Early days — 3
3. To Walthamstow via Lea Bridge — 5
4. 1934 – a brief season at The Stow — 11
5. Walthamstow speedway is silenced — 21
6. The Wolves move on — 25
7. Return of the Wolves — 27
8. 1949 – An indifferent start — 31
9. 1949 – Sustained improvement — 45
10. 1950 – Southern Shield frustration — 55
11. 1950 – League disappointment — 65
12. 1951 – Falling Short in the Shield — 81
13. 1951 – Dark times for the sport — 93
14. Farewell to Walthamstow speedway — 101
15. Farewell to Walthamstow Stadium — 107
16. The Walthamstow riders — 109

Appendices:
1: Results and scorers — 130
2: League tables — 156
3: Riders' statistics — 158
4: Walthamstow statistical highlights — 162
5: Walthamstow track records — 163
6: Walthamstow riders in World Championship and other meetings — 164

The programme from the last ever speedway meeting at Walthamstow Stadium.
(Courtesy Keith Corns)

1. The growth of Walthamstow

Walthamstow is located 6.5 miles north-east of the City of London, between the River Lea to the west and Epping Forest to the east. Along with Chingford and Leyton, it formed the new London Borough of Waltham Forest under local government reorganisation in 1965, having been part of the county of Essex prior to that. From the mid–1800s onwards, the area was transformed from a country parish, separated from London by marshes, to a dormitory town containing high density residential streets and industrial development, eventually becoming part of Greater London.

In the latter half of the 19th century the area saw growth in the building trade as the local population increased. At that time there were many small traders, but by the turn of the century industrial development took place on a larger scale. At the end of the First World War there had been a significant increase in electrical engineering and in the manufacture of motor vehicles. In 1897 there were 96 factories and workshops registered for inspection. Walthamstow Urban District Council reports show this figure increased to around 250 by the start of the First World War, with a dozen firms by then employing over 300 workers each.

By 1919 Walthamstow was the second most highly developed industrial area in south-west Essex, after West Ham. During the inter-war years industrial growth accelerated, particularly in the north-west of the town, with such development benefitting from the enhancement of road links on completion of the North Circular Road in 1930. Although several industrial premises suffered bomb damage during the Second World War there was rapid recovery in the late 1940s. There was also an influx to Walthamstow of businesses whose premises elsewhere had been destroyed.

Industrial development was matched by a changing housing landscape in Walthamstow and neighbouring areas, particularly after the coming of the railway to Lea Bridge in the 1840s. Formerly characterised by large houses occupied by city merchants, new roads were created to facilitate the development of speculative housing. Residential development gathered pace after the railway extended to Chingford in the early 1870s, with many houses built before 1914, including in Empress Avenue. Residential development continued during the inter-war period, with housing in Rushcroft Road dating from around 1930, at about the time Highams Park estate was built.

By the 1930s there were more than a dozen open sports grounds on the northern side of Walthamstow, mostly owned by London companies for use by their employees and it was on the site of one of these that a stadium would be developed, between Empress Avenue and Rushcroft Road. As with industry, the housing stock suffered extensive bomb damage during the Second World War and from 1946 onwards there was much rebuilding. Together with provision of new municipal housing estates, the growth of Walthamstow and the expansion of London continued.

Census figures show that the population of Walthamstow doubled between 1871 and 1881, to over 22,500, then more than doubled again to over 47,000 just 10 years later. This rapid expansion continued and by 1901 the population had increased to just under 98,000. Growth continued, but at a slower rate, until in 1931 the town boasted 132,972 residents, more than enough to provide a good level of support for any local sporting enterprises. The most prominent at that time was Walthamstow Avenue Football Club, a successful amateur team. The impact of the Second World War was significant and in 1951 the population of Walthamstow had dropped to 121,135.

Apart from sporting activities at Walthamstow Stadium, Walthamstow Avenue FC developed after the Second World War to become one of the country's leading amateur teams. They won the FA Amateur Cup in 1952 and 1961, and in 1953 held Manchester United to a draw at Old Trafford in the FA Cup. The replay was held at Arsenal FC, and Manchester United won 5–2. The team disbanded in 1988, although a newly formed club with the same name played in the early 2000s before merging with another club. Walthamstow FC was formed in 2018, again following various club mergers, and now represent the borough in senior football.

This publicity for the Christmas 1951 speedway dance shows the stadium with the famous facade.
(Courtesy Keith Corns)

2. Early days

The opening of speedway tracks in London and neighbouring Essex proliferated from 1928 onwards, following an organised meeting which took place at High Beech in Epping Forest, just six miles north of Walthamstow, in February of that year. This form of dirt-track racing had been developed in Australia since the end of 1923 and several of their riders came over to pioneer the sport in Britain, where good money was able to be earned. By 1930, official test matches took place between England and Australia as the sport boomed in this country.

The High Beech circuit staged dirt-track speedway until 1932 and then again between 1937 and 1950. By the early 1930s speedway became firmly established in the capital, with tracks at Crystal Palace, Harringay, Lea Bridge, Stamford Bridge (until 1932), Wembley, West Ham and Wimbledon. Speedway started at New Cross in 1934 when the Crystal Palace team relocated there. The sport also featured at Dagenham in Essex and other tracks had a brief existence in the capital, including White City, Catford, Crayford and Greenford. The Lea Bridge track was the nearest speedway circuit to Walthamstow, being just over two miles away, with Harringay 4½ miles to the east and West Ham 10 miles to the south.

In 1929, a year after the sport spread across the country, league racing began. Teams from the Midlands and the south competed in the Southern League, with northern teams in the English Dirt Track League. Eight of the 12 teams in the Southern League were in London. Birmingham Hall Green withdrew from the league with a third of the season gone. The teams from the capital were Crystal Palace, Harringay, Lea Bridge, Stamford Bridge, White City, Wembley, West Ham and Wimbledon. Birmingham Perry Barr, Coventry and Southampton were the provincial teams in the league.

Membership of the Southern League was expanded to 14 teams in 1930, although Birmingham Perry Barr withdrew after a handful of matches. Hall Green returned, joined by High Beech, Leicester Stadium and Nottingham, with White City (London) dropping out. The English Dirt Track League became the Northern League, starting off with 16 teams and ending the season with 13. Wembley and Belle Vue took the honours in their respective leagues.

Both leagues had less members the following year when Wembley and Belle Vue retained their titles. Six teams competed in the Northern League, in which only Belle Vue and Leeds completed their fixtures as Glasgow and Leicester Super failed to go the distance. The Southern League also suffered withdrawals by Harringay, Leicester Stadium and Nottingham, although the remaining matches of the first two were taken over by a Belle Vue reserve team (which raced as Manchester) and Coventry respectively.

League membership was drastically reduced for the 1932 season as the north and south combined to form the National League, comprising just nine teams. Belle Vue and Coventry were the sole representatives from the north and the Midlands. With Harringay having pulled out the year before, five London tracks were left, at Crystal Palace, Stamford Bridge, Wembley, West Ham and Wimbledon. The Southampton team relocated to Lea Bridge during the season and rode as Clapton Saints. Plymouth entered league racing to take the total to nine. For the first time, a league season was concluded with all member teams having completed their fixtures. Wembley won the title, with Belle Vue third behind Crystal Palace.

Belle Vue topped the 1933 league table, ending the season 16 points ahead of second placed Wimbledon. Stamford Bridge had closed after the stadium owners opted to run greyhound racing instead of speedway. Sheffield and Nottingham joined the league to increase membership to 10 teams, just half of which were now based in the capital.

A 1934 Lea Bridge programme. (JSC)

3. To Walthamstow via Lea Bridge

Lea Bridge Stadium opened for speedway in 1928, with Ernest J. Bass promoting on behalf of Motor Speedways Limited. The team competed in the Southern League from 1929 to 1931, at which point Ernie Bass held the position of secretary of the National Speedway Association (Southern) Limited. Motor Speedways Limited incurred the wrath of the National Speedway Association in 1932 when it allowed betting on racing. Betting was against the rules of the Association and *The Daily Herald* reported on a meeting it held on 19 February. Following the meeting, the Lea Bridge promoters were called upon to give an undertaking within seven days to comply with the rules, which they subsequently failed to do. The *Leicester Evening Mail* published details of a letter from the Auto-Cycle Union (ACU), pointing out that if public betting, including by totalisator, takes place at any licenced speedway track, the track licence is immediately revoked. The ACU was reportedly pleased to note that the Association was taking active steps to enforce the rule. It was widely reported in the press that the Wembley and Crystal Palace promotions had been quick to distance themselves from the idea of betting on speedway.

At a meeting with the Association on 26 February, the Lea Bridge management proposed a compromise whereby the venture would be called Tote Track Racing, rather than speedway. However, as reported in *The London Daily News* on 27 February, a resolution was passed that further membership of Lea Bridge would be detrimental to the interests of the Association and Motor Speedways Limited – the Lea Bridge Promoters – would cease membership at midday on 2 March. The promoters of Lea Bridge responded by saying they had withdrawn from the Association in any event.

Crowds dwindled at Lea Bridge and the venture only lasted until the end of May. Meanwhile, after Southampton announced closure at Banister Court due to inadequate support, the promotion agreed a lease at Lea Bridge to complete the season. Promoter Charles Knott elected to race as Clapton Saints so as not to have any association with the early season unlicenced activities. The ACU confirmed that a licence would be issued for the use of the track if the Lea Bridge promoters were not involved.

Clapton Saints continued at the track in 1933, with Charles Knott joined by Tom Bradbury-Pratt, operating as Lea Bridge Speedways Limited, before moving again in 1934, this time three and a half miles west to Harringay. When Sheffield closed at the end of the 1933 season, most of the team moved to Lea Bridge for 1934. The venue was once more under the control of Motor Speedways Limited, with Ernie Bass at the helm. Agreement was not reached between the parties on the amount to be paid for the Sheffield licence and so the figure was determined by a Speedway Control Board court of arbitration on 4 January. *The Daily Independent* reported the decision was that Motor Speedways Limited would pay Lea Bridge Speedways Limited the sum of £250. At a further meeting on 9 February, when the transfer of the licence was approved, the Control Board decreed that it would not be in the best interests of the sport for the track to operate on Saturday as this would be the same day of the week as neighbours Harringay. The options offered to Lea Bridge were Monday, Wednesday, or Friday, with Wednesday being chosen.

1934 Lea Bridge team: Squib Burton, Chun Moore, Wally Hull, Dicky Case, Eric Blain, Tommy Gamble, Jimmy Baxter (manager), Dusty Haigh. (JSC)

Lea Bridge duly competed in Division One of the National League, but attendances no doubt suffered due to the enforced change of race night from the traditional Saturday to Wednesday for 1934. A considerable number of fans who had supported the Clapton team were also said to have followed their idols to Harringay when the team relocated there for 1934. No meeting was staged at the Lea Bridge track on 20 June, following which the ACU issued a press bulletin saying that the Control Board had approved a scheme for the complete reorganisation of Lea Bridge Speedway.

The race night was changed to Friday and management was placed in the sole control of Fred Mockford, the New Cross promoter, who had been assisting the Lea Bridge promotion. Five home meetings were staged on Fridays before a shock announcement was made by the Speedway Control Board (SCB) on 27 July 1934. They said that the Lea Bridge licence had been revoked and speedway there would cease immediately. The reason given for closure was an alleged unsatisfactory situation, with the track unable to pay its way following poor team results and a slump in attendances.

The team did carry on, however, as the SCB arranged to transfer operations to a new track, still to be constructed, at Walthamstow's greyhound stadium. It was believed that the new track could be laid within two weeks and work was to be carried out day-and-night to ensure this timescale was feasible. Arrangements were made by the SCB for the riders to be compensated for the loss of one home fixture. The changes instigated by the Board did not initially meet with the approval of the promoters' association and such was the tension between the parties over the matter that a breakaway from the SCB and the ACU was a possibility for a while.

Walthamstow Grange Football Club used part of the Myrtle Grove sports ground, off Chingford Road, from 1919 onwards, playing in the Spartan League East Division. Greyhound racing was introduced to the site in 1929. At that time the venue was bounded by Empress Avenue, a residential street of terraced dwellings, on the south side and undeveloped land to the north, on which residential development took place around 1930. In addition to the site of the stadium, within a quarter of a mile there were a dozen other playing fields and sports grounds located either side of Chingford Road.

In 1931, Walthamstow Grange FC folded and the ground was subsequently sold for £24,000 to a Mr Webster, who operated the site as a small greyhound track. Webster proceeded to acquire another part of the site, occupied by Minerva Sports Club, towards the end of 1931. Both parts of the site were used for greyhound racing in 1932. An iconic Art Deco parapet entrance was built in 1932, together with a clock tower and totalisator board designed and built by Thomas & Edge Limited of Woolwich.

William Chandler, who had held shares in Hackney Wick Stadium, purchased the whole site from Webster in June 1933. The stadium was developed with what was known as The Senior Club on the first and second bends, together with covered accommodation along both straights. The back straight had one large stand, with the home straight having another Senior Club under the upstairs ballroom.

With the closure of the speedway operation at Lea Bridge Stadium, the team relocated to the Walthamstow Stadium, just over two miles to the north. There the new speedway track was laid inside the greyhound circuit. The track work was duly completed in two weeks, enabling the 1934 season to be completed by the Walthamstow Wolves speedway team, with the reluctant blessing of the promoters' association. Home meetings were staged on Thursday evenings. A was 305 yards, with banking on the bends. It was claimed that the venue could accommodate 30,000 spectators, although newspaper advertisements for early speedway meetings claimed there was covered accommodation for 40,000. Although the stadium was in an area of mixed housing and industry, development had taken place on the north side and it was now wedged between two residential roads, Rushcroft Road and Empress Avenue, with the River Ching between the stadium and the gardens of houses in the latter. This proximity to housing inevitably led to conflict with neighbouring residents.

At the time speedway was brought to Walthamstow, all the other London tracks still operating were members of the National League Division One, with Clapton having moved to Harringay and Crystal Palace to New Cross. Birmingham Hall Green and Lea Bridge had entered the competition before the move to Walthamstow, but Coventry, Nottingham and Sheffield were out. Division Two comprised reserve teams from seven of the nine teams.

The Daily Mirror initially reported information from the SCB that William Chandler, Walthamstow Stadium owner, would be in charge, but a few days later Mr RS (Dicky) Maybrook was announced as track manager. He had held the post of general manager of International Speedways Limited and had been clerk of the course at Harringay, Stamford Bridge and Wimbledon.

Of the riders who moved from Lea Bridge to Walthamstow, Cyril (Squib) Burton, Walter (Chun) Moore, Eric Blain, Walter (Wally) Hull and Herbert (Dusty) Haigh had been with Sheffield the year before. Dick Case had joined Lea Bridge from Coventry, after spending the three previous seasons with Wimbledon. Jack Bibby completed the regular septet after Tommy Gamble had moved to Hall Green. Following the relocation, Case assumed the captain's role, taking over from Burton.

The team tracked by Lea Bridge from the beginning of the season was lacking in heat leader strength. By the time of the move to Walthamstow, Dick Case had provided 40 race wins in league matches, with the rest of team managing just 34 between them in 330 starts. The 25-year-old Case was clearly the leading rider in the Lea Bridge team which switched to Walthamstow. He had achieved third place in the Star Championship Final at Wembley two years earlier and was a member of the Australian test team.

Cyril 'Squib' Burton, a 26-year-old England international, was one of the most experienced riders in the league, having been riding since 1928. He began the season as captain, riding at number one, but with Lea Bridge he managed only six race wins from 51 rides. In league racing, Squib's best years were between 1929 and 1931, with Rochdale, Leicester Stadium and Lea Bridge. He suffered serious injuries, including a fractured thigh, in a crash involving Ron Johnson. He was riding for England against Australia in a test match at Leicester Super in July 1931. The collision occurred when Burton's engine seized as he was leading in the opening race. Johnson was close behind and unable to avoid him. Johnson's machine also clipped Burton's head, knocking him unconscious. On making a comeback, Burton was with Sheffield for two seasons, without producing his best form, although another broken leg in a crash at Wimbledon in June 1932 was a major setback. In fact, he was not expected to resume racing, but eventually returned in May 1933. He had a disappointing spell on his return to Lea Bridge, which was contributed to by mechanical problems and several falls.

Eric Blain, a 28-year-old Englishman, had five years' experience of riding speedway. After representing Liverpool and Sheffield in the Northern League, Eric left Sheffield to join Crystal Palace during the 1932 National League season. He had proved to be a steady performer and continued to make progress when he returned to Sheffield in 1933. The team's switch to Lea Bridge for 1934 did not suit him. His league average fell to less than half of that achieved in the previous year by the time the move was made to Walthamstow. Herbert 'Dusty' Haigh, an experienced 28-year-old English rider, represented Halifax, Belle Vue and Sheffield before moving to Lea Bridge. Dusty had rediscovered his form following the move after a couple of disappointing seasons, the highlight being a maximum 18 points against Wimbledon in a National Trophy match. The scoring of 27-year-old Wally Hull had been impressive during his time with the Manchester clubs, Belle Vue and White City. He represented England in 1930, but his scores dipped in 1932 and 1933 during spells with Wimbledon and Sheffield. His struggle for top form continued following the move to Lea Bridge. Prior to the switch to The Stow, he had only gained three race wins for the team in official matches.

Steve Langton arrived in Britain from Australia in 1930 at the age of 20 and after a number of promising performances at non-league Portsmouth, he joined Southampton for the following season. He continued to make steady progress when Southampton relocated to

Lea Bridge, racing as Clapton Saints, during 1932. However, he then missed the 1933 season in Britain. Form deserted him on his return to Lea Bridge in 1934 and he struggled to make an impression.

Although only 22-years-old at the beginning of the 1934 season, Walter 'Chun' Moore had already gained experience with Manchester White City, Belle Vue and Sheffield, as well as having a brief spell at Lea Bridge with Clapton Saints in 1932. His progress was slow and he remained a lower order rider in the team.

Australian Jack Bibby was 23 years old when switching to Walthamstow. He was a newcomer to British speedway in 1934 and following some good results in second half events, he made his first appearance for Lea Bridge at the end of May. After scoring seven points in a promising debut, he then found points hard to come by. He failed to score in 17 of his 28 rides in team fixtures in June, before showing steady improvement in July.

Two other Australian junior riders, Clem Thomas and Fred Tracey moved to Walthamstow with the Lea Bridge team. 22-year-old Thomas was one of the smallest riders in speedway at just five feet two inches tall. He had made a sensational start to his career riding at the Melbourne track in Australia and looked to have a bright future in the sport. Tracey suffered misfortune before setting sail from Australia. He lost two fingers when they were caught in the chain as his bike ran over him after he crashed at the Melbourne track in January.

Race averages at the time Lea Bridge closed showed that the scoring of Burton and Blain was significantly down from the previous season. Hull was showing improvement, but still not up to the level of his 1932 season at Wimbledon. Haigh's improvement cancelled out the disappointing scores by Squib Burton, but Moore was also below par. Steve Langton's performance had been very disappointing compared to his achievements with Clapton Saints in 1932. He failed to register a single point in his first eight league meetings, although his number of rides from reserve were limited. Jack Bibby and fellow Australian newcomer Clem Thomas were brought into the team, with Bibby's scores improving after a slow start. Reg Stanley had more previous experience and had also been given a couple of league outings. Moore, Blain, Langton, Bibby, Thomas and Stanley all averaged less than a point a ride in their league appearances for Lea Bridge. The absence of strength in depth only added to the problems caused by lack of top end scoring power to support Case.

The nine teams competing in the National League met each other home and away twice during the season. Lea Bridge had already travelled twice to Wembley, Harringay and Hall Green in south Birmingham, so these destinations were not in the fixture list for Walthamstow.

The 'Star Championship', an individual championship sponsored by *The Star* newspaper, was to be competed for at Wembley by two riders from each of the National League teams, determined by an eliminating event at each track. The winner at Wembley would receive £100. However, as Lea Bridge closed before being able to stage an eliminator, the National Speedway Association took the decision to nominate Dick Case and Dusty Haigh to represent Walthamstow. This decision was taken as the Final was due to be held on 23 August, before which Walthamstow would have staged only one home meeting, on 16 August.

The building work at the Stadium to create the speedway track.

The opening ceremony: Vic Huxley, Dick Maybrook (Manager), Mrs Meston, Mrs Huxley, Captain FW Meston MC (General Manager). (Both photos courtesy Peter Lush)

4. 1934 – A brief season at The Stow

August

The newly formed Walthamstow Wolves began with a National League encounter at New Cross on Wednesday, 8 August, just six days after the final Lea Bridge match, at Wembley. The team was rooted to the foot of the league table with eight points from 22 matches, courtesy of two home wins against Birmingham at Lea Bridge and home and away successes against Plymouth. Nine of the last 10 league meetings had been lost and the team was six match points adrift of Birmingham and Plymouth with 10 league fixtures still to be raced.

New Cross was also a new speedway venue in 1934, with promoter Fred Mockford having moved the Crystal Palace team there at the beginning of the season. Speedway at Crystal Palace had become unviable due to a proposed massive rent increase. The track was also hindered by a lack of lighting which ruled out evening meetings. The spectacle of speedway raced under lights makes it look much faster than daylight meetings, adding to its appeal. Measuring 262 yards per lap, the New Cross circuit was the smallest in the league. Riding as Lea Bridge, the Wolves team had lost an earlier league encounter in May by 38–16 at the Old Kent Road track, south of the Thames in south-east London. On this occasion, Walthamstow suffered a similarly heavy defeat, by 36–17.

The home team provided race winners in seven of the nine heats, with Tom Farndon and Ron Johnson to the fore. Farndon and Johnson were formidable opponents, having finished first and second respectively in The Star Riders' Championship, the forerunner of the World Championship, in 1933. Farndon had also defeated Australian star Vic Huxley to become British Match Race Champion a week earlier, although Huxley was carrying an injury.

Dick Case carried on where he had left off with Lea Bridge, top scoring with seven points, including a race win. Eric Blain was the other heat winner for the Wolves, in totalling five, but Squib Burton had a very disappointing meeting, mustering just one point in three rides. Bibby, Haigh, Moore and Thomas all contributed a single point to the team total. Haigh had been in a run of good form, having scored 43 points in his previous six league outings. His meagre return at New Cross was a disappointment. Haigh had the misfortune to fall in his first ride, but remounted to earn a point after Moore had a broken chain.

Point scoring opportunities were missed as Squib Burton also took a tumble in his first ride, with the Wolves trailing by four points after three races. Jack Bibby pulled up with a broken chain in the next heat and the same problem caused Haigh to fall in the fifth race. Eric Blain fell in the sixth heat and Clem Thomas did likewise in the following race. Chun Moore fell again in the first attempt to run the penultimate race, with Haigh and Nobby Key unable to avoid running into him. Moore was badly shaken and was replaced by Thomas in the rerun.

Dusty Haigh would have been relieved to enjoy a spell of success in the sport. He and his wife had endured an appearance at a bankruptcy court in Huddersfield on 8 May, following the failure of their short-lived venture as owners of a millinery business in the town.

Just under a week after the defeat at New Cross, the Wolves travelled a few miles down the road on 14 August for the second league visit of the season to West Ham. After the tight New Cross track, the riders experienced the extreme of the large 440 yards Custom House track. For the second match in succession, Walthamstow were well beaten 36–17. West Ham had won the previous encounter, against Lea Bridge, by a margin of a dozen points, when Squib Burton had been absent from the visiting team. With Burton included on this occasion, Walthamstow would have hoped to run the home team closer, but it was not to be. After a second place in his first ride, Case suffered a blown engine when ahead in his next race and failed to score. He then withdrew from his last heat. The home team took maximum points in seven of the nine heats.

Burton top-scored for the visitors with six points and Haigh won the only race he completed, but again support was lacking. Burton's performance was very encouraging, and he was only inches behind Wilkinson, the race winner, in the sixth heat. Jack Bibby also suffered mechanical gremlins and did not take his third ride. As his partner, Case, was also out of the race, the Wolves tracked only one rider; reserve Clem Thomas came in. Thomas gained second place behind the unbeaten Bluey Wilkinson when the other home rider, Eric Gregory, failed to finish. Walthamstow secured their only heat win, 4–2, in the final heat after West Ham's Arthur Atkinson's engine failed. Australian test star Bluey Wilkinson scored maximum points for the Hammers and received good support, with Gregory the only home rider failing to record a race win.

The confidence of the speedway authorities was borne out when the first meeting was staged at Walthamstow just 20 days after the announcement of the closure of Lea Bridge. Wimbledon were the visitors. The meeting, on Thursday, 16 August, was well attended. *The Daily Mirror* and various other newspapers suggested a crowd of 25,000, the *Daily Telegraph* gave a more conservative estimate of 15,000. The *Walthamstow Guardian* reported that 11,000 spectators were present. Even the lower of these figures would have been very pleasing for the promoters, particularly after the poor crowds at Lea Bridge in the closing weeks there. Press advertisements for the meeting said that the imposing stadium provided covered accommodation for 40,000 spectators.

Admission prices were set at 1/3 (one shilling and threepence), 2/6 and 5/-, with children charged 7d (seven pence). In addition to spacious stands, features advertised included the new type of track surface, marvellous lighting, visible pits and ray timing of races. The new team race jackets, featuring a white star on a plain background, were available for the first time for this meeting. In the two previous matches the teams had raced in plain red race jackets. Match programmes cost 4d and the front cover proclaimed that Walthamstow was "the 'Goodwood' of speedway racing", no doubt inspired by Wembley's claim to be "the 'Ascot' of the speedways".

Things did not go as smoothly as management and riders would have hoped on opening night. The track surface consisted of decomposed granite, sourced from Leicestershire, rather than the usual cinders. Reports described the track as very slick, with most of the riders having trouble in controlling their machines on the bends. Press reports claimed that all the visiting riders were carried from the track on stretchers at some point during the evening. Wimbledon's Syd Jackson did not even take part in the match after falling and crushing a finger during the Grand Parade.

There was little between the teams throughout the league match and after the penultimate heat the scores were tied at 24–24. Walthamstow delighted the home fans by securing the league points with a 5–1 heat score in the final race. The success by Burton and Moore was made easier as they only had one opponent to face, in the form of Wimbledon reserve Fred Leavis. Wal Phillips was out of the meeting after suffering a collar bone injury in a first ride fall and Geoff Pymar was also ruled out of the deciding heat with mechanical trouble.

The victory was the result of a solid performance by the home riders. Dick Case again led the way, losing out once, to Gus Kuhn, who in turn was defeated only by Dusty Haigh. After a fall in his first ride, Squib Burton won his other two, showing something of his old form. Eric Blain won his first race but failed to score after that.

Wimbledon had won an earlier encounter at Lea Bridge by an eight-point margin. They would almost certainly have triumphed in this match, but for Australian test star Vic Huxley having been ruled out for the rest of the season. He had been in outstanding form, winning 75 percent of his races and topping the league averages, before sustaining a leg injury when falling in the test match at New Cross. The injury was slow to heal, with doctors advising that a lengthy rest from the sport was essential to prevent permanent damage. Huxley, a pioneer of the sport, was at the meeting and performed the official opening of the track.

Dick Case won the first race on the new track in a time of 72.63 seconds. This was bettered by Claude Rye, before Gus Kuhn set the fastest time of the match with 72.01 in the eighth heat. Some top names were booked to appear in a second half event for 'The Goodwood Trophy' and the fastest time of the night was recorded by the Belle Vue and England star Joe Abbott, with 70.64 seconds. Also taking part were Tom Farndon and Ron Johnson from New Cross, Harringay's Norman Parker, along with Belle Vue's Frank Varey and Max Grosskreutz. Farndon won the event, which consisted of four heats, two semi-finals and a final. Case and Abbott were given an opportunity to establish a record for four laps from a flying start. Case went first and set 70.48 seconds, but Abbott showed his liking for the track by recording 70.03.

There was a break from league fare on 23 August when West Ham were the visitors for the second meeting at Chingford Road in a challenge match for the Essex Championship. The fixture clashed with The Star Championship Final at Wembley, in which Dick Case and Dusty Haigh were competing. Both were eliminated in a semi-final. The Hammers were even more below-strength because Bluey Wilkinson and Tommy Croombs were riding in the Wembley event. Tiger Stevenson was also missing due to an injury the previous evening at New Cross. Two days earlier, Dick Case had represented Australia in the fifth and deciding test against England at West Ham, contributing 8+1 as his country won 57–50. He had enjoyed a successful series, scoring 45+7 points in five tests.

With the Essex Championship match run over 18 heats, the home team were no match for the visitors who won 65–39. Chun Moore and Wally Hull both notched two heat wins, but again there were disappointing scores from Blain, Bibby and Langton. Squib Burton started well with five points from his first two outings, before a fall in his third brought his scoring to an end.

West Ham took the lead in the third race and steadily pulled away until the result was beyond doubt with four heats left. Arthur Atkinson, Jack Dixon and Eric Gregory reeled off 12 heat wins between them and scored five points more than the entire Walthamstow team in a one-sided match. Atkinson beat Joe Abbott's record with a time of 70.49 in the first race, before Dixon went even faster with 70.06 in the eighth heat. The last three races were rain-affected, with the winning time for the final heat being more than 20 seconds slower than for heat 15 as track conditions deteriorated. With West Ham winning so comfortably, it was fortunate that the Essex Championship was not a two-leg tie.

The six tracks from the capital competed for the London Cup, sponsored by the *Evening News*. Walthamstow received a bye to the last four, where they were drawn against New Cross. They were very much the underdogs as New Cross had already inflicted three heavy defeats on Lea Bridge/Walthamstow. The first leg was at the Old Kent Road on 29 August. New Cross provided all 18 heat winners in a one-sided affair, easing to an emphatic 69–38 win. The Wolves riders had no answer to the home stars, with Tom Farndon and Stan Greatrex scoring 18-point maximums. Ron Johnson scored 17+1, beaten only by his team partner Joe Francis. Dick Case top scored once more for his team, with 11 points from six rides. The home team would have scored even more but for several falls by second string riders when well placed. The *Daily Mirror* reported that the processional racing was so uneventful that many supporters left the stadium long before the last race was run. Chun Moore fell when challenging Tom Farndon for the lead in the final heat and was hit by his team partner Dusty Haigh. Although battered and bruised, Moore took second place in the rerun. This was the second time in consecutive visits to New Cross that Moore and Haigh had collided.

Just 24 hours later, the return leg was staged at Walthamstow Stadium, before a crowd of around 12,000. It was a formality that New Cross would progress to the final, with the home side well beaten. Farndon, Johnson and Greatrex again outscored the entire Wolves team in a 65–41 win. Stan Greatrex achieved the remarkable feat of scoring an 18-point maximum in both legs. Case, Burton and Blain each won a race, but the visitors supplied the other 15 heat winners, emphasising the weakness in the home team. Haigh and Moore were below par, both suffering the effects of their falls in the away leg. New Cross progressed to the Final with a 134–79 aggregate win. They beat West Ham in the Final, with the Hammers missing the injured Tiger Stevenson for both legs.

After difficulties with the Walthamstow track on the opening night, work had been carried out by mixing in decomposed granite with a coarser grain, as used on the Pennycross circuit at Plymouth. According to the *Evening News*, the track stood up very well after heavy rain and there were no serious crashes.

The track held up so well, in fact, that the previous track record was beaten seven times. Ron Johnson set the new clutch start record time of 68.52 seconds. In a triangular match race Dick Case set a new flying start record of 67.35 seconds, defeating Tom Farndon and Jack Parker in the process.

September

A return to league action on 6 September failed to bring a change of fortune for the Wolves as they suffered a four-point defeat at home to near neighbours Harringay, in front of around 13,000 spectators. Jack and Norman Parker provided five of the visitors' six race wins. For Walthamstow, Case and Burton shone with eight and seven points respectively, but the rest of the team struggled to make an impact. Haigh was disappointing with just three third places. Chun Moore and Eric Blain continued to find points hard to come by in league racing.

As an added attraction, teams representing North and South London met in the second half of the meeting, with the South victorious. The North comprised Walthamstow and Harringay riders; the South included riders from Wimbledon and New Cross. Ron Johnson again showed his liking for the Walthamstow track – he scored a maximum nine points for South London. The promoter was providing attractive fare for the spectators, which compensated to some extent for the indifferent performances of the Wolves team.

When Walthamstow Wolves visited Wimbledon on 10 September, they had only won one league match, a narrow success in the home meeting against the same opponents. Lea Bridge team's visit to Plough Lane in south-west London at the end of April had resulted in an eight-point defeat. Vic Huxley, the Wimbledon captain, had led the home team's scoring with a maximum nine points on that occasion. However, the visitors were hopeful of a close encounter this time because he was unable to ride due to injury. Huxley did a farewell lap of the track before the meeting because he was returning to Australia the next day to recuperate.

The Wolves' hopes were dashed in two disastrous opening heats as the Dons went 10–1 ahead. In the first race Dick Case fell and Wally Hull was no match for the home pair, Claude Rye and Wally Little. The second heat was even worse for the Wolves because Squib Burton crashed when trying to pass Gus Kuhn on the last lap and Chun Moore's machine failed to last the distance. Burton was ruled out of the rest of the meeting with a shoulder injury.

Benefitting from a fall by Geoff Pymar and an exclusion for Syd Jackson due to a starting offence, Walthamstow only slipped a further six points adrift by the end of the meeting to lose 34–19. The usual failing of lack of heat winners persisted, as Wimbledon provided the first rider home in seven of the nine heats. Case recovered from his first race mishap to notch five points from two rides and Haigh provided the only other success for the Wolves. Wally Hull had a disappointing match, with just two third places on returning to one of his former tracks. Eric Blain gained two second places, but on both occasions one of the Wimbledon pair was out of the race. With five of the 10 Walthamstow league fixtures now completed, added to the results when competing as Lea Bridge, the team was still firmly rooted to the foot of the table.

It was an unlucky 13 September for Walthamstow when New Cross visited for a league encounter. Even the most optimistic home supporter would not have expected the match to go to a last heat decider after the heavy beatings handed out by their opponents in their previous meetings. Things had gone well enough until the last race, with the Wolves providing four heat winners, two each from Case and Burton. Ron Johnson continued his fine form at the track in winning heat one from Case after a rerun was needed.

Left: Dusty Haigh and Squib Burton when they were riding for Sheffield in 1931. (JSC)
Right: Dick Case riding in 1936. (JSC)

Left: A 1934 Walthamstow programme.
Above: A supporter's badge.

An advert for a Walthamstow meeting. (Courtesy Peter Lush)

In the first attempt, his bike reared at the start and he collided with Case. Johnson's machine was badly damaged, forcing him to complete the match on a spare.

Burton performed well, first defeating Stan Greatrex and then Johnson. With Case heading home Tom Farndon, the match swung first one way then another until the visitors were two points ahead after the penultimate race. The unbeaten Burton was partnered by Chun Moore in the decider. Moore had picked up a couple of third places in earlier rides. Their opposition was provided by Farndon, who had dropped a single point, and George Newton, who had scored just one when defeating Hull. The home supporters hoped that Burton would remain unbeaten and if Moore could get the better of Newton, the match would finish all square. It was not to be, however, as Burton and Moore collided just after the start of the race. Both home riders fell to gift the visitors the match 30–23.

Once again, the visitors' top three scored as many as the whole Walthamstow team put together. The third top scorer for the home team was Eric Blain, with just three points. The wooden spoon was now looking to be a certainty as the Wolves had to meet the top two teams, Belle Vue and Wembley, in three of the last four league matches.

The second half of this meeting was a match between Pioneers and The Rest. Tiger Stevenson of West Ham joined Case, Farndon, Greatrex, Moore and Blain for The Rest. The pioneers of the sport in 1928 in Britain were represented by Australian test stars Ron Johnson and Bluey Wilkinson, together with four Englishmen, Burton, West Ham rider Tommy Croombs, Gus Kuhn from Wimbledon, and Nobby Key from New Cross. The Pioneers won 28–26 in a close fought affair.

In mid-September, the Walthamstow management announced that plans were in hand for the 1935 speedway season. Case was returning to Australia for the test series against England and would be on the look-out for promising talent to recruit. According to *Reynolds's Illustrated News*, trials were also being held at the Chingford Road track in an attempt to discover new local riders, with the intention of forming a Second Division team for the next season. In 1934 the National League teams, apart from Plymouth and Lea Bridge/Walthamstow, had entered reserve teams in a Second Division, but it transpired that there would not be a reserve league in 1935.

Birmingham met Wembley in Round One of the ACU Cup, with Wembley progressing to join the other seven National League teams in Round Two. The ties were a straight knock-out and West Ham were overwhelming favourites when drawn at home to the Wolves, with the meeting on 18 September.

West Ham's Tiger Stevenson fell in the opening heat and then again in heat six, when Walthamstow's Eric Blain was unable to avoid him. Stevenson retired from the meeting with an injured shoulder. Eric Gregory was also missing for the Hammers, having suffered concussion after a crash when racing in Denmark. Even so, West Ham cruised to an emphatic 66–37 victory in the 18-heat match. The Wolves were still in contention after the seventh heat, trailing by just three points, but it was one-way traffic after that. The Hammers won six of the remaining heats by a maximum 5–1 scoreline. Case fought a lone battle, with an impressive 14 points from his first five rides. Even he then ran out of steam and failed to score last time out. Moore won his first race, but added just a single point from his remaining four rides. Haigh was the visitors only other heat winner, although five further outings yielded a meagre two points. Burton had a night to forget, with his points coming from three third places in five races. For West Ham, Wilkinson, Wal Morton and Croombs all registered double figure scores. Their reserves, Arthur Warwick and Stan Dell, recorded three heat wins between them, emphasising the difference in strength between the teams.

The opposition was tougher than ever when Belle Vue, the league leaders, visited Walthamstow Stadium on 20 September. The home team were completely outclassed, losing 36–17. This was the heaviest home league defeat of the season for Walthamstow/Lea Bridge. Case was their sole heat winner, beating the strong pairing of Frank Charles and Joe Abbott. Case had the misfortune to fall when attempting an outside pass to take the lead against fellow Australian test star Max Grosskreutz in the penultimate heat, but still finished joint top scorer with Squib Burton on five points.

Grosskreutz and Bill Kitchen scored maximums for Belle Vue, and were well supported by England internationals Joe Abbott, Frank Charles, Frank Varey and Bob Harrison. Kitchen lowered the track record to 68.42 seconds in beating Case in the opening race. It was just as well for Walthamstow that Belle Vue's top rider, Eric Langton, was missing due to injury, otherwise the margin of defeat might have been even greater. Haigh endured a miserable time against one of his former teams and failed to score in the match. He crashed in the first attempt to run the fourth heat when Kitchen fell in front of him. It was reported that Haigh had been knocked out, but although he took part in the rerun, he fell again. Kitchen was unscathed and won the rerun. Haigh was badly shaken and pulled out of his final ride. Moore completed only one race, with a fall and machine problems in the others.

Three riders made attempts to lower the flying start track record for four laps in the second half. Grosskreutz went first and set a new fastest time of 66.89 seconds. Kitchen and Case were unsuccessful in their attempts to better the new record, clocking times of 68.40 and 67.61 respectively. This was followed by a match race in which Case beat Grosskreutz.

A junior match was staged between Walthamstow and Harringay in the second half of the meeting, although it did not feature any new faces. The Walthamstow team was Steve Langton, Clem Thomas, Reg Stanley and Fred Tracey. All had appeared in the Lea Bridge/Walthamstow team at various times during the campaign and they defeated their local rivals 14–10. To complete a full evening of 22 races, a scratch event was staged and dominated by visiting riders, with Charles defeating Parker, Kitchen and Harrison in the final.

Two days after the heavy home defeat by the Aces, Walthamstow travelled to Manchester on 22 September for the return, on a wet track which gathered puddles in the last three heats. As expected, the Wolves were soundly beaten, this time 40–14. This was their heaviest away league defeat of the season and was also the only meeting for which Walthamstow travelled outside London in 1934.

The scores were level after the second heat, when former Belle Vue riders Hull and Moore raced to a 5–1 heat success against Oliver Langton after Joe Abbott dropped out of the race with engine trouble. Belle Vue provided the other eight race winners, however, with Kitchen, Charles and Harrison all unbeaten by the opposition. Both teams were missing their top rider, with Eric Langton out injured for Belle Vue and Case away riding for Australia in a challenge match against London at Harringay. Grosskreutz was also missing from the home side because he too was in the Australian team. Belle Vue adequately covered for their absent Australian star, but Walthamstow were severely disadvantaged. As the Australian riders were not on official international duty, it is inexplicable that the challenge match took precedence over a league fixture. With such strength in depth, it surprised few people when Belle Vue went on to retain the league title which they had won in 1933, although the Wembley Lions were just two points adrift in the final table. The Aces continued their winning ways in the next two seasons, eventually taking a fourth consecutive title in 1936.

After their opening ride success, Moore and Hull added only one further point for the Wolves. Haigh had ridden for Belle Vue in 1930 and 1932, but track knowledge did not assist him on this occasion as he scored just a single point. Burton fared no better and had another disappointing match.

West Ham paid a second visit to Walthamstow Stadium, this time for a league encounter, on 27 September. Tiger Stevenson had not recovered from injury, but the Hammers team was still strong enough to provide the first man home in six of the nine heats. There were also solid contributions from support riders and the Wolves slipped to yet another home defeat, this time 32–21. The margin would have been greater still had not Wilkinson had an engine failure when in the lead in one heat. In the same race Burton also suffered mechanical failure and failed to finish.

Eric Blain was absent from the Wolves team, with his car having broken down on the way to the track. Jack Bibby replaced him and Clem Thomas came in as reserve. The home team's woes continued in the first race when Case fell, allowing the visitors to take the heat 5–1. Just three points separated the teams after four heats, but only Case offered any real resistance thereafter. He won two races, but Haigh was the only other Walthamstow rider to register a heat win.

October

The Wolves were due to host Wembley Lions in the final meeting of the season at Walthamstow on 3 October until rain forced a postponement to the following week. The curtain then came down on a disappointing season in terms of results when the visitors romped to an emphatic victory, 32–22 on 10 October. The evening did not go well, with the stadium affected by electrical gremlins. The starting gate malfunctioned causing a delay and then failed completely after the second heat. Races had to be started on a light. Further delays tested the crowd's patience when the track lights failed temporarily as the fifth heat was completed.

Case had mechanical trouble in the first heat, although he picked up a point as Wembley's Les Bowden fell. Ginger Lees was in fine form for the visitors and in addition to scoring a maximum, he lowered the track record when he won the opening race. The season and the pre-war era ended with the Walthamstow track record standing at 67.26 seconds.

Once again, the home team's downfall was an inability to provide race winners. Case won twice and Wembley provided the first man home in the other seven heats, even though Australian star Lionel Van Praag had already returned home for the winter. George Greenwood was also absent from the Wembley team due to injury. Haigh provided support with three second places, beyond which the contributions were disappointing. Moore, Hull and Burton chipped in with just two points each. The wooden spoon had been inevitable when Walthamstow inherited a set of poor league results from Lea Bridge. Unfortunately, the results at the new track were very much the same.

The riders' scores show the weakness in the team, with only Case consistently able to match the top riders from opposing teams. The remainder of the team generally averaged little better than third place per ride, or three points per match. Burton was particularly disappointing as his league average dropped by over two points per match from the previous season. Haigh, Hull and Moore all saw their form dip after the move from Lea Bridge to Walthamstow.

Although unsuccessful on the track, with just one victory in 10 league matches and no cup wins, the move from Lea Bridge to Walthamstow had been a worthwhile one. The venture was much better supported than Lea Bridge had been, a fine stadium had been developed and the racing was of good quality.

Preparations were being made with a view to tracking a competitive team in the 1935 season. On 3 October, the *Daily Mirror* reported that Phil Hart, Bill Clibbett and Mick Murphy had all been transferred from Plymouth to Walthamstow. Plymouth had finished just one place above the Wolves in the table and dropped out of the league for the following season.

Sadly, the dark cloud of protest by neighbouring residents had hovered overhead throughout the short season, regarding the use of the stadium for both speedway and greyhounds. Things came to a head before the year was out.

5. Walthamstow speedway is silenced

The staging of speedway at Walthamstow Stadium in 1934 met with the immediate disapproval of neighbouring residents and opposition intensified during the ensuing months.

Within days of speedway activity commencing at the stadium, on 16 August 1934, residents decided to hold a meeting to form a plan of action to bring it to a halt. According to press reports, the meeting took place on Sunday, 31 August and was attended by more than 100 people. One of the meeting organisers described the noise from the speedway as resembling heavy bombardment by artillery. Those present agreed an injunction should be sought against the organisers of the Walthamstow Speedway, because of the "nuisance and annoyance which supplements the existing annoyance of the greyhound racing."

On 9 September, a court application was made on behalf of the residents' group for an interim injunction, primarily to restrain the holding of motor-cycle speedway races, but objections to the broadcasting of music through loudspeakers on the ground were also specified. As the civil courts were on vacation during August and September the case could not be heard immediately, so pending the hearing representatives of the parties conferred and an agreement was reached whereby the number of speedway meetings would be limited and the noise of the loudspeakers would be modified or toned down.

The court action was eventually heard on Friday, 7 December 1934 by Mr Justice Clauson in the Chancery Division of the High Court in London. The plaintiffs were three owner-occupiers of houses in Rushcroft Road and Empress Avenue, Chingford. They claimed an injunction against William Chandler, the promoter of Walthamstow Stadium, Chingford Road, 'to restrain him from holding upon the premises any speedway or dirt track or other motor races, or any dog or greyhound races, racing, or race meetings, and from broadcasting music or making announcements by means of sound amplifiers or loudspeakers.'

The barrister for the residents argued that following construction of the track a large number of meetings had been staged in August, causing a very serious nuisance and disturbance by way of noise, fumes and odours, with further distress caused in the neighbouring roads by unruly and noisy crowds, including trespassing in gardens and indiscriminately parking cars. Cheering, shouting and other noises by the crowds attending meetings were also cited, as was the whining and barking of dogs. In fact, there had been just three speedway meetings in August, four in September and one in October, amounting to eight in all. He referred to the interim agreement made at the initial application to the court and asserted that no measures had been taken to alleviate the nuisance, as nothing could be done to silence the noise of the machines or prevent the fumes from the exhausts. Further, nothing had been done to remove the nuisance from the noise of the loudspeakers, with the whining and barking of dogs also being just as bad as before.

The defence denied that any nuisance was being created and emphasised that the district was not a residential one, having been developed commercially. It was also claimed that the police had addressed the issue of car parking and had it well in hand.

Before adjourning the case until the following Tuesday, Mr Justice Clauson contradicted the opinion of the plaintiff's barrister by commenting that it appeared clear that certain things had been very much better since a sensible arrangement was made on 9 September. He went on to suggest that perhaps the number of speedway meetings held during the year might be reduced, thereby diminishing the noise. Of course, this was not strictly valid as the level of noise would remain the same, only the number of occasions on which the residents would be subjected to it might differ.

The defence barrister pointed out that tracks were now limited to staging no more than 104 greyhound meetings per year following the passing of the 1934 Betting and Lotteries Act. Evidence was given that before Mr Chandler took over there had been two dog tracks on the site, with many more dogs kept on the premises and they had dog racing then every day, including Sundays, without any objection from the residents. It was only when the stadium was being developed that they paid any heed. The stadium manager gave evidence that the largest attendance for a greyhound meeting was 2,000, with the stadium having a capacity of 30,000.

He expressed a willingness on behalf of his client, Mr Chandler, to see if an arrangement could be made to end the litigation, but Counsel for the residents doubted whether they would accept any speedway at all at the stadium.

On resumption, the court heard evidence from a number of residents, with details of how some had to go out each evening to avoid the disturbance from speedway and dogs, and some had children whose sleep was delayed causing them to be absent from school the next morning. One resident claimed that meetings took place nine times a week, on three afternoons and every evening except Sunday. Conversely, some witnesses told the court that the noise did not trouble them at all, with one Rushcroft Road resident saying that since Mr Chandler had taken over the stadium there had been a complete change, with the loudspeaker not in the least affecting her peace and quiet. A chartered surveyor engaged by Counsel for the residents submitted an opinion that the nuisance caused by greyhounds on the site reduced the value of neighbouring houses by 20 to 25 percent and, furthermore, the impact of the speedway noise made it impossible to put any value at all on the properties. Other opinion provided by a local member of the Auctioneers Institute was that the value of properties in the immediate vicinity of the stadium was diminished by 10 to 15 percent.

The judgement of Mr Justice Clauson on Wednesday, 12 December, as widely reported in the press, was:
- After the Stadium was altered for dirt track racing, there must have been, to some extent, more noise than there was at the time Mr Chandler's predecessor was conducting it.
- The machines used for dirt track racing had no silencers, and, accordingly, did make a great deal of noise. It was quite clear that races with motor cycles without silencers must be stopped in some form or other.
- While the loudspeaker did constitute an actionable nuisance, some steps have been taken since September to reduce the noise to such an extent as not to be a nuisance.
- Some of the spectators had whistles and rattles, which had been used to add to the general hilarity, and, at the same time, the general din. These adjuncts to racing are quite unnecessary for anyone's enjoyment, and can quite easily be stopped.

Mr Justice Clauson said that he was satisfied there had been a nuisance to the extent he had indicated, but he was not disposed to grant a form of injunction which would prevent the use of the stadium for greyhound or dirt track racing altogether. The hearing was adjourned to enable Counsel to consult on the form of the order, following which an undertaking was given on behalf of the defendant, William Chandler:

(1) Not to use loudspeakers of any amplification above 65 for music and 70 for announcements, and not to install loudspeakers outside the stands.

(2) Not to permit to race motor cycles which are not fitted with effective silencers within the meaning of the Motor Car Act.

(3) Not to permit any person within the Stadium to use rattles or whistles, or other noise instruments.

(4) Not to hold speedway meetings between 15 October and Easter in any year, and not to hold more than one speedway meeting in any one week before 25 July. After that date not to hold more than one speedway meeting in any week in which there are more than two greyhound race meetings. In any case, after July, not to hold more than two speedway meetings in any one week.

(5) Not to hold more than one dirt-track practice in any one week between the hours of 10.30 am and 1.30 pm.

(6) Not to hold either greyhound or speedway meetings on Sundays.

Mr Justice Clauson stated that, with these undertakings having been given, the Court did not think it right to grant an injunction. However, Mr Chandler was ordered to pay the plaintiff's costs.

All but one of the undertakings could be put into effect fairly easily, but the requirement to fit silencers to all bikes being used at the stadium was a different matter altogether and effectively ruled out the continuation of speedway at Walthamstow at that time. As part of the defence, Counsel had put the onus on others to resolve the issue of noise from speedway machines by stating that, in regard to the speedway racing, there was necessarily some noise, but the trouble was that the body controlling the sport permitted the use of machines without silencers, and if only that state of affairs could be changed the trouble would disappear. This statement nudged Mr. Justice Clauson in the direction of undertaking (2).

On 13 December 1934, the *Daily Mirror* published an article expressing concern for other speedway tracks in light of the judgement. TW Loughborough, secretary of the Auto-Cycle Union, said that the decision would no doubt affect other stadiums. He added that, about Walthamstow, a visiting team would now have to go to the expense of securing the same sort of silencers as the home riders or not go at all.

By 10 January 1935 the 'silencing' question was reported to be at an advanced stage, with the Speedway Control Board in possession of three silencers which it was believed would address the requirements of the Walthamstow judgement. In mid-January these silencers were being tested. On 1 February 1935, the newly constituted Control Board granted permission for the Birmingham team to transfer to Harringay and indicated that a licence would be approved for a new track at Hackney Wick, but this was dependent on the outcome of the Walthamstow 'silencing' question. The indication was that Hackney Wick could replace

Walthamstow if the noise matter could not be resolved and brought to a satisfactory conclusion. In due course, the licence was transferred and Walthamstow Wolves became the Hackney Wolves from the 1935 season onwards.

Fans who had supported the Wolves at Walthamstow, as well as followers from Lea Bridge, could easily follow the team to Hackney if they wished, with the Waterden Road track just over three and a half miles south of the Chingford Road stadium and one and a half miles from Lea Bridge.

During the period of uncertainty over the future of the team the Walthamstow management had continued to prepare for a further season at The Stow, but their plans suffered a blow at the end of January. Negotiations had been taking place with Harringay for the services of 26-year-old Charlie Blacklock, but news was received that the rider had been fatally injured in a track crash on 27 January in his native New Zealand.

Although there was to be no more speedway racing at Walthamstow Stadium before the war, greyhound racing flourished in the late 1930s and in an immediate post-war boom for the sport. By that time, the greyhounds were kennelled off-site and neighbouring residents only had race night inconvenience to consider. So long as the stadium remained there was always a chance that speedway might return one day.

6. The Wolves move on

Lea Bridge had a league speedway team from 1929 to 1931. The team did not enter league racing the next year, when a failed attempt was made to run meetings in which betting was permitted, against the rules of the speedway authorities. In 1932, the Southampton team relocated to the Lea Bridge stadium after their track closed and they rode under the name of Clapton for the remainder of the season, continuing in 1933, before moving on again to Harringay in 1934. The Sheffield track closed meanwhile and the former promoter of the Lea Bridge team secured the services of most of their riders for the 1934 league season. After the subsequent failure to last the season, with the team relocating to Walthamstow, a new home was required for 1935 due to the noise-related difficulties at The Stow. The next move was to a new track at Hackney Wick greyhound stadium, still with the 'Wolves' nickname.

Of the Walthamstow riders, Case, Burton and Haigh formed part of the new Hackney team. Case stayed with Hackney for three years before the team dropped to Division Two for the 1938 season. He joined Wembley in 1938 before retiring, although he was tempted to make a comeback with Hackney the following year to replace the injured Frank Hodgson. His return, in a World Championship Qualifying Round, lasted just two races, after being injured in a fall first time out. Remarkably, he came out for a second and final ride, which he won. Three years earlier, Case had finished joint eighth in the first World Championship Final at Wembley. He ran training schools at the Rye House track in Hertfordshire before and after the War, providing Walthamstow with two very good riders for the 1949 team.

Burton retired from racing after a poor season with Hackney in 1935, hampered by further injuries along the way. Speaking after his retirement, he recalled that during his racing career he suffered 14 fractures. He was not lost to speedway, however, as he returned to manage Leicester Hunters in 1950, a position he retained until the end of 1961. Haigh performed well for Hackney, but was tragically killed in a track crash when riding against West Ham in May 1936. He had won his first three rides and was leading in his final outing when he lost control and fell in front of the following riders, succumbing instantly to head injuries.

Reg Stanley and Wally Hull made a few appearances in reserve matches and second half events at Hackney. Hull eventually returned to Belle Vue, one of his former teams, midway through the season. He remained with the Aces until 1948. Clem Thomas spent only one season at Hackney, riding occasionally as a reserve, without making significant progress. Back in Melbourne, Australia, he initially announced his retirement from speedway in November 1936 at the age of 24, but then reappeared on the track 12 months later.

Eric Blain moved back north in 1935, having a few early season outings for Belle Vue in Division One. He met with more success when dropping down to the Provincial League the following year with Liverpool and moved with the team to Manchester, as Belle Vue Merseysiders, in 1937. Blain finished with a disappointing season back at Sheffield in 1938. Chun Moore had rides at a handful of tracks in 1935 and met with little success as a reserve at Belle Vue over the next three years before finishing. He had his best season with Nottingham in the Provincial League in 1936 and was a useful middle order rider at Norwich the following year.

Jack Bibby had few opportunities at Hackney and failed to secure a regular team spot. He gained experience at non-league Cardiff and then joined Plymouth in 1936. After making progress there, he later linked up with Bristol, where he enjoyed a good year in the last pre-war season. His best season was his second with Sheffield in 1947 and he remained a steady scorer there for two more years before missing the 1950 season with a broken leg. A comeback with Ashfield and then Cardiff in 1951 proved unsuccessful.

Fred Tracey returned to Australia after his season with Lea Bridge/Walthamstow, making a brief reappearance in the UK with Coventry after the war. He subsequently promoted successfully at the Maribyrnong track in a suburb of Melbourne, Australia. Perhaps he gained some useful ideas from the noise issues at Walthamstow in 1934 because he was commended for the way in which his track was run. A move to take legal action against the previous speedway had been led by Mr Jaffray and Mr Broad of Newstead Street. The *Sunshine Advocat* newspaper reported after the opening meeting at the track in November 1951 that these gentlemen had complimented Fred Tracey on the way the meeting had been conducted, with noise reduced by 50 percent, leaving all parties happy. Residents in the vicinity of the track were pleased with the early finish and the orderly way in which the crowd departed. One resident commented that he was able to listen to his radio without interference from the speedway.

Case was the last member of the former Walthamstow team to leave the Hackney Wolves when he moved to Wembley for 1938. Phil Hart, Bill Clibbett and Mick Murphy had been lined up to join Walthamstow from Plymouth. All three joined Case, Burton and Haigh at The Wick. Murphy struggled at times and switched to West Ham part-way through the season. Clibbett spent three years with the Hackney Wolves, where he was a solid middle order rider, before transferring to Bristol. Hart found it difficult to retain a team place and was often as a reserve, until he moved to Nottingham midway through 1936. After the next two seasons with Hall Green, he returned to Hackney for 1939 and enjoyed a successful season.

In each of the first three seasons of National League membership, the Hackney Wolves finished fifth in a league of seven teams, six of which were based in London. On dropping to Division Two in 1938 the team finally found success by winning the league title after swapping riders and the track licence with Bristol, who moved into the top division from the former Provincial League. The Wolves were destined to finish in mid-table when the 1939 season was halted by the outbreak of the Second World War. It was another 25 years before speedway returned to Hackney, but the Wolves name was replaced by the Hawks on reopening.

7. Return of the Wolves

Many factories in Walthamstow manufactured items for the war effort, with F Wrighton & Sons Limited switching from furniture to production of de Havilland DH98 Mosquito fighters and bombers. Between 1940 and 1945 the enemy bombing campaign caused a great deal of devastation in the area, as the air raids particularly targeted industry. Between September 1940 and June 1941, during the Blitz, more than 700 bombs were dropped in the district of Waltham Forest. Walthamstow Stadium car park suffered damage when hit by a high explosive on 16 September 1940. This followed a close call eight days earlier when a high explosive fell on a footpath just to the east of the stadium, between Empress Avenue and Cavendish Road. An unexploded shell then landed on the stadium on 20 September. Walthamstow Avenue football ground was less fortunate and took three direct hits on 17 September.

Wartime speedway had been staged at a few tracks, most notably at Belle Vue in Manchester. Only Belle Vue ran meetings regularly during the war. In London, two meetings were held at Crystal Palace in March and April 1940, with West Ham defiantly carrying on until mid-May, at which point the track had hosted six meetings. With many people unable to see much live sport during the war years, it was natural that crowds flocked to see it when restrictions were lifted, and speedway was no different to any other in this respect. There were still some difficulties, one of which arose early in 1947 when the government contemplated banning midweek sport, although the idea was dropped before the start of the speedway season. The government had concerns about the effect of midweek sport on productivity in industrial areas as the country recovered from the war years. This may have influenced Speedway Control Board thinking when considering applications for licencing of some of the proposed new venues.

Speedway returned to the capital when five meetings were staged at New Cross in June and July 1945. Tracks in Bradford (Odsal), Bristol, Exeter (Alphington), Glasgow (White City), Manchester (Belle Vue), Newcastle and Sheffield also staged meetings in 1945. League racing recommenced in 1946, with two leagues of six teams. The National League saw six teams compete, with Belle Vue and Odsal joining four London teams: New Cross, Wembley, West Ham and Wimbledon. The Northern League also had six teams in Birmingham, Glasgow, Middlesbrough, Newcastle, Norwich and Sheffield. Additionally, Bristol, Eastbourne and Rye House staged open meetings. Speedway took place on grass/dirt circuits at Bell End (Holbeach), Eastfield (Peterborough), March and Wisbech. The season was a great success in terms of attendance figures, which served to inspire would-be promoters to look at re-opening other former venues, as well as finding new ones. According to the *Bristol Evening World*, figures reported to the Speedway Control Board showed that 6,623,587 spectators attended at tracks throughout the country in 1946.

Harringay re-opened and joined the National League Division One in 1947. The National League incorporated the Northern League tracks, and three divisions were formed as speedway boomed. From 12 teams in 1946, the leagues grew to 23 tracks in 1947. All the active London tracks were in the top division, racing in front of massive crowds. No changes were made to Division One membership for 1948, but with the other two divisions expanding, the number of league tracks increased to 27. Fans witnessed speedway at Wigan and Cradley Heath for the first time, with Exeter and Tamworth supporters getting their first taste of league speedway. In the early post-war period, the SCB received and refused applications for new tracks at numerous other venues.

The sport had still not reached its early post-war peak in terms of league membership. Although some ventures were short-lived, there were 33 league teams in 1949 and then 34 in 1950. Attendance figures for the 1949 season reached somewhere in the region of 12 million. A sign of things to come was the withdrawal of Southampton from Division Two during the 1951 season, when 36 teams had started in three divisions. By 1952 the Third Division had been replaced by the Southern League and the number of teams across the country had reduced to 32 after Long Eaton folded mid-season. The post-war speedway boom was over, although the same five London teams continued to operate in Division One as in 1947. Throughout the early post-war return of the sport, there was no re-opening of the track at Hackney Wick, which had shut down at the start of hostilities in 1939. When Walthamstow returned to the sport the old nickname of Wolves was adopted.

During the 1948–49 season in Australia, noise complaints had led to a requirement for silencers to be used on speedway bikes in Sydney. Wimbledon rider Alec Statham had welded a silencer to his bike to comply with the requirement and used the same machine in the opening meeting of the 1949 season at Wimbledon. However, silencers were still not a common or mandatory feature of speedway in Britain and were not required until 1977.

Walthamstow Stadium had not remained completely silent. At the beginning of May 1948, the *Sunday Mirror* reported that American Midget Car Racing would be touring the UK, with Stamford Bridge and Walthamstow the first two destinations named. It was announced soon afterwards that special tracks were being laid at these venues, as well as at The Valley, the home of Charlton Athletic Football Club. American millionaire Henry (Bob) Topping, husband of film star Lana Turner, was one of the promoters of the venture. Mr Topping and Ms Turner were in England on their honeymoon at the time. The cars had drivers from America throughout the tour, which was originally intended to last for 10 weeks, with six meetings a week. However, the Home Office gave permission to run for a trial period of only 30 days.

The car racing started on Thursday 13 May 1948 at Stamford Bridge after the first trials had been held at Walthamstow. Unsuitable tracks and negative publicity saw the series end after only three weeks. A particularly scathing assessment of the spectacle in *The Westminster and Pimlico News* described the first event at Stamford Bridge as being greeted with ironic applause and cries of "bring on the greyhounds", as the event "had thrills but lacked spills". According to the *Sunday Dispatch* there was an attendance of around 50,000 for the first staging at Stamford Bridge, but two weeks later only 3,000 turned up. The final meeting of the tour took place at Walthamstow on Friday 4 June, following which the cars and track equipment were transported back to the United States. Bob Topping and his partners in the failed venture were said to have lost between £75,000 and £100,000. This is equivalent to £3 million to £4 million in 2023.

The judgement of Mr Justice Clauson on Wednesday, 12 December 1934 relating to noise from speedway machines was also worded to cover other forms of motor racing. Perhaps the authorities viewed the transient nature of the car racing at Walthamstow Stadium as something which the residents could bear. In any event, the judgement was disregarded when the bikes returned, still lacking silencers, in 1949. However, when permission for speedway to relaunch at the track was granted by the local authority, under the terms of new planning legislation that became operational at the start of July 1948, it was a conditional permission, granted for a three-year period, to end on 31 October 1951.

Speedway journalist Basil Storey described the close season of 1948–49 as an unhappy time for the sport, largely because of the lack of information forthcoming from the SCB to begin with, then because of unpopular decisions eventually reached. From the 1948 season, Wombwell closed, and the Middlesbrough team moved en-bloc to Newcastle, with promoter Johnnie Hoskins having taken his contracted riders from there to a new track at Ashfield in Glasgow. Meanwhile, the continuation of the sport at Sheffield and Fleetwood had also been in doubt for a while.

The *Daily Mirror* reported on 24 November 1948 that five new tracks would be competing in league speedway next season, at Glasgow (Ashfield), Halifax, Liverpool, Oxford and Walthamstow, with 20 applications for new track licences having been submitted. News from the meeting of the SCB on 21 December provided an early Christmas present for speedway fans in north-east London when the make-up of the National League Division Two for 1949 was announced. Walthamstow were one of 11 teams included. Other newcomers to the Second Division were Ashfield, Coventry, Cradley Heath and Southampton. These teams joined existing league members Bristol, Edinburgh, Glasgow, Newcastle, Norwich and Sheffield. Consideration of an application from Fleetwood to continue in the Second Division was deferred, but eventually approved. Bristol, the Second Division champions in 1948, felt aggrieved at being denied promotion when second placed Birmingham were accepted into the top league. There was no system of promotion and relegation in operation between the speedway divisions based on league positions in the previous year.

The decisions announced by the SCB following the meeting were met with dismay in south-west England, where the applications from Exeter and Plymouth to move up from Division Three were rejected. Promoters of the second and third tier teams had voted in favour of the elevation of both teams. Exeter had convincingly won the Third Division in 1948 so had particular cause to feel unjustly treated. The promoted teams, Cradley Heath, Southampton and Coventry, had finished second, third and eighth respectively in the previous season, with Plymouth seventh and Walthamstow not even competing since 1934.

The SCB decisions were described as baffling in the south-west, with the *Western Daily Press* publishing details from the deliberations. Initially, the promoters met the SCB on Monday 20 December for 4½ hours, agreeing to form a Second Division with two sections of nine teams each, on a north and south split. Plymouth and Exeter were to be in the southern section, as would Walthamstow. When the Board met again the following day, it reversed the decision and decided to continue with Second and Third Divisions. Billy Eastmond, the Exeter manager, told the *Western Daily Press* that he thought it grossly unfair to overlook Exeter and Plymouth and yet allow Walthamstow to come straight into the Second Division. Mr Eastmond added that when he asked the SCB chairman, Colonel RVC Brook, what importance was attached to Exeter's Third Division championship win, he was told "nothing". Jim Wolfenden of Fleetwood was equally surprised to learn that a decision on Fleetwood's participation in the division had been deferred as he had been led to believe that it was assured beforehand. The Midlands press commented that the omission of the Devon clubs from Division Two was due to the tracks being geographically misplaced for a competition with the three Scottish clubs. In early February the Exeter promoter, WTJ Eastmond, was told by the SCB that they rejected his plea for promotion because they considered attendance figures at the track were not sufficient to enable payment of the higher prize money rates in Division Two. The Board later disclosed that concerns had been expressed about the number of loan riders at Exeter and considered that the track would be unviable if these riders were recalled by their parent clubs.

Walthamstow would be the only London team in the division, in stark contrast to the short season in 1934, when six of the nine teams in the top tier were London-based. As soon as membership of the Second Division was confirmed, it was announced that Walthamstow speedway would be managed by 39-year-old Wally Lloyd. He was a recently retired speedway rider who began his career at the Birmingham Hall Green track in 1928. Before the War he rode for nine teams in 11 seasons: Birmingham Perry Barr, Crystal Palace, Lea Bridge, Southampton, Clapton, Hackney Wick, Wembley and Wimbledon. Before retiring, he spent three post-war seasons with Belle Vue.

On 5 January 1949, Walthamstow confirmed the signing of Wilf Jay, who had ridden for Newcastle in 1948. Two days, later the transfer of Dick Geary from Fleetwood to Walthamstow was announced. Geary had been Fleetwood's top scorer in 1948, but lived in London and wanted a club nearer home. Further signings of Bill Osborne, from Bradford, and Dick Shepherd, from Hull, were made by mid-February. £2,400 was spent in the transfer market on these four team members. Fred Tuck, a tall scorer with Bristol in 1948, was then linked with Walthamstow. Southampton also asked about him, but he eventually stayed put.

Another decision by the SCB in early February was that all new tracks must have cinder surfaces, as part of a move towards standardisation. Where existing tracks were formed of decomposed granite or sand a decision would be made by the Board's technical sub-committee on what the minimum loose riding surface should be. Other news in February was that a parliamentary agent had been appointed to aid the SCB in its efforts to reduce the Entertainment Duty levied on speedway. The rate of duty was between 45 percent and 48 percent, with the exact rate varying on a scale according to each club's admission prices. In support of the fight, speedway followers throughout the country were asked to sign organised petitions. A committee of MPs arranged to send a deputation to the Chancellor of the Exchequer, with a member of the SCB and a track promoter included in the group.

In previewing the season, Basil Storey said Walthamstow would succeed, as London fans had become tired of watching the same handful of teams over and over in Division One. The opportunity to see new riders and teams in Division Two would be an exciting prospect. It was because of this that the other London-based teams, all in Division One, did not embrace the reopening of Walthamstow with open arms.

Walthamstow Stadium was well-served by public transport, being accessible by four bus routes and six trolley bus services. Trains were also available to Hoe Street station, later renamed Walthamstow Central.

8. 1949: An indifferent start

When the Mayor of Walthamstow, Councillor Miss D Wrigley, officially reopened the track for speedway in 1949, she hoped that the Wolves would be a howling success. Although it was generally felt among the speedway press that a good squad had been assembled ahead of the new season, there were various factors which might impact on its success or otherwise.

Five members of the team had previous experience of league racing and were expected to form a competitive spearhead. However, the riders making up the balance of the team were all new to league racing and were an unknown quantity. Three Wolves riders had ridden in the pre-war era. Wilf Jay had enjoyed success in the second tier of speedway with Norwich before and after the War and was expected to be a leading rider with the Wolves. Dick Geary also had some experience just before the War with West Ham, as well as making a few appearances for Glasgow and Sheffield. Charlie May rode at Southampton before the War and made a couple of appearances as a reserve.

Dick Geary was the top ranked acquisition, but he had broken his arm in a crash at Tamworth in October 1948 and was not recovered sufficiently to ride in the Wolves team for the first four meetings. Wilf Jay was an established leading rider at Second Division level and Charlie May had been a reliable scorer at the same level in 1948. They were expected to receive good backing from the less experienced Bill Osborne and Dick Shepherd, both having performed well in the Third Division. If the team was to have a successful season, rapid progress would be required from the newcomers, two Englishmen and two Australians.

Ted Argall took the place of Geary in the main part of the team for the opening matches. Both Argall and Harold Bull had limited experience on Australian tracks and were likely to take time to adapt to racing on the smaller British circuits. Bull started the season at reserve with Reg Reeves. Harry Edwards took the other spot in the main body of the team.

The *Speedway World* newspaper ran a training school in the winter of 1948. Sessions were held at Rye House and High Beech, giving novices the opportunity to develop their skills on two very different tracks. Of the 145 riders given trials, 28 were rewarded with contracts with teams at the beginning of 1949. Reeves and Edwards were products of the training school, with Walthamstow speedway manager Wally Lloyd also reporting that he had taken on Ed Williams and Harry Du Paauw, although neither rode in official races at the track.

When speedway returned to Walthamstow, various changes were evident compared to the previous time racing was staged there in 1934. The straights had been shortened, so the post-war track was considerably smaller at 282 yards to the lap. It was now only 20 yards longer per lap than the tiny New Cross circuit. On the death of William Chandler in 1946, the venue passed to his eight children in equal shares. Charles Chandler, the eldest, became the managing director. In the interim period, improvements had been made to facilities and the grandstands had been further developed. The team race jackets now featured three horizontal red 'Wolves'. For 1949, the traditional toss of the coin to choose starting gate positions was dispensed with and the visiting team now had the choice of starting positions before every heat, with a choice of gates one and three or two and four. Also introduced for 1949 was the requirement for clutch levers to be ball-ended as a safety measure. The ball had to be not less than one inch in diameter and to be brazed or welded on to the clutch lever. Additionally, the clutch lever had to be cut down so as not to exceed five inches in length from the fulcrum to the end of the ball.

Referring back to the issues of 1934, the match programmes carried a reminder to spectators that rattles and noise instruments were strictly prohibited in order to keep noise levels down. Supporters were invited to enjoy themselves at the weekly dances in the Senior Club after the meetings, when all riders were in attendance. In order to limit the volume of the public address system, a light was illuminated on the starting box to indicate that an announcement was about to be made. Spectators were advised to be quiet in order to hear the announcements. The Hall Green track in Birmingham had closed at the end of the 1938 season, with one of the factors being increased threats of legal action by residents over noise levels. Even when the track was operating, conditions imposed by the city council when granting an entertainments licence were restrictive. Like Walthamstow, there were houses in roads adjacent to the track. Birmingham Council specified that only essential loudspeaker announcements could be made, music and community singing by spectators was not allowed, with no rattles or bells permitted to be used either in the stadium or the surrounding streets. The Walthamstow management took great care to ensure that noise levels were kept to a minimum to avoid a repetition of the problems encountered in 1934.

As the 1949 season began, fans were invited to join the Walthamstow Supporters' Club. Membership cost 2/6 (2 shillings and sixpence), inclusive of a badge. Weekly dances were held in the Senior Club after the completion of racing. Membership of the Senior Club cost 21/- (21 shillings) a year and subscribers were also entitled to access the Junior Club on the popular side of the track. The annual charge for membership of the Junior Club was 2/-, but admission to the popular side of the track was cheaper. Merchandise was available from kiosks, with photographs of riders priced at 6d and rosettes in team colours at 1/9. Stickers for cars were free of charge and pennants were available priced 3/6 for cars and 2/6 for cycles and motorcycles. Jack Buck from Leyton was the club secretary, assisted by area secretaries Miss E Dowding and Mr Hill, both from Walthamstow. Supporters were encouraged to roar on the team with a war cry of '1, 2, 3, 4, who are we for, W O L V E S, Wolves.'

April

After completion of the reopening ceremony, Walthamstow Wolves battled to a draw against newly promoted Southampton on Monday 4 April. The visitors had finished third in Division Three in 1948, since when they had lost their top rider, Alf Bottoms, recalled by First Division Wembley in exchange for Roy Craighead. The Wolves badly missed the absent Geary, although they could have won, but for a series of falls. Charlie May fell twice and Wilf Jay once. May and Jay dropped only one point between them in their other rides. In one race, May led into the first bend, but thinking he saw a red light he slowed, letting the other three riders past him. He then realised that the red light was a restaurant sign.

The Australians, Argall and Bull, failed to master the track and fell in three of their combined five rides. Wolves led by two points going into the final heat but, after Jay fell, the experienced Saints duo of Jimmy Squibb and Tom Oakley looked certain to take the maximum points needed for victory in the match. Debutant Harry Edwards then rode brilliantly to pass Oakley in the race for the line, thus ensuring a share of the match points. Bob Oakley set the fastest time of the meeting when he won heat 12 in 66.2 seconds.

There was an element of confusion when Jay and Shepherd came out wearing the wrong helmet colours in the opening heat. This resulted in Shepherd being announced as the race winner instead of Jay, an error spotted and recorded by the *Speedway Gazette* reporter. The error was not noted by other publications and records continued to contain the error.

George Burrows, managing director of the firm of brokers which handled accident insurance for the Speedway Riders Association, was at the opening meeting and was concerned regarding the last bend, which caused the riders some difficulty. Although admitting that the spills added to the thrills, Burrows made the point that his company would prefer the thrills and spills to not involve injuries.

Conditions were dreadful for the return match at Southampton the following day, and the Wolves slipped to a 23-point defeat in heavy rain. Walthamstow riders managed to win only three races and were no match for the home stars Bob Oakley, Roy Craighead and Cecil Bailey, who between them outscored the visitors. Bill Osborne gave a promising performance to top the Wolves scorers with eight points. It was inevitable that most races were won from the gate and after a track inspection by the ACU Steward the second half was abandoned.

On 8 April, the Wolves had another heavy defeat, this time by 20 points at Cradley Heath, who were also newly promoted from Division Three. Only Wilf Jay and Charlie May offered any significant resistance to the home team, with the inexperienced quartet of Edwards, Reeves, Argall and Bull gathering only five points between them. This time the Wolves managed four race wins, two by Charlie May who was top scorer with 10. The lack of race winners was a concern, showing that the team needed Geary to quickly return and that it may still require further strengthening. Rising star Alan Hunt was impressive for Cradley Heath and won all his races with ease.

Three days later, on 11 April, Sheffield were the next visitors to Walthamstow Stadium, advertised as The 'Stow but popularly described as 'The Stow' without the apostrophe. It was clear before the season started that Bristol, Norwich and Sheffield had the strongest teams in the division. Still without Geary, the home team put up a good fight before going down to a three-point defeat. Walthamstow had signed the experienced Arch Windmill for £400 from First Division Wimbledon in time for the meeting, but were denied permission to include him by the SCB. Windmill was another Wolves rider with pre-war experience, having performed well for Hackney. His post-war outings for Wimbledon were mainly inauspicious because he usually occupied a reserve berth. However, he had one particularly memorable occasion, in a match at Wembley in May 1947. The Lions were leading the league table at the time and the Dons were struggling near the bottom. A home win was on the cards as Wembley led by eight points with six heats left. Arch had already beaten the home star Bill Kitchen in his first ride before partnering Norman Parker to a maximum heat win in the ninth race. The Lions came back to once more lead by eight points, with just three heats to go. Windmill won two of those heats to end the match unbeaten by the opposition, becoming a club legend as Wimbledon snatched a one-point success.

Against Sheffield, Wilf Jay and Charlie May both accumulated 11 points and received good backing from Reg Reeves. The meeting could have provided the Wolves with a first league success, but for a fall by Dick Shepherd. He was leading in heat 11 when his bike lifted and threw him head-first into the fence on the pits bend. Shepherd suffered head, neck and back injuries, which ruled him out for the rest of the season. In the re-run Osborne and Semmens dead-heated for second place behind Allott and what had looked like a 4–2 race success became a three-point reverse. To make matters worse, Shepherd had to be replaced by a reserve in his final ride. In that heat the home reserves were paired together and went down to a 4–2 defeat.

A report in *Track News Weekly* commented that Australian Ted Argall made a hash of things in every ride, falling three times during the evening. He was clearly having difficulty coming to terms with a small track. Jack Bibby had a mechanical failure in the fifth heat and, with the Sheffield rider out of the race, Bill Osborne was given an ovation by the crowd when he walked his bike home for a point after falling. Bibby was the only rider from the regular 1934 Wolves team to return to Walthamstow after the War. However, because of the significant change to the size of the circuit he gained no benefit from his previous racing experience there.

The strength of the Norwich team was evident in a 32-point home win when the Wolves visited The Firs on 16 April. The Stars provided 12 of the 14 heat winners, with both Paddy Mills and Phil Clarke scoring maximums. Wilf Jay and Reg Reeves were the only Wolves riders to win a race. Harold Bull was dropped from the Wolves line-up for this meeting as Dick Geary made a welcome return to the side. Geary struggled to have any impact, however, with just three third places in four outings. Windmill had been given SCB permission to ride, although only as cover for Dick Shepherd, who was still in Whipps Cross Hospital.

With Geary and Windmill in the team for the visit of Newcastle two days later, the home team secured an emphatic 48–16 win. Newcastle had a solid group of riders supporting star men Jack and Frank Hodgson, but could not deny the home team their first victory of the season. Geary recorded a good second place in his first ride, but faded to score only four, the same as home debutant Windmill. Geary's arm was causing him some difficulty in handling his machine, whereas Windmill had problems with his motor. Bill Osborne lost control and collided with Frank Hodgson as he attempted an inside pass on the Newcastle rider in the first heat. Osborne sprained his ankle and was replaced by the reserves in his last two rides.

The lesser lights in the Walthamstow team were improving. Reg Reeves was paired with Charlie May in the main body of the team and scored six points, and three bonus points for following his race partner home in a scoring position. Harry Edwards impressed with seven points from three rides and Ted Argall, mounted on a new machine, had his best meeting to date with four points and a bonus. Bonus points in team events are used in assessing race averages and calculating payments to riders but are not included in the match scores. They are awarded when a rider finishes in a scoring position immediately behind his team partner and were introduced to encourage pairs to race as a team rather than against each other. Team-mates can also ride together to block overtaking manoeuvres by following riders.

With no time to rest after the Newcastle encounter the Wolves were on their travels to Glasgow for a meeting the next day, 19 April, against Ashfield Giants and then White City the following day. A defeat by 12 points against the Giants was followed by a 20-point reverse at the hands of the Tigers. Walthamstow had the honour of providing the opposition at the opening of the Ashfield track. They got off to a bad start when Wilf Jay was left at the tapes in his first heat and the Wolves trailed 10–2 after two races. Jay and Charlie May put up spirited resistance, accounting for half of their team's score between them, but Dick Geary continued to struggle and managed a single point. There was no stopping Ken Le Breton, who was undefeated for the home side.

May and Jay were defeated just once each at White City, a track which, at 440 yards, was almost twice the length of their home circuit. Although White City had very long straights, it had bends not dissimilar to The Stow. Walthamstow made a better start to lead by two points after the third heat, before the home team took control and ran out easy victors. The home riders adapted better to a track made difficult by heavy rain and Will Lowther led the scoring, also dropping just a single point.

There was a good following to watch the Wolves take on Coventry at Brandon on Saturday 23 April. This was the nearest fixture Walthamstow had to a local derby in the Second Division, but the distance between the two tracks was still over 90 miles. The supporters had a grand day out, leaving Walthamstow by coach at 11.30am, taking tea at the Brandon Hall Hotel at 5.30pm, arriving at the track in time for a 7.30pm start. The day was rounded off with an organised supper in the Bees supporters' club before the return journey.

The travelling fans were rewarded by their team putting on a good show, going down by a narrow margin of six points. Wilf Jay was in fine form as he recorded a 12-point maximum and equalled the track record time of 76.6 seconds in his second ride. May and Osborne gave good support on this occasion, but Geary continued to struggle and managed only two points.

By the time that Norwich visited The Stow on 25 April, there was good news that Dick Shepherd had been discharged from hospital. There was optimism that he might return to take his team place before the end of the season, but it was not to be.

Against strong opposition the Wolves came close to winning the match when leading by a point going into the final heat. They lost the race 5–1 when the visitors led from the tapes against Reg Reeves and Jay, who was struggling with flu-like symptoms. With Jay out of sorts and scoring only four points, Arch Windmill stepped up and recorded his best score to date with nine. For Norwich, Paddy Mills and Phil Clarke were unbeaten by the home riders. Mills also set a new track record of 65.8 seconds. Dick Geary took three rides, but failed to score. In his six meetings to date he had notched 13 points from 22 rides. As he had averaged nearly 10 points per match in the league in 1948, it was clear that his form was the biggest single factor in the lack of success for Walthamstow. At this stage the Wolves had one win and a draw from four home matches, with no reward from six away meetings.

The team was clocking up the miles, as further fixtures at Fleetwood on 27 April and Sheffield the next day completed a gruelling schedule of eight meetings in 13 days. This may have accounted for the lacklustre performances which resulted in heavy defeats by 24 and 27 points respectively.

At Fleetwood, the match was as good as over after three races, with the home team already 10 points ahead. Dick Geary scored five points, but was a shadow of his former self on his return to the track where he had previously been the leading scorer. For the Flyers, Wilf Plant and George Newton scored maximums and Ernie Appleby was unbeaten by the opposition, as the home team provided 12 of the 14 heat winners. The Fleetwood riders were certainly flying as the previous track record was beaten eight times during the match.

The next evening the top three riders for Sheffield were instrumental in leading their team to a decisive win. Bruce Semmens, Stan Williams and Len Williams were all undefeated by the opposition as the home side supplied the winner in 13 heats. Only Jay and May gained any credit for their performances for Walthamstow. Ted Argall fell in his first ride and broke his leg which ruled him out for the rest of the season. Dick Geary was disappointing, managing three third places on one of his former tracks.

May

A long overdue second victory was hard-earned when Ashfield visited The Stow on 2 May, with the Wolves triumphing by just five points. The home team was a single point in front after the penultimate race. Then, Wilf Jay and Charlie May took the lead from the start to secure the match points. Success had appeared unlikely when the away team led by nine points after two heats, as Jay and Reeves both fell in the first race, before Osborne was excluded for a starting infringement in the second. The Giants still led by two points after heat 12, but successive 5–1 heat wins, first by Osborne and Edwards, then by Jay and May, snatched victory for the Wolves. Osborne carried on despite great pain from an ankle injury following a collision with Alec Grant in his second ride.

With Argall injured, Harold Bull was named in the programme as his replacement, but did not arrive in time and Harry Edwards took the reserve rides. He responded with one of his best performances to date, scoring four plus three bonus points. Geary showed glimpses of better form, winning his first race and picking up two further points when second to Ken Le Breton in his final outing.

An article by Dick Geary in *Speedway World* in May described the difficulty he was experiencing in controlling his speedway machine, due to lack of strength in the arm he had broken at the end of the previous season. He was still having treatment, but found that the hectic schedule following his return had hampered his progress. Team captain Geary added that he expected to improve and mentioned that Bill Osborne had also been carrying an ankle injury after his collision with Newcastle's Frank Hodgson. Harry Edwards was said to be still slowly regaining health and fitness after suffering malnutrition during four years as a prisoner of war in the Far East.

After a few days rest, the team took a break from league racing to visit third division Hull for a challenge match on 7 May. Hull had a good home record and held their visitors to a draw. Charlie May had a subdued time, scoring only four points. Jay, Reeves and Osborne scored well, but the most pleasing performance was by Dick Geary, equal top scorer with nine points. His four races included two wins, although his cautious riding was reflected in the fact that they produced two of the three slowest winning times of the match.

A strong Cradley Heath team visited Walthamstow in a return to league action on 9 May and the match saw some odd events. In the first race, Les Beaumont, the Cradley Heath captain, caused the race to be stopped when he crashed on the last bend of the first lap. The ACU Steward ordered a rerun, but instead of excluding Beaumont, as the cause of the stoppage, allowed a reserve, Geoff Godwin, to replace him. Godwin took second place, but fortunately the incorrect application of the rules by the steward did not affect the match outcome; the Wolves won by six points. Harold Bull was again programmed as second reserve for the home team, but was replaced in both rides by the other reserve, Harry Edwards. Edwards had his best meeting to date, with two wins in his nine-point return. The *Speedway World* reporter insisted that the substitutions were against the rules and Bull should have ridden.

Charlie May had a successful meeting, winning all his rides, including two in the second half Cradley Scratch Race event. He received good support from Jay, Osborne and Edwards. Unfortunately, Dick Geary gained only one point and that was in his last ride when he beat Les Beaumont.

The Supporters' Club held its first social evening and dance at Grove House, High Road, Leyton on Thursday, 12 May, enjoyed by over 200 members. Also in attendance were manager Wally Lloyd, riders Ted Argall, Harold Bull, Harry Edwards and Reg Reeves, together with Cliff Watson of West Ham. Ted Argall was unable to participate in the dancing because he was on crutches, with his broken leg in plaster. The event made a profit of £7/8 and this was handed over to the injured riders, Argall and Dick Shepherd.

The early season rush of team fixtures eased and the next event at Chingford Road was a best pairs event on 16 May, won by Les Jenkins and Ken Adams from Third Division Hanley (Stoke). Two home pairings tied for second place. Harry Edwards scored nine and Bill Osborne added eight to total 17 points. This was matched by Charlie May and Dick Geary, with May beaten only by Jenkins in scoring 14. May was on top form and four days later he set a new Leicester track record of 74.4 seconds on his way to winning a World Championship Qualifying Round with a maximum 15 points.

With Belle Vue away to Bradford on their usual Saturday race night, Walthamstow and Sheffield were booked in to face each other in a 12-heat challenge match with six-man teams at the Manchester track. The meeting on 21 May resulted in an easy win for the Wolves, 42–20. Dick Geary was comfortable on the big track and was only beaten once by an opposing rider in four races. May and Edwards also shone in a meeting which saw the first appearance for the Wolves of Belle Vue rider Jim Boyd. Boyd, considered to be a small track specialist, joined Walthamstow on loan and made his league debut in a 42–42 draw at home to Fleetwood two days later, on 23 May. He had started riding before the War, gaining useful experience with Southampton as well as impressing in meetings at non-league Oxford.

Following his run of poor scores, Dick Geary was relegated to a reserve slot for the Fleetwood encounter and he responded by recording a win and a second in his two rides. Jim Boyd top scored with nine points and although only providing five heat winners, the team scored solidly throughout to collect a league point. Charlie May took a heavy fall in his first outing and missed another ride as a result. Although badly shaken and having a swollen ankle, he was able to ride in the final heat, which he won. With Jay coming in third, the two-point deficit was wiped out. Jay was below par and scored only six points. Fleetwood owed much to their top order riders, Wilf Plant scoring a maximum and Norman Hargreaves being beaten only by May in the crucial last heat.

George Newton scored well for Fleetwood after a first ride engine failure, setting a new track record time of 65.4 seconds while defeating Boyd in the heat eight. Newton had the support of a large contingent of fans from New Cross, his previous club. Newton was a member of the New Cross team which won the National League title in 1938 before illness ruled him out of speedway for 10 years. On his return to New Cross in 1948 he was again a member of a league championship winning team.

Walthamstow now had a stronger team than that which started the season. The experience and scoring power of Boyd made up for the loss of Dick Shepherd; Geary was beginning to score well having come into the team in place of Bull and Windmill's scores were an improvement on the contributions from Argall. A trip to Bristol for a league encounter on 27 May immediately brought the Wolves back down to earth. The strong home side emphatically won by 36 points. Jim Boyd was the solitary heat winner for the visitors. Putting the result into context, the Bristol Bulldogs team was invincible at home and had already scored 60 points or more in defeating Fleetwood twice, Newcastle, Edinburgh, Coventry and Ashfield. In the second visit of Fleetwood the home team had dropped just a single point in the match. Sheffield had been the only visiting team to put up much resistance at Knowle Stadium and they still lost by 55 points to 29. It was unsurprising that Bristol ended the season 10 points clear of second placed Sheffield in the league table.

A visit the following day to Third Division Rayleigh gave the Wolves an opportunity to regain some confidence and they won the challenge match by a point. Harold Bull made a rare appearance in place of Charlie May. Boyd top-scored again, Arch Windmill was paid for maximum points and Geary had two wins in his total of eight. Jay had a disappointing meeting with four from three rides and his form had dipped over the last few matches. Ted Argall and his wife accompanied around 200 members of the Supporters' Club to the meeting.

Several teams had been looking to strengthen and there were suggestions that Bill Kemp might be on the verge of transferring to Walthamstow from Cradley Heath, but he preferred to ride another season in the Third Division and joined Oxford instead. At the same time, Charles Ochiltree, the Coventry manager, was contemplating making an offer for Wilf Jay. Jay had impressed when scoring a maximum in the league encounter at Brandon.

At the end of May, it was revealed that police were looking for a man who had been collecting door-to-door donations of 10 shillings from residents, supposedly with a view to funding an injunction against Walthamstow speedway. The management of the club might have feared a repeat of the situation which arose in 1934, but nothing came of it.

Walthamstow were drawn against Southampton in the National Trophy, with the first leg on Monday 30 May and the return at Banister Court the following day. In the league encounters at the beginning of the season, the Saints had come out well on top overall, but the cup clashes promised to be much closer. Not only did the Wolves race to an emphatic 19-point win in the first leg, but they also triumphed in the away match, by four points to progress to the next round.

Walthamstow Wolves 1949: Charlie May, John Deeley (Manager), Arch Windmill, Jim Boyd, Benny King, Bill Osborne, Harry Edwards, Reg Reeves, Dick Geary (on bike) (JSC)

Ray Duggan (Harringay) and Benny King (Walthamstow) at Green Lanes in the London Cup on 12 August 1949. (JSC)

Charlie May was the star for Walthamstow, following up his score of 16 from six rides at home with a paid maximum from five races in the return. Jim Boyd also rode well in the first match, scoring double figures from six outings, before stunning the Southampton fans with an 18-point maximum the next night. The performance of Harry Edwards at Banister Court was remarkable. He was unbeaten in his two rides despite having a high temperature and acute stomach trouble. The rest of the team gave good support over the two legs and the results suggested that the Wolves might start to climb from their lowly league position.

At the end of May the Supporters' Club announced that a small party, selected at random, would be invited to the Senior Club after each meeting, the proviso being that they must be over 18 years of age, possess a membership card and badge, as well as having purchased a match programme. The party would have a reserved table in the ballroom and could join in the dancing.

June

Edwards had almost a week to recover before the next meeting, at home to Newcastle on 6 June. All of the home riders contributed well except Wilf Jay in a 50–34 win against his former team. Charlie May led the way with a maximum, supported by Boyd with a double figure score. Boyd would almost certainly have been unbeaten by the opposition, but for a fall in his first ride, although he remounted to score a point as Close had also fallen. Jay ran two last places and managed just three points. He was soon to return to Newcastle, known in 1949 as the Magpies, in an exchange deal involving Benny King. King impressed as top scorer for his side with nine. The Wolves' success in this meeting was due to providing 11 heat winners and filling most of the minor places.

George Newton's track record time of 65.4 seconds was equalled twice during the match, first by Charlie May in the third heat and then by Jim Boyd two races later. June saw the record beaten three times in successive weeks by different home riders, showing that they had mastered their own circuit.

Frank Arthur, Australian speedway promoter and a former leading pioneer rider, was at The Stow for the Newcastle match. He was visiting the country with a view to putting together a team to tour Australia during the winter and was accompanied by *Speedway News* editor RM 'Sammy' Samuels.

In the return match at Brough Park two days later, on 8 June, Walthamstow celebrated their first away league victory, by two points. Charlie May and Jim Boyd were now a potent spearhead, both scoring double figures. The partnership of Wilf Jay and Reg Reeves was solid, although Reeves recorded two race wins and outscored his more experienced partner for the second meeting in a row. Dick Geary managed two third places and struggled again. This was disappointing after he had recorded three second places behind his team partner in the home meeting. The victory saw the Wolves record their first double in the league, following closely on the National Trophy home and away successes against Southampton.

Although changes were being considered, the first announcement was a surprise when Dublin-born Tom Turnham transferred from Third Division Liverpool to the Wolves. Turnham was living in Hoe Street, Walthamstow, at the time but before he had an opportunity to appear for the team he moved again, this time on loan to Third Division Rayleigh. In his limited appearances for Liverpool, Turnham had averaged just three points per meeting.

A qualifying round of the World Championship was staged at Walthamstow on 13 June. The winner's cheque was taken by a meeting reserve. This was the first time this had happened in the history of the championship; Jim Boyd was the successful rider. He had not joined Walthamstow in time to be entered for the qualifiers, but came in for George Craig, who was ruled out with broken ribs. Norwegian rider Leif Samsing took part in the meeting, but failed to impress, scoring two points. Three days earlier, Charlie May had bad luck in his qualifying round at Cradley Heath, a broken footrest meant he failed to finish his first heat and he missed his second as well. He came back strongly to score eight points from his other three rides. For the second week in succession the track record was equalled, this time by Bob Baker of Third Division Hull in heat two. His name was only in the record books for a few minutes, however, with a new record of 65.2 seconds being set by home rider Jim Boyd in heat five.

Edinburgh was the destination for the next league meeting for the Wolves on 18 June. This was Wilf Jay's final appearance for Walthamstow and he started well with two race wins, beating home stars Clem Mitchell and Dick Campbell, before finishing with a third place and a last. Jay explained that he was disappointed with his form at Walthamstow and felt that a move back to Newcastle would revitalise him.

He did not enjoy the journey to the north-east London track from his Rotherham, Yorkshire, home and this was another factor in his request for a move. Charlie May rode well to record double figures, inflicting the only defeat on Australian star Jack Young in the process. It was yet another disappointing match for Geary as he managed just two third places, with the Wolves defeated by six points.

An epic battle with Cradley Heath in the second round of stage two of the National Trophy began at Walthamstow on 20 June. The competition consisted of three stages, third division teams contesting stage one, the winner going through to stage two. The Division Two teams entered at the second stage, with the winners going on to join the Division One teams in stage three. A fine performance resulted in a 25-point lead for the home team to take to the return leg.

The meeting was full of incident, beginning with Walthamstow debutant Benny King setting a new track record of 64.8 seconds in the opening heat. The race should have been stopped as Eric Williams fell and lay on the track for a while after clipping his partner's rear wheel. Wilf Jay's wish to return to Newcastle had been granted, much to the dismay of Charles Ochiltree, Coventry's manager, who believed that a deal was agreed for him to move there. At the last minute, the Magpies management offered an exchange deal including King plus a fee of £400, which Walthamstow immediately accepted. This arrangement suited King and Walthamstow, as the former West Ham rider was based in London and a rider-exchange ensured that the Wolves would not be a man short. Benny King had been due to move to Newcastle at the beginning of the season with the former Middlesbrough team, but in early April he asked the SCB to arbitrate because he wished to ride for a southern team. He eventually rode in a few meetings for Newcastle, including the league match at Walthamstow when he was top scorer.

An eventful heat 11 saw Jack Arnfield fall, with Bill Osborne laying down his machine to avoid him. Alan Hunt fell and tried to push home, but a damaged wheel chain stopped him, leaving Charlie May to finish the race alone. Harry Edwards and Eric Williams collided in heat 17, with Edwards excluded. Williams attempted to push his bike for a point, but was excluded when he was lapped. Charlie May was outstanding for the Wolves, winning five races after finishing second to team partner Jim Boyd first time out. Boyd was also unbeaten by the opposition after a fall in his first heat. King's remaining rides were less eventful as he totalled eight points.

The after-meeting gatherings were popular with riders from other tracks. After the Cradley Heath match the dance was attended by Wembley's Split Waterman and Bruce Abernethy, along with Malcolm Craven from West Ham, Buck Whitby of Birmingham and Rayleigh's Charlie Mugford. The Wolves riders were also present.

The Wolves team would have been confident of progressing to the next round of the competition when they travelled to Dudley Wood for the second leg four days later, but cruel luck in the final heat left the aggregate scores level, meaning the tie needed to be replayed. May gave another superb performance in scoring 17 points, losing only to Australian Jack Arnfield. He, in turn, had only been beaten by May prior to the eventful final heat. In the deciding race, Arnfield and Williams faced May and King. Williams had also ridden well, dropping two points to the opposition in his five rides, with King having a steady, if unspectacular, match to score eight points. The home team went into the race one point ahead on aggregate and just needed to share the heat to win the tie. May led from Arnfield and Williams, which was sufficient for Cradley Heath, but Arnfield tried an outside pass and fell. With the race now looking like a 4–2 win for the visitors; the outcome would have been a one-point overall success for them. King then had the misfortune to have an engine failure and pulled out of the race to leave the aggregate score level at 105–105.

Although the next home match on 27 June saw a resounding victory over Edinburgh Monarchs by a 32-point margin in a meeting described by *Track News Weekly* as an unexciting encounter, it did feature some events worthy of note. Benny King showed his liking for his new home track and had his only defeat in his final ride when Dick Campbell registered one of just two heat wins for the visitors. The other success for the Monarchs was provided by Jack Young in the penultimate race. The future double world champion had a quiet match and scored a meagre five points. May made a poor start in the final heat and was in so much trouble on the first bend that he found himself the length of the back straight behind. Riding superbly, he missed taking second place behind his team partner by a fraction. He was otherwise unbeaten as he scored double figures for the eighth match in a row.

All the home riders scored well and but for some misfortune, the winning margin could have been even greater. Reg Reeves dropped two points through engine failure in one race and Bill Osborne had a broken chain when leading Young off the last bend in heat 13.

Charlie May faced veteran Wembley and England star Bill Kitchen in a special match after the interval and triumphed by two races to nil, setting a new track record of 64.0 seconds in the process. Kitchen had been one of the top riders in the country in the immediate pre-war and post-war seasons until he broke his arm injury in 1948. He was still riding well enough to finish sixth in the 1949 World Championship Final and May's performance against him underlined his good form at the time.

At Sheffield, however, on the last day of June for their second league encounter, the Wolves put up a much-improved performance but still lost by 12 points. Five Walthamstow riders each won a heat, but Sheffield were particularly strong on their own circuit and the meeting was virtually decided by heat 10. Dick Geary's up-and-down form continued as he finished as second top scorer. The bigger tracks seemed to cause him less trouble than the small circuits with tight bends.

July

Walthamstow gained a useful first leg advantage against Cradley Heath in the replay of the National Trophy tie when the teams met again on Monday 4 July, this time coming out on top 62–44. After an extremely hot day, the track was very dry to begin with and the meeting was marred by several falls. There was a hosepipe ban in force in the area and the track staff were unable to water the track. Clouds of dust obscured the view of the action, particularly on the pits bend, but then rain came to the rescue part-way through the meeting.

Phil Malpass was excluded from the first race after bringing down Dick Geary, who aggravated his arm injury in the crash. Geary fell again in his second race and after a pointless third ride, pulled out of the meeting. Malpass was also shaken and failed to score in the match. Harry Edwards and Alan Hunt collided in heat 11 and their machines became entangled. As Edwards lay against the safety fence, Hunt skilfully steered both machines clear of the fallen rider. Earlier, Hunt pushed his bike for 50 yards in the fifth race when his engine failed, but he was excluded after being lapped. He had won his first race, but was exhausted following his exertions and added only three more points to his total.

After heat 13, the home team led by just four points, before securing an emphatic win by scoring maximums in four of the last five races after the rain came. Cradley's Jack Arnfield won his first five races, but fell when leading heat 18. Charlie May was ill with a high temperature and did well to only drop a single point in his first three rides, before a last place in his final outing. Two days later May, still feeling unwell, was eliminated from the World Championship in a qualifying round at Glasgow White City, despite winning three races and beating Jack Young and Sweden's Olle Nygren in the process. An exclusion for a starting offence in his first ride and an engine failure in his fourth cost him dearly.

In the return leg of the cup replay on 8 July, the Heathens wiped out the first leg deficit before the meeting had reached the halfway point and went on to win by 34 points on the night. None of the Wolves team shone, with only two race wins, courtesy of May and Osborne. Arnfield and Hunt were in scintillating form for the home team, both being unbeaten by the opposition in six rides.

Walthamstow made up for the disappointment of their display in the National Trophy by thrashing a weak Coventry team 67–17 in a league encounter on 11 July. Remarkably, the Bees took the lead by winning the first heat 4–2, but they had no answer to the home team's onslaught thereafter, every race being won 5–1. Dick Geary and Benny King were the Wolves riders who tasted defeat in the opening race. This was only after Coventry's Bob Fletcher hit the fence causing Geary to take avoiding action, allowing Ed Pye to take the lead. Harry Edwards won all of his races, setting the four fastest times of the match in the process, although afterwards he was quick to praise the team-riding skills of his race partner Jim Boyd. Edwards and Reg Reeves were fully justifying the faith shown in them by the management at the start of the year. Charlie May was on top form after recovering from a bout of influenza. Coventry finished the season at the bottom of the league table.

Dick Geary and Harold Bull were both commended by the SCB for their actions during the meeting. The Control Board Bulletin dated 20 July said that both had shown gallant conduct in quickly and skilfully laying down their machines to avoid running into fallen riders. The bulletin added that the commendations had been entered on their records.

With half of the league fixtures completed by Walthamstow, seven meetings had been won, two drawn and 13 lost. The improved performance of the team was reflected in only three defeats in the last 10 league matches, whereas just one of the first 12 was won. The poor start saw the Wolves still in the lower reaches of the league table on 11 July, with only Newcastle, Ashfield and Coventry having less match points. Bristol, Sheffield and Norwich were well ahead of the rest at the top of the league, with Bristol looking clear favourites for the title even at that stage.

Prospects for the second half of the year were promising, with Edwards and Reeves continuing to impress in their debut season. Charlie May had increased his average by over two points per match from the previous year and increased scoring power had been provided through the introduction of Boyd and Windmill to replace the injured Shepherd and Argall. Dick Geary's recent scores had also improved, with his average over the last seven league matches being double the figure achieved in his first 12 meetings.

8. 1949: Sustained improvement

The Wolves lost by a single point on a second league visit to Southampton on 12 July. Harry Edwards continued his fine form by winning his first two races and Walthamstow supplied the majority of heat winners in the match. Charlie May recorded yet another double figure score, although Geary struggled once more and contributed just two points. With Wolves needing maximum points from heat 14 to win the match, the race was rerun after Southampton's Bill Rogers fell. Benny King took first place by passing Tom Oakley, but it was not enough as May had his first defeat when finishing third.

In the return fixture against the Saints six days later, Bill Osborne had machine problems and finished pointless from two rides. The rest of the team scored well, with Boyd, May and Geary leading the way as Southampton were beaten by 19 points. Walthamstow provided race winners in 11 of the 14 heats. The team was becoming a force to be reckoned with on their own track. The visitors were weakened by the absence through injury of recent acquisition 'Wild' Bill Rogers. Although fairly successful back home in Australia, Rogers had an injury-hit career in Britain during pre-war and post-war spells with Wimbledon, Bristol and Belle Vue, rarely showing his best form consistently.

Another inter-track challenge was staged in the second half of the meeting on 18 July, this time against First Division New Cross, represented by Eric French and Jeff Lloyd. Charlie May and Jim Boyd lost by a single point over two heats. French sped to a new track record time of 63.8 seconds in the first heat, in which both May and Lloyd fell. Harold Bull notched a rare win in a scratch race, but his opposition was modest. His main claim to fame at this stage of his career in the United Kingdom was that he was a cousin of the Australian superstar Vic Duggan and his brother Ray.

Bristol Bulldogs eased to an 18-point win when Walthamstow paid a second visit to Knowle Stadium on 22 July, but the Wolves team posted the equal highest score by a visiting team during 1949 to date in league meetings. The total of 33 points might have been better still, but Reg Reeves had a heavy cold and missed his final ride. Benny King had an off-night and Dick Geary struggled again on the small track.

Three days after the impressive result at Bristol, a home meeting took place against Norwich Stars on 25 July. The Stars were then third in the league table and had been narrow victors in the first league encounter at The Stow. Wolves continued to show improvement as the visitors were emphatically beaten 55–28. Sole consolation for the visitors was gained by Bob Leverenz when he scorched around the track to set a new record time of 63.8 seconds in the opening heat. This feat demonstrated the Australian's talent. He was more used to longer tracks and spent a very short time in the sport. He was only added a further three points after this as the home riders dominated, winning 11 of the 14 heats. On this occasion the Stars' riders, Leverenz apart, seemed to experience difficulty in coming to terms with the track, which was only two-thirds the size of their home circuit at The Firs.

An encouraging performance by Dick Geary saw him record two heat wins. Team manager John Deeley appreciated the difficulties which Geary was dealing with in nursing his injured arm. He acknowledged that it was wise for the rider not to take unnecessary risks. On this occasion, Geary gave a glimpse of his true ability when his machine stalled at the beginning of his third race. He made up 75 yards before only narrowly failing to take third place. Jim Boyd led the home scorers with a maximum and Charlie May dropped a single point to the opposition, losing to Phil Clarke in his first ride. Reg Reeves was also beaten only by Clarke of the visiting team in the same race. Geary and Benny King formed a strong opening pairing and the home team had no weak links.

Rayleigh had a Third Division engagement in The Potteries against Hanley on the last Saturday in July and to provide a meeting to fill the gap at The Weir, a challenge match was staged between Walthamstow and Southampton. In six earlier clashes the teams had proved to be fairly evenly matched, but on this occasion the Wolves achieved a resounding 32-point victory. Boyd led the way with a second successive maximum. Such was the strength of the Wolves performance that second-string riders Harry Edwards and Reg Reeves outscored the top Saints rider, Bob Oakley. Oakley eventually transferred to Wembley Lions and went on to finish third in the 1952 World Championship Final.

The winning Walthamstow team was presented with a Challenge Trophy by BBC sports commentator Raymond Glendenning, who had followed the sport since the pioneer days in Britain. It was reported that over 500 Wolves fans had travelled the relatively short distance of 27 miles to Rayleigh to support their team.

In July the Supporters' Club were pleased to add scarves and propelling pencils in Walthamstow colours to the stock of items available to purchase from the track kiosks. Disappointingly, the proposal to form a motorcycle section of the club did not meet with sufficient interest and the idea was discarded. Other initiatives to engage with the fans were explored, one being a cricket match to take place at The Stow, pitching riders and officials against members of the Supporters' Club. Charles Chandler agreed to captain the former team, with Phil Sugden of the *Walthamstow Post* and editor of the Walthamstow programme to take on that role for the supporters' team. Also announced by the club in August were a series of dances during the winter, to be held at the Royal Forest Hotel in North Chingford.

August

Confidence was high when league title favourites and small track specialists Bristol Bulldogs paid their first visit to The Stow on Bank Holiday Monday afternoon on 1 August. They were duly handed only their fifth league defeat of the season, 46–37. Wise, Salmon and Mountford were again in good form for Bristol, but three of the away team failed to score, whereas the home team performed solidly throughout. The points scored by first-year league riders Reeves and Edwards laid the foundations for the success. Bristol's cause was not helped by their riders falling in five of the heats.

Two days later, the in-form Wolves team, with just one away league success to date, travelled to Glasgow and defeated the Tigers by six points. Only the strong Bristol team had previously returned from the White City track with the league points. This success was founded on another solid team effort, with six of the Wolves riders recording race wins. Support for the top three of May, King and Boyd particularly came from an impressive Reeves and an improved performance by Geary.

Reports in the press suggested that due to poor attendances and financial unviability the Hull track was soon to close and concerns were also expressed over the future of Sheffield. In contrast, the evening of 8 August saw what the press described as 'a record crowd' enjoy warm weather as Harringay of the First Division provided the opposition at Walthamstow in the first leg of a London Cup tie. According to the Walthamstow management, the attendance was 21,000. The outstanding Australian, Vic Duggan, who won the British Riders' Championship in 1948, was missing from the Harringay line-up due to injury. Both teams were otherwise at full strength, although Charlie May was unwell with a heavy cold.

Even without their star rider, Harringay were still expected to win, but Walthamstow continued their rich vein of form to win 55–52. A three-point advantage was never likely to be sufficient and Harringay duly won the return leg at Green Lanes on 12 August by 12 points. Walthamstow fought hard, however, still being one point ahead on aggregate with 11 of the 18 heats completed. After Geoff Pymar top-scored for Harringay in the first leg, Lloyd Goffe did likewise in the return. All the Walthamstow riders performed well in the two meetings and with a bit more luck a shock might have occurred. Dick Geary fell twice when second and in another heat Charlie May fell when leading. Added to these misfortunes, Harry Edwards pulled out of the second leg after two pointless rides and an x-ray later revealed he had chipped an ankle bone. In both of his rides Edwards had been leading early in the race, but could not hold on.

Cradley Heath made a fourth visit of the season on 15 August, following the earlier league meeting and two National Trophy matches. Again, the visitors were comfortably defeated, with support lacking for young English star Alan Hunt who scored 11, being beaten by May in one race.

Again, all the home riders contributed useful scores, the lowest being the reserves, Windmill and Osborne, with four points each. Edwards had recovered to top score with double figures, beaten only by Hunt for the visitors.

May and Boyd took on the Birmingham pair of Australian Graham Warren and American Wilbur Lamoreaux in another two-heat challenge in the second half of the Cradley Heath meeting. The result was a draw as Warren impressed with two wins while the home riders kept Lamoreaux behind.

Good form continued to be displayed two days later as the Wolves took both league points following a 43–41 win at Fleetwood's Highbury Avenue Sports Stadium. The home team supplied nine heat winners in 14 races, but Walthamstow's success was once again due to a solid performance throughout. Boyd, Geary and Edwards joint top-scored with eight points each. Geary particularly enjoyed this return to his former track.

Meetings in Division Two involved a significant amount of travelling and for Walthamstow it was on to Edinburgh to meet the Monarchs on 20 August. The visiting men and machines were not at their best and the Wolves were heavily defeated, 61–22. Boyd and Reeves were top scorers, with a modest five points each. May was completely out of touch and failed to score in his four rides. Such was the power of the home team that future world champion Jack Young was fourth top scorer with nine points.

Revenge was taken against the Monarchs' Scottish neighbours Glasgow White City two days later when Walthamstow returned to form on their home circuit. A 14-point success was founded on another solid performance throughout the team, as five riders recorded heat wins. Boyd, King and Edwards were particularly impressive. Glasgow's Junior Bainbridge was beaten once, finishing behind Boyd in heat 11. Boyd completed a paid maximum.

In a bid to add glamour to the second half programme, the Glasgow match featured a race between Division One stars Ron Clarke, Bill Longley, Oliver Hart and Bert Roger. New Cross riders Longley and Roger then met Benny King and Harry Edwards in an inter-track match race in which the points were shared. Then Boyd teamed up with May to defeat Clarke and Hart from the Bradford-based Odsal. The Walthamstow management was testing their riders against top-flight riders, probably trying to gauge what strengthening their team needed to survive in Division One against their London neighbours. These 'experiments' continued to the end of the season.

Walthamstow were invited to take on First Division Birmingham at Perry Barr on the last Saturday in August, albeit their star riders were not included in the Brummies team. Three coachloads of Wolves supporters travelled to watch the match. This was another long day out, departing at lunchtime and arriving back at The Stow at 2.15 on Sunday morning. There was a lengthy stop at St Albans for refreshments on the return journey, however, when supporters also met up with the riders. The Wolves put up a good performance before going down to a 14-point defeat. The home team was strong enough to provide 11 heat winners in the 14 races, which illustrated the difference in standard between the two divisions. Walthamstow continued their recent trend of scoring solidly throughout the team.

Undeterred by the lack of sufficient interest in forming a Motorcycle Section, the Supporters' Club sought to establish an Angling Section in August, with membership open to all registered supporters on payment of an annual fee of 5/-.

The recent heavy defeat at the hands of Edinburgh was avenged when the Monarchs visited The Stow on 29 August, as the Wolves triumphed by 22 points. All the team members contributed to the victory, with Boyd, King and May to the fore. Jack Young and Dick Campbell impressed in scoring 20 of their team's 31 points between them, but support was sadly lacking from most of their team-mates. Graham Warren and Wilbur Lamoreaux represented Birmingham in a two race second half inter-track match and won 7–5 against May and Boyd.

September

By the end of August, Walthamstow occupied a comfortable mid-table position in the Second Division. Of the last eight league matches, seven had been won and just one lost, at Edinburgh. September proved to be an equally successful month, with five league successes and a single defeat, an unexpected reverse at Ashfield, who were in the bottom but one position, above Coventry, in the table.

The first success of the month came at home to league leaders Sheffield on Monday 5 September. Emphasising the progress made by the team, the match was won emphatically by 20 points. A remarkable feature of the score-chart was that Geary, Boyd and May were restricted to 11 points between them. Benny King showed fine form to score a maximum for the first time and Edwards dropped a single point, to Len Williams, in his opening ride.

Wilf Jay (Walthamstow), Jack Hodgson and Frank Hodgson (Newcastle). (JSC)

Left: Cyril Cooper (Fleetwood) and Arch Windmill (Walthamstow) at The Stow. (JSC)

Right: Harry Edwards riding for Walthamstow against Coventry. (JSC)

Although Boyd managed a below par four points, he had reason to celebrate as his loan from Belle Vue had been made into a permanent transfer. A fee of £1,000 was paid by the Wolves management and this proved to be a sound investment. He had the misfortune to take a heavy fall attempting to take the lead in his third ride, causing the race to be stopped and he was excluded from the re-run.

May had a disappointing match against Sheffield and after trying a new frame, he scored his only points in winning his third race on the track spare. He complained of feeling unwell and withdrew from the second half of the meeting. Arch Windmill had just recovered from illness. Despite this, both he and fellow reserve Bill Osborne were unbeaten by visiting riders. In a second half inter-track event, Dent Oliver and Louis Lawson of Belle Vue beat Boyd and King 7–5. Oliver impressed in winning both races.

A week later, on 12 September, Coventry visited The Stow. Although bottom of the league table, the Bees had been strengthened by signing Les Wotton from Wimbledon and Roy Moreton from Cradley Heath. The visitors put up a spirited performance before losing by 14 points. King continued his good form and top-scored, receiving excellent support from Edwards, Reeves and Boyd. Geary struggled again and scored a single point. May fared worse and after completing a second pointless ride he dismounted from his machine before collapsing. After medical attention, it was finally announced to the public that he had been in poor health for some time. He clearly needed a break from racing to fully recover.

On 19 September Fleetwood were the next visitors to be sent home pointless as Walthamstow won easily by 41 points, even without top rider Charlie May. Geary again enjoyed racing against his former team and won two races. Windmill stepped up in place of May and dropped only one point to a visiting rider. Bull had two good rides, with Fleetwood star George Newton, a former world finalist, the only Flyer to finish ahead of him. Apart from that race win, Newton had an unhappy evening and failed to score in three other outings. All the home team registered good scores and Reeves was undefeated by opposition riders. Wembley stars George Wilks and Bob Wells, the latter substituting for Freddie Williams, beat Boyd and King in an inter-track challenge in the second half. Wilks won both heats.

Ted Argall had hoped to return to racing, but in mid-September it was found that although his fracture had healed his muscles had wasted and his leg was not strong enough. This ruled him out for the rest of the season. In view of this he booked a berth to sail home to Sydney, Australia, on 20 September. An update on the progress of Dick Shepherd confirmed that his injuries, which had initially caused paralysis to his arms, also ruled him out of a return in 1949. The Wolves then suffered a setback when May took a break from racing in order to recover from the illness which had dogged him for a while. Other significant news in September was that in order to comply with a directive to move to uniformity of track surfaces, a change to red shale was being considered at The Stow.

With May still absent, the Walthamstow team travelled to Plymouth to face a West of England team on Thursday 22 September. The Plymouth team was engaged in a league fixture at Oxford and so the opposition for the Wolves was a mix of Exeter and Bristol riders. The visitors were advertised as Walthamstow ahead of the meeting, although the programme and subsequent reports labelled the team as London. Despite being beaten 56–25, a bright spot for the Wolves was Windmill's performance, promoted from reserve in place of May. His top score of 10 points included two heat wins. Geary completed four rides, but did not score.

The Walthamstow riders regained their best form for the visit to Brandon on 24 September and defeated Coventry 47–36 to record their fourth away league win of the season. May returned to the team and struggled as he registered two points. Boyd delivered an immaculate maximum and was well supported by King with 10. Windmill kept his team place, with Geary dropping down to reserve where his poor returns continued. More Wolves followers were enjoying the away trips and nine coach loads made the journey to Coventry.

Two days later, Glasgow White City were well beaten, 56–27, as the impressive run of Walthamstow's home performances was extended. Only Gordon McGregor and Jack Hodgson were a match for the home riders, who all scored well. Geary returned to the number one position and after a pointless first ride, rallied to be unbeaten by the opposition in his other races. May also appeared to be on the road to recovery after his illness and recorded two race wins using his new bike frame.

The crowd was disappointed when the injured Jack Parker was unable to ride in match races against Birmingham's Graham Warren. George Wilks stepped in to replace the Belle Vue man and took the first heat before Warren levelled in the second run. Warren won the decider after Wilks fell on the pits bend on lap three as the two riders battled wheel-to-wheel.

A better performance might have been expected when Walthamstow visited Ashfield on 27 September, with the Glasgow team in a lowly league position and the Wolves comfortably in mid-table. However, the home team had recently held title favourites Bristol to a draw and were in good form. After their recent successful run, the 22-point margin of defeat was a big disappointment for the Wolves team. May and Windmill were their only race winners. Ashfield's 'White Ghost', Ken Le Breton, famously clad in his white leathers, recorded an effortless maximum and fellow Australian Merv Harding returned a paid maximum.

The Supporters' Club continued to grow and in September 40 new members were enrolled by Miss Flanders and Mr Brown, the new Edmonton and Tottenham branch secretaries. The date set for the cricket match at The Stow was 2 October. Phil Sugden of the *Walthamstow Post* was likely to be ruled out due to ill health, but Lewis Gale, the *Post* photographer and a former club cricketer was named as a replacement. Unfortunately, the match did not take place. Two hundred members of the Supporters' Club attended the World Final at Wembley on 22 September.

October

The next month started brightly for Walthamstow with a draw at Newcastle on 1 October. The match might have been won, but for two pieces of misfortune. Harry Edwards withdrew from the meeting after a shoulder injury when he fell in his second ride and then Reg Reeves, who had dropped one point to the opposition in his first three outings, stalled at the start in his final ride when favourite to win the race. The Magpies took the opportunity to cancel out a four-point deficit leaving the match to be decided in the last heat. King duly won the race, but May was unable to split the home pair of Close and Lawson.

Walthamstow programmes from 1949. Left against Norwich in a league match and right against near-neighbours Harringay in the London Cup.

The highlight for the visitors was Geary's sparkling form. He joint top scored with Boyd on 11 points. For Newcastle, former Walthamstow star Wilf Jay recorded his best score to date, also scoring 11.

The home team made no mistake against Ashfield two days later, notching a 25-point victory despite Edwards being unfit to ride, King having a heavy cold and Boyd nursing a sick motor. Bull stood in for Edwards and continued his run of good scores since being given another opportunity. May was unbeaten by a visitor and Geary recorded two more wins in a total of seven. Geary's last place against Merv Harding and Willie Wilson was the only race in which a home rider failed to score. After falling in his first race, Ken Le Breton was untroubled in reeling off three wins. A second half inter-track event was staged against Eric French and Jeff Lloyd of New Cross. The home pairing of May and Boyd were relegated to the minor places in both races.

In the final three league matches which followed, Walthamstow suffered emphatic defeats on each occasion, although none of the results was a surprise. In the first one, on 7 October, the Wolves travelled to Dudley Wood where they had lost heavily three times to Cradley Heath. The pattern of the previous encounters was repeated as the Wolves slipped to a 30-point loss. Only a fall for Alan Hunt and mechanical troubles for Les Beaumont and Phil Malpass prevented an even bigger margin between the teams. Walthamstow failed to provide a single race winner.

At Norwich, on the next evening, the outcome was similar as the home team won 56–28 and secured third place in the division. The Wolves riders were outpaced on the large Firs circuit, as Bob Leverenz and Ted Bravery won four races each. May was the sole heat winner for the visitors and top scored with a modest six points.

At The Stow on Monday 10 October, the Wolves completed their league programme with a 49–35 home defeat against the league champions, Bristol Bulldogs. The champions supplied 11 of the 14 heat winners, with Roger Wise registering a maximum. Edwards ended the league season on a high note by top scoring with nine points for Walthamstow.

The team was invited to Third Division Rayleigh for another challenge fixture on 15 October, but failed to repeat their triumph there against Southampton earlier in the season, losing by eight points. Jim Boyd and Reg Reeves both won two races for Walthamstow, but the support from the other team members was inconsistent.

To finish the season at The Stow, the Wolves entertained First Division Belle Vue Aces in a challenge match on 17 October. May had one ride without scoring, but solid performances from the rest of the team resulted in a win by three points. The visitors struggled on the small track, except for star rider Jack Parker, who won all his races in the match except one when he was excluded. In his first ride at The Stow, Parker equalled the record time of 63.8 seconds. King won the final of a second half event for home riders and Louis Lawson did likewise for the visitors, beating Parker in the final. Prizes for these events were presented by Lois Green, the Australian film star.

The season was still not over as the team was invited to Leicester and then Oxford for challenge matches. At Third Division Leicester, the Wolves lost by eight points. Boyd scored a maximum and Harry Edwards displayed a liking for the track with two wins in a total of nine. In the meeting at Cowley, the visitors took on the combined forces of Oxford, Bristol and Cradley Heath, rather surprisingly coming out on top 43–31. Although Alan Hunt and Jack Mountford registered double figure scores, they were matched by Boyd and Edwards, the latter pair receiving marginally better support from their colleagues on this occasion.

As the season ended a Supporters' Club darts team was formed, with fixtures arranged. A series of West-End theatre visits was also planned. A more expensive outing under consideration for July 1950 was a boat trip to France. It was planned that members would embark at Gravesend for Calais aboard the *Royal Daffodil*, with lunch and tea on board at an inclusive cost of 35/-, payable by weekly instalments. The first dance, on 12 October, proved to be a great success, with Reg Reeves receiving praise for his role as Master of Ceremonies. A second dance at the same venue in Chingford was arranged for 17 November, with Phil Sugden as MC. Club membership at the end of the season was in the region of 3,000 and average attendances at The Stow were reported to have exceeded 10,000. However, the *Stenner's Speedway Annual* said that attendance levels at the track had been disappointing in 1949.

Season's end

After a slow start to the campaign Walthamstow had rallied well and a respectable sixth place league finish was entirely satisfactory. There were many successes among the riders recruited for the Walthamstow post-war revival. Boyd was top man and received excellent support from May and King in leading the scorers. King matched the scoring of Wilf Jay after the exchange deal with Newcastle. Edwards and Reeves were two of the most impressive first year riders in the division. The loss of Shepherd to injury so early in the season was a huge blow, but one which the team successfully overcame with shrewd signings. Both Windmill and Osborne were dependable lower order riders, although more might have been expected of the latter after his fine performances with Hastings in 1948. The inability of Geary to fully overcome his arm injury was a huge disappointment and a rider who had been expected to finish at the top of the scorers struggled. He was eventually relegated to reserve. Of the Australian newcomers, Bull seemed more likely to succeed. The unlucky Argall's broken leg followed a series of crashes as he struggled to master the smaller British tracks.

Shortly after the season ended, the Walthamstow general manager Wally Lloyd resigned, allegedly after a disagreement with Charles Chandler. Various sources said that Lloyd and Chandler had disagreed on the 'present and future policy of the club', but did not go into detail. In fact, Lloyd had been approached during the season by some Irish businessmen about opening of a track in Northern Ireland. He followed up their invitation to manage the new venture after leaving Walthamstow. He was succeeded by John Deeley, who had been the team manager. The roles of general manager and team manager were then combined.

As the year drew to a close the SCB met on 22 December and announced that for 1950 the Second Division would be regionalised, with north and south sections. Walthamstow would be joined in the southern section by six other tracks, Coventry, Cradley Heath, Norwich, Plymouth, Southampton and Yarmouth. At that stage, the proposal was for the teams to meet once home and away during the first seven weeks of the season after which the north and south sections would amalgamate. The northern section was to comprise Ashfield, Edinburgh, Fleetwood, Glasgow White City, Halifax, Hanley (Stoke), Newcastle and Sheffield. A prime reason for regionalisation was to reduce travel costs. In the 1949 season, Walthamstow had travelled over 2,000 miles to and from away meetings by the end of April alone. A 'local derby' for Walthamstow in the 1949 league involved journeys of over 90 miles to Coventry and over 100 miles to Norwich.

Following the successful introduction of Edwards and Reeves to the Wolves team in 1949, Walthamstow again looked to use the training facilities at Rye House in the winter. The Hoddesdon circuit in Hertfordshire promised to be a hive of activity. Former Walthamstow captain Dick Case and Eric Chitty of West Ham were running training schools each Tuesday and Thursday, Walthamstow were to have use of the track on Mondays, Wembley on Wednesdays, and Harringay on Fridays. Walthamstow needed to look for emerging young talent as the average age of the regular team in 1949 was 31 years.

10. 1950: Southern Shield frustration

At the beginning of February 1950, the Court of Appeal rejected an appeal from Hastings Speedway against an injunction preventing the sport being staged at Pilot Field on noise grounds. As with Walthamstow in 1934, it was felt that the sport could perhaps have continued if silencers were fitted to the speedway bikes. Don Clarke, writing in the *Sunday Mirror*, commented that the SCB would not allow this and thought that without the vibrating, crackling snarl of the racing engine, speedway would become as tame as a church bazaar. John Wick, the editor of *Speedway World*, reminded readers that a local rule in Sydney, Australia, required the fitting of silencers to machines and this had satisfactorily addressed the noise issue there.

News emerged in March that former Walthamstow general manager Wally Lloyd was set to manage a group of tracks in Ireland and would also be riding once more. Lloyd took up a position and also rode at the Dunmore track in north Belfast throughout the season. He enjoyed a reasonable degree of success, albeit against mainly junior standard opposition. However, there was no 'group of tracks' and Dunmore was the only one to operate in Northern Ireland in the 1950 season.

In mid-March, the Wolves riders took part in practice sessions at The Stow, giving them an opportunity to experience the new red shale surface and the introduction of standardised concrete starting areas. The starting area was the brainchild of Coventry manager Charles Ochiltree. Another significant change for the new season was the introduction of a narrower tread tyre, aimed at improving the quality of racing. The tyre was initially brought in for a trial period up to 23 April.

There were some arguments about the new tyre in the early weeks of the season. However, its supporters could point to the breaking of several track record times. During trials at training schools in February and March, the riders using the new tyre thought that they would wear out faster than the old ones and this would push costs up. By mid-April, the Speedway Riders Association (SRA) members were considering taking strong action against using the new tyre. Odsal's Oliver Hart refused to use it after falling twice in one race in his opening meeting. As riders attempted to get the best out of it, a protest at Hanley (Stoke) resulted in a Fleetwood rider having to replace a tyre which had been doctored by cutting grooves in it. At an SCB meeting on 20 April, it was decided to allow riders to choose whether they used the old or new tyre. The SRA welcomed the move, with a ballot of members indicating that 80 percent favoured reverting to the old broad tyre.

Standardisation of the starting areas had been decided during the winter, with the design specifying concrete, grooved every two inches across the width. An exception was immediately made at New Cross, where diagonal grooving was allowed to create a diamond pattern, after excessive 'snaking' from the start had been reported. The starting areas were originally to have been provided by approved makers, intended to keep costs down. This standardisation caused problems with interpretation, with many tracks opting not to use the approved design and in April a protest was lodged by Harringay because the Birmingham design had grooves cut to form rows of oblong boxes. However, the area had been inspected and passed by the SCB before it was used.

Major changes were agreed between the promoters and the SRA about payment rates. The SCB approved the rates at a meeting in early March. The changes saw a reduction in starting money and an increase in point money. It was believed that the new rates would make for keener racing, particularly for third place, as well as forcing riders no longer up to standard to retire from the sport. For Walthamstow, in the Second Division, the new rates were 15 shillings a start in all meetings, 32s 6d per point in league matches and World Championship qualifying rounds, 25s per point for second half events and 30s per point in 18-heat cup matches and 20-heat National Trophy matches.

March

Walthamstow staged a behind-closed-doors practice on Thursday 16 March. There were encouraging performances by all the riders present. Geary, set to continue as team captain, seemed to have overcome the injury difficulties which held him back in 1949. He recorded a time of 50.2 seconds for three laps, bettered only by Boyd and King with 49.4. Shepherd, recovering from serious injury, was not far off their pace, with 51.0. The fastest time over four laps was recorded by May with 66.2, just ahead of Reeves who clocked 67 seconds. Edwards and Windmill were using new frames and both had some difficulties. Bull rode steadily and Bruce Gardiner improved once he became accustomed to the track. Bert Edwards, Harry's brother, created a favourable impression. Manager John Deeley hoped that Les McGillivray might join the Wolves from Rayleigh.

April

Looking ahead to the new season, the Walthamstow speedway management challenged views expressed during the winter about low crowds. They thought that the team was already attracting numbers sufficient to justify elevation to the First Division. The Supporters' Club secretary, Jack Buck, commented in the opening meeting's programme that attendances in 1949 averaged more than 10,000, with several meetings attracting 18,000 to 20,000. This, of course, meant that there must have been occasions when significantly less than 10,000 were present.

The aim of the Supporters' Club was to double membership to 6,000 during the 1950 season. Jack Buck outlined that there was a lot to be gained from being a member, including participation in a range of recreational activities. Dances continued to be organised, a fixture list had been drawn up for the cricket team, darts matches were ongoing at the *Royal Oak* public house at Higham's Park and the cycling club, which met at the same venue each Tuesday, arranged Sunday runs. After a few weeks, the cycling club changed its meeting venue to *The Popular Café* in Chingford, no doubt a healthier option. The darts club expanded its activities to include snooker, billiards and table tennis. A bowls club was formed and efforts were made at the beginning of the speedway season to set up a football team. In April a

Rayleigh branch of the club was established, with Vic Taylor appointed as secretary. He had previously been secretary of the Rayleigh Speedway Supporters' Club.

Newly promoted Hanley (Stoke) entertained Walthamstow in a challenge match to open their new season on 1 April. In previewing the meeting, the *Staffordshire Sentinel* newspaper expected the visitors to be one of the division's strongest teams. The Wolves' management was optimistic that both Shepherd and Geary would be fully fit and this would help the team. Two coach loads of supporters went to The Potteries, leaving Walthamstow at 10am.

Walthamstow romped to an easy 56–28 win, with Harry Edwards and May scoring maximums. The Wolves provided 11 heat winners in 14 races. Shepherd returned in place of the transferred Bill Osborne, otherwise the line-up was the same as the one which finished the previous season. Shepherd had shown no ill effects when practising at Rye House in the winter and made a promising start from a reserve berth. He won his first race and finishing third behind his race partner in the other. A feature of the second half races was the inclusion of four Swedish riders: Sune Karlsson, Thord Larsson, Dick Weider and Joel Jansson.

The regional competition for the Second Division teams took the form of the Kemsley Shield, Northern and Southern sections, more commonly referred to as the Northern Shield and the Southern Shield. The competition was sponsored by the *Sunday Chronicle* newspaper, part of the Kemsley group, with a prize of £400 for the winning team and £200 for the runners-up. In the first home fixture in the competition, Walthamstow swept Norwich aside with an emphatic 30-point victory on 3 April.

Boyd, Harry Edwards and May achieved double figure scores and received good backing from King, Shepherd, Reeves and Windmill. The only rider off the pace was Geary, who managed just one point and was replaced by Shepherd in his third ride. Reeves was shaken when he fell after rearing at the start of heat 13. In the next race, King was pushed wide on the first bend and careered headlong into the safety fence. His machine was damaged, but although battered and bruised, he won the re-run on a spare bike. Norwich badly missed their star rider Bob Leverenz, who had not yet returned from Australia. Their two race wins were both by Paddy Mills, whose real name was Horace Burke. Bull fell in a second half reserves race and dislocated his shoulder. It was immediately put back in place by Doctor Mackenzie, the track doctor.

In view of the changes for the new season, comprising a different track surface, a narrower rear tyre and a concrete starting grid, it was decided that a new track record would be established. The time of 65 seconds set by Paddy Mills in the opening heat of the Southern Shield match against Norwich on 3 April was bettered by Boyd in the following race and by May in the seventh heat, both Walthamstow riders recording 64.6 seconds. The new record time was a second slower than the previous record jointly held by Leverenz and Jack Parker. The programme for the following meeting did not claim the new time to be a record, however, instead describing it as 'the fastest time to date'. The riders were happy with the new shale track surface and there were no complaints about the new tyres.

On 8 April, the Wolves met Norwich in the return fixture at The Firs and exceeded expectations, winning 46–38 in front of a crowd of just under 14,000 fans. The Norwich team was widely tipped for honours and on this form, there was every reason to expect Walthamstow to be challenging strongly. Boyd and Harry Edwards were on top form, both scoring 11 points. They received good support, particularly from King and May, but Geary struggled again and failed to score. Members of the Rayleigh branch of the Supporters' Club travelled by coach to the home and away meetings with the Stars and 20 members of the Supporters' Club cycled from Walthamstow to Norwich to cheer on their team. A further 200 supporters travelled by coach. A party of supporters stayed overnight in Norwich before travelling on to Yarmouth the next day to spend time by the sea, returning in time for the home meeting against Southampton on Monday.

In Second Division terms, the meeting at Norwich was one of the shorter away trips for the Wolves supporters. Nevertheless, they left The Stow at 10am, arriving at 4.30pm. This allowed time for afternoon tea in the city before going on to the stadium. There a was a stop for supper on the return journey for these supporters before they arrived back in Walthamstow at 4am on Sunday.

Heavy rain made track conditions hazardous during the early part of the Easter Monday afternoon match as Walthamstow beat Southampton in the Southern Shield on 10 April. The visiting team forced six successive drawn heats as conditions eased, but victory for the Wolves was never in doubt. Boyd again headed the score-chart, but all the home riders contributed well. The attendance for the meeting was very poor, many people choosing to stay at home because of the atrocious weather. King fared best for Walthamstow with 11 points, but there were useful contributions from all the riders. Harry Edwards and Shepherd fell in their first rides, but apart from these races the Wolves had only one other last place in the match. With Geary concerned about his fitness and form, he asked to be relieved of the captaincy of the team and Boyd agreed to take it on. Steve Langton, who made one appearance for Walthamstow in 1934, returned to The Stow with the Southampton team and scored a single point.

Bill Osborne was an interested spectator at the match against Southampton, being side-lined with a broken leg, from his first meeting for Oxford. Without ever appearing for the team, Walthamstow asset Tom Turnham was transferred to Ashfield in April for a fee of £30. His stay with the Glasgow team was brief before he moved on again to ride with Wally Lloyd at Dunmore in Belfast. The remaining squad members embarked on a fitness programme, participating in physical exercise sessions on Thursday afternoons led by Fulham footballer Ron Lewin, a keen follower of the sport at The Stow.

The visit of Yarmouth in the next Southern Shield match on 17 April was eagerly awaited, mainly as the visiting team should have included teenage sensation Billy Bales. Sadly, Bales was doing National Service and often had trouble in getting time off for meetings. On this occasion, it was said that he got lost on his way to the track. Tip Mills was also absent due to influenza. The weakened visiting team was soundly beaten, 56–28. All the home riders scored well as the Wolves provided 12 of the 14 heat winners. Reeves and captain Boyd scored maximums. May had mechanical gremlins and a faulty clutch caused him to miss one ride. He ended up with just one point. The 'fastest time' was reduced to 64.2 seconds by Yarmouth's Bill Carruthers in the first race. This was equalled by Boyd in the following heat, before being set at 64.0 seconds by Boyd in heats six and eight.

In the opening heat of the Southern Shield match against Plymouth a week later, King narrowly defeated the Devils' star Peter Robinson in a thrilling duel. In doing so, he equalled the fastest time to date of 64.0 seconds. Three heats later, having familiarised himself with the track, the Plymouth rider set a fastest time of 63.4 seconds, which also beat the record set the previous year. A concern for Walthamstow was May's performance, with a single point for the second home meeting in a row. More bad weather affected the attendance for this meeting, but the fans who did not brave the cold and damp missed a thrilling meeting. The scores were level after the seventh heat before the Wolves pulled away in the latter part of the match to win by 18 points. Across the country, promoters were bemoaning the bad weather, which in some cases saw attendances of below half the expected figure.

A fighting performance saw Walthamstow achieve their second away win in the Southern Shield, this time at Southampton, on 25 April. The meeting was run during a heavy storm and the home riders adapted less well to the adverse conditions. The Wolves came from two points down at the halfway stage to win 47–37. Harry Edwards and May top scored with nine each, and received good support from Boyd and King in particular. Geary continued to have problems in difficult conditions and mustered a single point. The supporters' club arranged for 30 Wolves fans to fly to Southampton for this match, a highly unusual occurrence in the speedway world. Unfortunately, due to heavy snowfall and poor visibility, the return flight had to be cancelled and a coach was hastily arranged to transport the supporters back to London. Windmill had the misfortune to leave the road on his return journey, his vehicle had to be retrieved from a ditch.

With half of their Southern Shield fixtures completed, Walthamstow headed the league table, four points clear of Coventry and Cradley Heath, having also ridden fewer matches. It seemed at this point that the shield was destined for Chingford Road.

Riders were given the option of using either the new or the old tyre for the next Southern Shield match at Plymouth on 27 April. May was the only one who opted to persevere with the new one. Walthamstow went into the meeting with the proud record of having won all six meetings to date in the Southern Shield. However, they met their match on this occasion and were soundly defeated 58–26. The Wolves manager lodged a protest with the meeting steward about the rough state of the track. Boyd, who had taken over the captaincy from Geary, was top scorer for the Wolves with seven points. There was another single point return from May as his poor run of form continued. For the Devils Peter Robinson won all his races in untroubled fashion and Len Read was also unbeaten.

May

Following the disputes over the new tyre at the beginning of the season, the SCB issued a ruling that any track records set using the smaller tyre would continue to stand.

Recognising that meetings against First Division opposition attracted the best crowds, the newly promoted Bristol team was invited for a challenge match at The Stow on 1 May. With supporters enjoying the first meeting of the season to be run in good weather, the Bulldogs displayed the power which took them to the Second Division title the previous year. They won by 20 points. Billy Hole and Dick Bradley scored maximums for Bristol. Windmill's heat 13 win was the home team's only success in the match as the gulf in standard between the two divisions was underlined.

Walthamstow Wolves 1950: Jimmy Grant, Reg Reeves, Arch Windmill, Benny King, George Newton, John Deeley (Manager), Harry Edwards, Charlie May, Jim Boyd (on bike). (JSC)

The four Walthamstow riders who rode for Great Britain against Overseas at The Stow in 1950: Jimmy Grant, Jim Boyd, Reg Reeves, Benny King. (JSC)

George Newton (leg-trailing) and Reg Reeves. (JSC)

Left: Harold Bull and Reg Reeves working on the track at The Stow. The huge scoreboard used for greyhound racing can be seen behind them. (JSC)

Although most riders reverted to using the old gauge tyre for the start of this meeting, Boyd and King believed that they did much better on the smaller tyres. King changed to the smaller tyre after his first outing and then top scored with eight points. He felt that the new tyre gave an advantage at the starts. May injured his shoulder when he crashed in his last ride.

Having made such a good start to the Southern Shield campaign, the Wolves were shocked as they slipped to a one-point home defeat after leading Coventry by seven points with four races left on 8 May. Successive 5–1 heat wins put the Bees ahead and with the last two races drawn Walthamstow lost. The away riders adapted better to the wet track, which particularly affected the starting area, from which the Bees were invariably quicker away

May was unable to ride after his first outing when he scored points only because both Coventry riders failed to finish. He was still feeling the effects of an old injury and was replaced by reserves in his other three rides. King was the pick of the home riders with a maximum, but there was inconsistent support from his team-mates.

The third heat, in which neither Bees rider finished, was highly controversial. Lionel Levy was leading on the first lap when he fell, taking his partner Johnny Reason, down with him. Reeves and May passed the fallen riders as the meeting steward allowed the race to continue with the stricken riders lying on the track. As Levy and Reason made efforts to remount and rejoin the race, members of the track staff rushed on and removed their machines. The steward should have stopped the race in the interests of safety. The track staff should have been reprimanded for preventing riders from restarting, as well as placing themselves in danger in the process.

The match might have been won but for two falls for Harry Edwards, the second when chasing Reason for first place in heat 12. Geary had held second place in the fateful 12th heat, but was unable to keep Reason behind him. Then in the final race, when replacing May, Geary held third place for much of the race until he was passed by Roy Moreton. Moreton also overtook his partner to finish in second place. These two races ultimately proved the difference between winning and losing the match. This defeat virtually ended the Wolves' hopes of winning the Southern Shield unless the team could spring a surprise by winning at Cradley Heath or Yarmouth.

Following the meeting both Geary and Dick Shepherd made written transfer requests. The directors, management and riders held a meeting, at which the requests were accepted. Shepherd had never fully returned to his best form following the serious injury at the start of the previous season. Geary, still hampered by his arm injury, was ill at ease on the small Walthamstow track. Having been expected to lead the scoring when he joined the Wolves in 1949, his fitness problems had seen him slip to reserve.

The downturn in the fortunes of the Wolves team continued at Yarmouth in the next Southern Shield match the following evening. They lost 48–35. This was a match Walthamstow might have expected to win, but instead Yarmouth managed their first victory of the season. The meeting saw the first home appearance in 1950 by Billy Bales, who scored seven points from three completed rides. Boyd fought a lone battle as he scored 10 points against a solid Bloaters team. Harry Edwards was programmed at number one for the Wolves, but was not fit to ride after his crash against Coventry, leaving the Wolves a rider short. Windmill pulled out of the meeting after a heavy first race fall to worsen the visitors' plight. Remarkably, there was only a point between the teams after nine heats, before Yarmouth raced to three maximum heat wins in the remaining five races.

In mid-May, Fleetwood's George Newton made an official transfer request, following which an exchange was arranged which saw him move to Walthamstow with Geary returning to his previous club. The *Daily Herald* reported that Walthamstow had also paid £700 as part of the deal. Newton started riding as a 19-year-old at Crystal Palace in 1932. He caused a sensation when he equalled Vic Huxley's West Ham track record in only his fourth London Junior League outing. Several sources incorrectly describe his record-breaking ride as occurring on his debut. He had already ridden in home and away matches with Stamford Bridge, as well as the home match against West Ham. It was, however, his first appearance at Custom House. His spectacular leg-trailing style thrilled spectators wherever he rode. When the Crystal Palace team relocated to New Cross in 1934, Newton's new home track matched his stature, both being tiny. It was at the Old Kent Road circuit that his career rapidly developed. He scored 16 points on his England debut against Australia at Wembley in 1936. Later that year he rode in the inaugural World Championship Final.

Newton made his Wolves debut in the 14-point defeat at Cradley Heath in a Southern Shield encounter on 13 May, notching a disappointing three points. A positive note was that his points came from a heat win, in which he inflicted the only defeat of the match on Cradley star Alan Hunt. This was only the second time that Hunt had been beaten by a visiting rider at Dudley Wood during the season to date. Newton reared and fell at the start of his final race, but was unhurt. Some might have questioned the wisdom of spending the considerable sum of £700 in replacing Geary with Newton, a veteran rider who was out of the sport for 10 years due to ill health before he made a comeback with New Cross in 1948. He had suffered from tuberculosis and had a lung removed. His liking for the circuit had been shown, however, when he was track record holder at The Stow for a while in 1949.

Harold Bull made his first appearance of the season for Walthamstow in this meeting, replacing Shepherd, but he failed to score. May, who had ridden exceptionally well on previous visits to Dudley Wood, continued to disappoint and managed only two points. Walthamstow were unable to take advantage of the home team's misfortune in losing two of their top riders, Jack Arnfield and Gil Craven, by the sixth heat. Both were taken to hospital with concussion after heavy falls.

Two days later, the Wolves gained revenge when they beat the Heathens by 36 points at The Stow in the return Southern Shield encounter. The visitors were without the injured Arnfield and gave a subdued performance. All members of the Wolves team contributed useful scores. Particularly pleasing was the 10-point return by May and nine points for Newton in his first home appearance. Bert Edwards made his Walthamstow debut and was unbeaten by the opposition in two reserve rides. Alan Hunt was the only opposition rider to defeat May and Craven was the only visitor to get the better of Newton. Hunt took first place in the final heat to be Cradley's sole race winner.

Another poor away performance saw the Wolves beaten by 30 points at Coventry on 20 May before a crowd estimated to be around 20,000. This included 200 Walthamstow supporters. They had another late return, with coaches not arriving back at The Stow until 3am. Boyd top-scored again, with eight points, but Newton, May and Harry Edwards managed only four points between them. Newton had an eventful evening. His engine seized in his first ride and then he had a burst tyre in another race. Les Hewitt, who was originally due to link up with Walthamstow in 1949, recorded a maximum for the Bees and Lionel Levy was also undefeated by a visiting rider.

Walthamstow went into the meeting as leaders of the Southern Shield table, but with Cradley Heath defeating Southampton on the same evening, they replaced the Wolves at the top of the table. The dip in form which had seen the team lose five of their last six matches, after winning the first six, cost them dearly as they slipped to third in the final standings.

First Division Birmingham provided the opposition in a challenge match on 22 May and surprisingly lost by seven points. Only Australian star Graham Warren with a maximum, and Geoff Bennett – beaten once, by Boyd, got to grips with the small circuit. May showed some better form to joint top score with nine points for the Wolves. Newton also rode well, but fell in a controversial incident in his third race. Visiting rider Ron Mountford failed to pull out of the race after being excluded and Newton then fell in attempting to pass him. Reserve Bert Edwards retired after losing a chain in his first race and was substituted in his other ride, but the rest of team made useful contributions. Warren was in scintillating form and recorded four fast wins, including smashing the track record in his second ride with a time of 62.6 seconds. Such was the Birmingham rider's speed that he finished about 100 yards ahead of second placed George Newton in this race.

Walthamstow met Yarmouth home and away in The National Trophy knock-out competition at the end of May. The home team won each time. After an emphatic 24-point first leg win, the Wolves held their hosts to just seven points in the return to progress to the second round. A National Service overseas posting prevented Billy Bales from riding in the tie and this severely affected Yarmouth's performance. At The Stow, King excelled for the Wolves in scoring 17 points, beaten by his partner, Jim Boyd, in one ride. Boyd was beaten once by an opponent when giving second best to Reg Morgan. Newton fell in his first race and pulled out of the meeting with mechanical problems after one further ride. According to manager John Deeley the attendance at Walthamstow was the best of the season to date for the Bank Holiday Monday afternoon meeting.

A good all-round team performance in the away leg was enough to secure the aggregate success. Boyd, King and Reeves all returned double figure scores at the tricky Caister Road track. The reward for the Wolves was a second-round tie against Southampton Saints.

11. 1950: League disappointment

At the beginning of June, Walthamstow were looking for a new rider to bolster the squad. Ted Argall had joined Rayleigh towards the end of May and Harold Bull moved to St Austell, leaving the Wolves with nobody to back up the regular team members. Rumours circulated linking Walthamstow with Coventry's Bob Fletcher, Plymouth's Peter Robinson and Yarmouth's Reg Morgan, although none of them came to The Stow. Bad weather continued to concern promoters and First Division Odsal reported that gates were down to the extent that a loss of £2,000 had been made on the season to date.

Top end strength saw the Wolves ease to a 51–33 win over Sheffield in the first match of the league campaign on 5 June. The home team provided 12 of the 14 heat winners, with maximums from Boyd and King. Reeves scored 11, finishing second to team partner Newton in one race. Newton was inconsistent, picking up only one point from his other three outings. Sheffield's cause was not helped by their captain, Jack Chignell, falling in his first two rides. The second one saw him carried off with a leg injury, although he did complete the match. Boyd was on his way to completing the evening unbeaten before his engine blew up when leading the second half final. Both Wolves reserves, Windmill and Bert Edwards, were using new engines, although their investment did not bring much reward on this occasion.

The first supporters' dance of the season took place in the stadium ballroom on Thursday 8 June, with Wolves riders Bert Edwards, Bruce Gardiner, Benny King and Arch Windmill in attendance. The remaining team members had other commitments. Phil Sugden from the *Walthamstow Post* newspaper again acted as Master of Ceremonies. Continuing the efforts to put the Supporters Club activities at the heart of the local community, a proposal was put forward to establish a swimming section. The club secretary and helpers worked tirelessly to ensure close contact between riders and the people who cheered them on each week.

Walthamstow were invited back to Sun Street, Hanley, for another challenge match on 10 June. The Potters avenged their heavy early season defeat by taking a one-point win. Walthamstow looked to have the match won as they led by 13 points with five heats remaining, but were then overwhelmed by their hosts. Reeves took the honours for the Wolves, with three wins in his double figure score. May, such a stalwart the previous season, floundered again and scored a single point. Ken Adams led the way for the home team with 10 points, losing only to Reeves of the visiting riders.

A challenge meeting against Second Division 'stars' should have provided a stern test for Walthamstow on 12 June, but an 11-point win was a fair reflection of the gap between the teams. Boyd was defeated by Johnny Reason in his first race before reeling off three wins, during which he equalled Graham Warren's track record in the 10th heat. King, Reeves and Newton also scored well for the Wolves. Harold Bull rode at reserve for the opposition and showed the benefit of regular racing with St Austell by recording a heat win over Windmill and Harry Edwards.

Walthamstow had beaten Southampton in the first round of the National Trophy in 1949. This time they met in round two, with the first leg at The Stow on 19 June and the return the next evening. The Wolves again came out on top over the two matches, building a substantial 26-point lead at home before going down by 10 points in the return.

The home leg on a rain-soaked track saw a welcome return to top form for May, who jointly headed the scorers with Boyd on 16 points. Both riders were unbeaten by the opposition in their six rides. Reeves gave an impressive performance with four heat wins in his 13 points. Captain Bob Oakley managed double figures for the Saints. The lead could have been greater except for a few mishaps. After winning heat one in a record-equalling time of 62.6 seconds, King failed to win another heat and had a seized engine when leading the penultimate heat. Two heats earlier, Newton fell when looking certain to partner May to a maximum 5–1 win. Bert Edwards characterised the determination of the home riders when he remounted after falling heavily in heat four and still managed to pip pioneer Phil Bishop, nicknamed 'The King of Crash', for third place. Reeves was even more impressive in the away leg, racing to five heat wins in a total of 16 points. He received solid backing from the rest of the team and progress to the next round was never in doubt.

With the home team engaged in a league fixture at Tamworth, the rivalry between Walthamstow and Southampton continued the next evening as Aldershot hosted a challenge match between them. The Wolves triumphed again, this time 45–39. The match was closely contested in poor weather and the scores were level at the halfway stage. Harry Edwards returned to top form with 11 points and Boyd again performed well with 10. Reeves went from heroic top-scoring exploits the previous night to finish bottom scorer with one point. Bob Oakley recorded a maximum for the Saints and after being pushed hard by Edwards, he set a new track record time of 68.2 seconds in heat one.

Walthamstow enjoyed a comfortable 15-point win at Sheffield on 23 June in a league encounter. Already without the injured Jack Chignell and Charlie New, the home team lost Bert Lacey in a first ride crash. He was taken to hospital with broken ribs and a dislocated shoulder. The Wolves took full advantage, scoring solidly throughout except for King who endured a rare off night. He seized an engine for the third time in a week. Leading the way for Walthamstow were two of the lesser lights, Harry Edwards and Reeves who both scored nine. Len Williams, standing in as captain of the Tars in Chignell's absence, scored a fine maximum, but in the second half scratch races was beaten by a visiting rider for the first time since 5 May. George Newton was the rider to achieve this feat.

The Wolves riders and supporters had a frustrating 560-mile round trip to Brough Park, Newcastle, on Saturday 24 June. Heavy rain intervened and forced the match to be abandoned after three heats. Bad weather and the counter-attraction of the Newcastle Town Moor Festival meant a very poor attendance for this meeting. For one of the longer journeys of the season, supporters left Walthamstow at midnight, not arriving back home until 9am on Sunday morning.

A week after beating Southampton in the second round, the Wolves took on Ashfield in the first leg of the Division Two semi-final of the National Trophy, and gained a substantial 25-point advantage. There were several impressive performances, with Boyd scoring 15 from six rides and Reeves dropping one point to the visitors in five outings. Bert Edwards won both his reserve rides, but Newton withdrew from the meeting without scoring after losing a chain his first race and falling second time out. Ken Le Breton with 16 points and Merv

Harding with 10 kept their team's faint hopes alive for the return leg. Le Breton equalled the track record time of 62.6 seconds in the first heat. Johnnie Hoskins, the Ashfield co-promoter, predicted before the match that if his team could restrict Walthamstow to a lead of 25 points, they would overturn it in the second leg.

Off the track, the idea of a light car and motorcycling section of the Supporters' Club had been resurrected in mid-April, with one of the proposals being to stage grasstrack meetings. Several of the club members proceeded to compete on the grass, the first occasion being on 4 June at Abridge, about six miles north-east of Walthamstow in the Epping Forest District. Three weeks later club riders participated in another grasstrack event, at Stanford-le-Hope in Essex, before returning to Abridge on 2 July. The club intended to recommend any promising riders to the speedway management for trials.

July

Financial problems at Third Division Tamworth worsened in mid-July, with attendances below 3,000 making the track unviable. After two riders, Eric Boothroyd and Brian Shepherd, were transferred, promoter Les Marshall undertook to carry on for the foreseeable future. The Long Eaton track was suggested as a suitable venue to take over the fixtures if Tamworth pulled out of the league. Newcastle had similar worries and other clubs, including First Division Harringay, were said to be monitoring the position in case Derick Close became available for transfer.

The supporters' Channel cruise took place on 2 July, with 200 members joined onboard by manager John Deeley and riders Jim Boyd, Bert Edwards, Harry Edwards, Benny King, Reg Reeves and Arch Windmill. Percy Chandler, a stadium director, also accompanied the group, along with his wife. Some of the riders also took along family members. The original idea of spending time in Calais was abandoned. Coaches left The Stow at 7.30am, with *The Royal Daffodil* sailing from Gravesend at 9am. The party was scheduled to arrive back in Walthamstow at around 11pm. Members of the motorcycle section of the club not on the cruise attended another grasstrack event at Abridge. As an incentive for the grasstrack riders from the club ahead of the next event at Abridge on 30 July, Phil Sugden, the *Walthamstow Post* editor, promised a trophy to be awarded to the best performer across the season.

After getting the league campaign off to a fine start with home and away victories over Sheffield, the Wolves were stunned as they slipped to a three-point home defeat to Plymouth on 3 July. The visitors provided the majority of heat winners, being well led by maximum scorer Pete Lansdale and captain Peter Robinson, who was beaten by Harry Edwards in the opening heat. That was Edwards's only success. He fell in his next ride on a track made difficult by rain. Just as Coventry had done earlier in the season, Plymouth took advantage of the Wolves riders' difficulties, particularly from the starts, when their home track was affected by wet conditions.

A second half series of match races was staged between reigning World Champion Tommy Price and Australian Graham Warren, a joint track record holder at The Stow. Price, of Wembley and England, was successful in the first heat, before the Birmingham rider came back to win the second and the decider in fine fashion. Warren equalled the record of 62.6 seconds in the second heat and established a new best time of 62.4 in the decider.

The day after the home defeat to Plymouth, the Wolves travelled to Glasgow to face Ashfield in the return leg of the National Trophy semi-final, in front of a reported record crowd of 23,000. The advantage from the home leg was still intact going into the final race as Walthamstow led by three points overall. Boyd and Edwards were then no match for the home pairing of Le Breton and Harding who both completed the meeting unbeaten by a visiting rider. Windmill won two races, but none of the other Wolves riders managed a heat success. After the disappointment of surrendering a sound position in the Southern Shield competition, it was another huge setback for Walthamstow after coming so close to reaching the divisional final.

Walthamstow had little difficulty in beating Edinburgh Monarchs by 20 points in a home league encounter on 10 July. King and Reeves returned double figure scores and Windmill won his first three rides. Bruce Gardiner, the South Australian Junior Champion, substituting for the injured Newton, failed to score. This was Gardiner's sole league outing for the Wolves and he finished the season early after breaking his leg in a track crash at Rye House on 6 August. He was leading his opening race at the Hoddesdon track by about 30 yards when he swerved and crashed. Despite having sufficient time to avoid him, the following rider ran into Gardiner as he lay prone on the track.

Consolation for the visitors came when Jack Young reduced the track record to 61.4 seconds when he beat King in the opening heat. King avenged this loss when he defeated Young in the final heat. Young was in exceptional form and had broken the Norwich record two days earlier on the way to scoring a 15-point maximum in a World Championship Qualifying Round.

George Formby, one of the entertainment world's biggest speedway fans, was present to witness a controversial meeting between Fleetwood and the Wolves on 12 July. The match was littered with incidents and disputed decisions by the meeting steward, with the large crowd becoming very aggrieved and agitated as the evening progressed. The outcome was a four-point win and two league points for Walthamstow. The most hotly disputed decision followed the exclusion of home rider Norman Hargreaves in heat five after a collision with Boyd. Reports suggested that the home rider attempted an inside pass on the second bend which caused Boyd to fall. However, back in the pits, the Walthamstow rider apologised to his opponent and admitted the collision was his fault. Nevertheless, the exclusion of Hargreaves stood.

Former Wolves rider Dick Geary had a mixed night, winning one race in scoring five points, whereas Newton, who moved to Walthamstow as part of the exchange deal, had his best match in his new colours and scored 11. Fleetwood were out of luck as Geary and Culshaw both had engine failures when heading for almost certain 5–1 heat wins with their partners.

The Walthamstow team was invited across the Irish Sea to Dublin on Sunday 16 July to take on Shelbourne at their track on the west bank of the River Dodder in Ringsend. Shelbourne were managed by Ronnie Greene, the promoter of First Division Wimbledon. He tracked a competitive team led by 17-year-old Ronnie Moore, the Dons' Australian-born sensation who went on to represent New Zealand, his adopted country, for most of his career. In fact, seven of the eight home riders regularly appeared for Wimbledon in the National League First Division. Moore was hard to beat at Shelbourne Park and scored a maximum. He led his team to an emphatic 54–30 victory.

Against such strong opposition, it was little surprise that the Wolves supplied just two heat winners. Boyd top-scored with nine points, but his team-mates struggled on yet another rain-affected track. Ahead of the visit to Dublin, it was announced that Jimmy Grant had joined Walthamstow from First Division Harringay. He rode in place of Bert Edwards in this match. Bruce Gardiner also rode as a reserve, in place of Newton. A group of Walthamstow supporters flew to Dublin for the meeting and had better weather conditions than for the Southampton trip earlier in the season.

In mid-July, rumours were circulating that May was on the verge of leaving Walthamstow, but manager John Deeley was quick to deny this. Harry Edwards was the only home rider not to win a race as the Wolves recorded a comfortable win over Fleetwood by 24 points on 17 July. However, Edwards did finish second to team partner May in securing maximum points in heat 12. Megs Jenkins, star of stage and screen, presented the trophy and cash prizes in the second half of the meeting. The event was contested by home riders and new signing Jimmy Grant won the final from King and May after Reeves fell.

The league meeting at Cradley Heath on 22 July was postponed due to rain as the season continued to be blighted by bad weather. The postponement was particularly frustrating for three members of the Supporters' Club who had cycled all the way there from Walthamstow. Another 60 supporters made the journey in vain by coach. Cradley Heath visited The Stow two days later. Although matches between the two teams were traditionally hard-fought affairs, they usually ended in emphatic home victories and this one was no exception. The Wolves won 59–25. Captain Jim Boyd scored a maximum and there were no weak links in the home side. The visitors provided little support for Alan Hunt, who scored 11, being defeated by Boyd.

Boyd tried out a new engine in the second half and broke a chain. Fortunately, no other damage appeared to have been done, but he still stripped and rebuilt the motor in time for the World Championship qualifier the following week. Although Boyd had taken the winner's cheque when brought in as a meeting reserve in 1949, the field was much stronger when this World Championship Qualifying Round was held on 31 July. Nevertheless, Boyd was a winner once again, this time with a maximum 15 points, four ahead of Scottish sensation Tommy Miller and reserve Jimmy Grant. For the second year running, a reserve for the meeting made a big impact as Grant replaced Ticker James. James fell in the first heat and was unable to take part in the re-run, and was ruled out of the rest of the meeting. Boyd recorded the five fastest times of the meeting and was presented with the prize of a cheque for £40 from the editor of the *Sunday Dispatch* newspaper.

August

Although his form could best be described as inconsistent, Newton was selected to represent Britain as reserve against Overseas in a Second Division level international match at Sheffield on 3 August. He was given two rides and scored three points.

Dick Shepherd had been limited to second half races at Walthamstow since May. At the end of July, his former Wolves manager, Wally Lloyd, invited him to Belfast to compete at Dunmore. Shepherd rode regularly at the track for the rest of the season and he won the Belfast Riders' Championship in August. He also rode for the Belfast Bees in team matches.

Walthamstow were drawn to meet First Division West Ham over two legs in the first round of the London Cup, sponsored by the *Evening News* newspaper. The first leg was at Custom House on 1 August and the return at Chingford Road six days later. The Wolves almost pulled off a giant killing act, for after losing the away leg by 24 points they triumphed in the return by 16 to lose on aggregate 112–104. In the first leg, before a crowd of 65,000, the scores were level after heat eight, but Walthamstow had no answer to Aub Lawson and Malcom Craven, who between them outscored the Wolves team over the last 10 races. With a massive following from Walthamstow, the match programmes were sold out well before the start.

For the return leg, a record crowd of over 20,000 was reported. The Hammers were in danger of being on the receiving end of a shock exit from the cup when the Wolves had reduced the overall margin to just four points with three heats remaining. Lawson and Craven came to life in heat 16 and took a 5–1 against the home pair of Boyd and Windmill. Before the visitors had time to draw breath, the Wolves hit back in the next race as King and Windmill overcame Chitty and Byford, to reduce the gap to just four points again. Needing maximum points from the last heat to force a replay, the home pair of Boyd and Newton were unable to stop Wally Green as he duly completed an 18-point maximum. For good measure, Aub Lawson took second place and the tie was won by the Hammers. Newton had a seized engine in this race, the fifth time this season when he had been struck by major mechanical gremlins.

Reeves, May and Boyd had led the scoring in the away leg, with double-figure scores from Newton, Boyd, Windmill and King, ably supported by a solid return from Reeves, taking the Wolves close in the second leg. The exit from the London Cup left Walthamstow with just the league title to challenge for in their quest for silverware in 1950. 17-year-old Reg Fearman, who went on to serve speedway as a rider, promoter, international team manager and Chairman of the British Speedway Promoters' Association in a long career, rode for the West Ham team in both legs of the London Cup tie.

At the beginning of August, Charles Chandler, the stadium's governing director, was taken ill and spent some time in hospital.

Having been long in the planning, the cricket match finally took place on Sunday, 6 August at The Stow. The team of riders and officials triumphed against the supporters' team. The success owed much to some fine batting by Ron Lewin and Percy Chandler, with Jim Boyd's spin bowling proving very effective. A highlight of the afternoon, which greatly amused the 2,000 or so spectators, was the sight of opening batsman Bert Edwards striding out to the middle wearing a top hat and frock coat.

On the same afternoon as the cricket match, the club's grasstrack riders ventured further afield, to Chelmsford, where Ben Bridgewater performed with distinction in securing two race wins and a second place. H. Salmon also took second place in one event. Another trip to the Chelmsford venue took place on 13 August and again the competitors were well supported by members of the motor cycling and light cars section. The club then returned to Abridge for a meeting on 3 September.

Walthamstow travelled to Glasgow for a league match on 9 August and went down by two points. Tommy Miller scored a maximum and the Hodgson brothers, Jack and Frank, both achieved double figures. The match was won for the home team by the contribution of reserve Ken McKinlay, who was given extra rides. Inconsistent form which dogged the Wolves team was again evident. On this occasion, the bulk of the scoring was done by May, Newton, Boyd and Grant. Reeves had an off night. Luck was against Walthamstow when King discovered his machine had a broken clutch countershaft before racing began. He was unable to repair it and pulled out of the meeting.

Once again, the Wolves riders could not match the speed of Australian star Jack Young. He scored a maximum in leading his Edinburgh team to a 48–36 win in a league encounter at Old Meadowbank on 12 August. Young also equalled the track record during the match. Jimmy Grant, Walthamstow's recent acquisition from Harringay, managed two points. May had extra rides as reserve and notched 10 points in one of his best meetings of the season. He was the only visiting rider to match the speed of the Monarchs from the start.

The return league match with Glasgow Tigers on 14 August resulted in an easy home win by 22 points. The lead was four points halfway through the match, before Walthamstow steadily pulled away. King and Boyd scored maximums and were well backed by Reeves with 10. Newton took a nasty fall and banged his head against the safety fence in his first ride. He failed to get going in his other outings and it would have been wiser for him to have pulled out of the meeting. Harry Edwards was unlucky to have a puncture in the first heat after hitting the fence, causing him to retire. Tommy Miller had a quiet evening for the Tigers and failed to win a race, mainly due to making poor starts in his heats.

Even without the injured Boyd, the Wolves overwhelmed Newcastle by 38 points on 21 August to take two more league points. Boyd had broken a collar bone in a crash in a second half event at Wembley a few days earlier and this caused him to miss the next round of the World Championship. Walthamstow took maximum points in each of the first three races and thereafter cruised to an easy victory. King, Reeves and Grant were unbeaten by an opponent and good support was provided by the rest of the team. Will Lowther was the only visitor to win a race, although he finished last in his other rides.

The last meeting in August at The Stow saw the Wolves entertain Yarmouth in the league. After a hard-fought match, the home team won by eight points, thanks to a maximum from stand-in captain King and double figure scores from Grant and Reeves. King was in a rich vein of form and his full score was his third in a row. Dry, slick track conditions prevailed because the track staff did not apply any water because of threatened rain. However, the rain did not arrive until after the meeting finished. The surface was not to the liking of May and Harry Edwards, which was reflected in modest points returns. In heat 13, Edwards and Yarmouth's Stan Page fell on the last bend in the tricky slick conditions. Both got up and pushed their bikes in a race to the finishing line, with Page getting there first in a time of 91.0 seconds. Newton was once more hampered by mechanical gremlins. King went on to pip Reeves to win another staging of the *Walthamstow Post* Trophy in the fastest time of the meeting in the second half. The trophy was presented by Mlle Daniele Viault, a young French visitor to Walthamstow.

Graham Warren and Rosalyn Boulter after Warren had won the second-half trophy on 19 September 1950. (JSC – Courtesy Graham Warren collection)

Left: Jimmy Grant riding for Walthamstow. He began his career at The Stow in 1950. (JSC)

Ken Le Breton (Glasgow Ashfield) and Jim Boyd (Walthamstow) in action. Le Breton was one of the stars of the Second Division and died in a track accident in Australia in January 1951. (JSC)

Two Walthamstow programmes from 1950. Left: a league match against Bristol; right: The Third Division Riders' Championship. (Courtesy Keith Corns)

At the end of August RM Samuel's editorial comment in the *Speedway News* called for measures to address difficulties brought about by falling attendances and diminishing interest in the sport from several newspapers across the country, where little or no coverage was given in some cases. Two principal suggestions involved creating two larger divisions in place of the current three, together with reducing pay rates for riders. He also said that a reduction in the high rate of Entertainment Tax levied on the sport would be highly beneficial, although very unlikely to happen.

September

At the beginning of September, there was talk that a fall in attendance figures was hitting some tracks hard. It was claimed that gate receipts at Third Division Tamworth were barely enough to cover payments to riders. Exeter had been forced to sell Hugh Geddes, their Australian star, to Swindon for £550 to enable the track to continue to stage speedway. Meanwhile a committee of First Division promoters was looking at pay rates, with it being almost certain that reductions would be recommended. All indications were that the immediate post-war boom was well and truly over.

Walthamstow started the month in fifth position in the league. With matches in hand over all their rivals, more success away from home could enable a title challenge to be mounted. After the unexpected home loss to Plymouth, there had been a string of comfortable wins on the Chingford Road circuit.

18-year-old Arthur Forrest scored a maximum for Halifax at The Stow on 4 September, but it was not enough to prevent the Wolves from winning by 13 points. Both Forrest and Edinburgh's Jack Young qualified for the World Championship Final to be staged at Wembley on 21 September, reflecting the improving standard of the Second Division.

Boyd returned after recovering from injury and to ease his way back, he replaced Bert Edwards at reserve. In an eventful fourth heat Boyd fell then Ray Johnson could not avoid his fallen team partner Vic Emms, leaving Windmill to finish the race alone. Boyd replaced May in this heat after May had fallen in his first ride. All the home riders made useful contributions and the meeting saw a welcome return to form by Reeves and Harry Edwards as they jointly top-scored with nine points.

In yet another rain-affected match, Reeves found the Tongham track not to his liking when the Wolves beat Aldershot by six points in a challenge match on 6 September. He stood down after one pointless ride and the four points gained by his reserve substitutes were enough to turn the match in his team's favour. Windmill enjoyed the conditions to top his team's score chart with nine points.

Hanley (Stoke) had developed into a solid team under the management of pre-war star Tiger Stevenson and claimed the league points in a 14-point win when the Wolves visited on 9 September. This was after the visitors had led by two points halfway through the match. Reeves excelled with 11 points, as May, Newton and Edwards totalled only two points between them. An eventful evening for Newton saw him fall in one race and twice pull out with machine problems.

Walthamstow recorded an important victory over league leaders Norwich in the home meeting on 11 September. The winning margin of 20 points was much more than expected and the home team was well led by Boyd and Grant. Both riders were unbeaten by the opposition. Windmill also rode well and dropped just one point from his three rides. Bert Edwards was given an opportunity in place of May who was suffering from recurring tonsillitis. The Wolves established a lead of 10 points after just five heats and the outcome of the match was never in doubt. Newton's awful run continued, with yet another mechanical breakdown and a fall as he failed to score.

After a bright start, in which Walthamstow led by four points after three heats, wet conditions spoilt the league meeting at Ashfield on 12 September. The Wolves lost heavily, 56–28. The visitors found the muddy conditions in torrential rain hard to master. The steward considered abandoning the meeting before the rain eased slightly. Newton won his first ride in the fastest time of the meeting, then fell in both his other rides. Grant and Reeves were the only other heat winners for Walthamstow, finishing as joint top scorers with seven points.

A large group of members of the Supporters' Club cycling section rode to Norwich for the match on 16 September. They travelled there on the Friday evening and stayed in the city before cycling back on the Sunday. Another 100 fans travelled to the meeting by coach. Meanwhile, the grasstracking members were in action at Stanford-le-Hope on 17 September. Ben Bridgewater again starred in this meeting, with three wins and a second place aboard his new machine.

Although the Walthamstow followers were hugely disappointed with the 66–17 annihilation of their team, they enjoyed great hospitality. The hosts provided the visiting fans with a meal at the stadium, such were the good relations between rival tracks in those days. Journeys by long-distance travelling supporters were slow and tiring. The meeting was disastrous for Walthamstow as they succumbed to the league leaders. Newton, a former Norwich track record holder, had four rides in the match and fell each time. Reeves, King and Boyd all had machine problems. The Norwich score might have been higher had not Littlewood dropped out of one race with engine failure when ahead of the visiting pair.

A win at The Stow over Hanley by 15 points kept alive the faint hopes of league success for Walthamstow two days later. Windmill moved up from reserve, changing places with Newton for this match and he celebrated by winning all four of his races. King and Boyd with 11 and 10 points respectively provided excellent support as the Potters were restricted to just three race winners. Managing Director Charles H Chandler decided that the proceeds of this meeting would be entirely given over to eight charities, seven nominated by the Mayor of Walthamstow, together with the Riders' Benevolent Fund.

A prize of a £50 silver trophy, provided by Mr Chandler, was put up for the winner of races between Belle Vue's match race ace Jack Parker and Graham Warren. Parker was a fine exponent of match racing and had dominated the monthly British Match Race Championship since 1946, winning 18 out of 21 events in which he competed, staged on a best of three basis. Deciding legs were staged on a neutral track when required. The prize money was often referred to as 'Parker's Pension'. Warren, who had shown a great liking for the Chingford Road track on previous visits, was also a former track record holder. With no regard for past reputation Warren overcame his rival in two straight runs, making a decider unnecessary. Parker led the wheel-to-wheel tussles on both occasions, but Warren had the speed and the skill to get by. The prizes were presented by special guest Rosalyn Boulter, a star of screen and stage, with West End and Broadway appearances to her name.

Undeterred by the previous difficulties they had encountered, the Supporters' Club arranged another flight to Southampton for the league match on 19 September. The total cost of the return flight, airport transfers, admission, programme and a meal amounted to £3/8 per person. This time the weather did not play havoc with the journey. The Wolves fans saw their team put on a good show, including taking an early lead before going down to an eight-point defeat. The teams were evenly matched and only home star Roy Craighead achieved a double-figure total. Reeves top-scored for Walthamstow, but King withdrew from the meeting after one pointless ride.

Any lingering hopes of winning the division title were dashed at Plymouth on 22 September, when the Wolves lost by four points to a Devils team missing two of their regular team members, Johnny Bradford and Bill Thatcher. Although Walthamstow gave a solid performance, they provided only two race winners. The visitors had no answer to Pete Lansdale, Len Read and Peter Robinson who won 11 heats between them. This was the seventh away defeat in a row, five of them in September.

On 23 September, 70 supporters travelled by coach when the Wolves visited The Abbey Stadium to meet Third Division Swindon in a challenge match. The team's away following continued to be strong, taking into account the distances and journey times involved. The match was won comfortably 51–33. The basis of this victory was a good all-round team performance, but it was encouraging that two riders who had joined the club in 1950 were to the fore. Grant led the scorers with 11 and Newton notched 10 points. The only disappointment was Benny King, who failed to score in four outings.

The international series between Britain and Overseas concluded at The Stow on 25 September, with the Overseas team victorious 65–42, taking the series by three wins to two. Before the meeting started, the riders were introduced to Donald Peers, a star of the West End and described as the greatest singing sensation of post-war years. Peers had agreed to become president of the Walthamstow Speedway Supporters' Club. Writing ahead of the match, speedway journalist Jim Stenner warned that the odds were very much in favour of the Overseas team as Britain were under-strength and would particularly miss the injured Arthur Forrest and Alan Hunt who was riding in a league match for Cradley Heath.

Four Wolves riders were included in the home team and all did fairly well. Boyd, King and Grant each scored 11 and Reeves chipped in with five. The Walthamstow riders were poorly supported by Peter Robinson, Phil Clarke, Stan Williams and Vic Emms, who managed only four points between them.

Jack Young once again displayed a great liking for the track, racing to an 18-point maximum and recording a time just outside his own track record in the first heat. Ken Le Breton was not to be outdone and as well as being unbeaten by the home riders, he bettered Young's record with a time of 60.6 seconds in the second heat. The record was now exactly five seconds faster than at the beginning of the 1949 season. The Australian trio of Young, Le Breton and Bob Leverenz won 15 of the 18 heats between them.

Walthamstow kept their hopes of a top three finish in the league alive with an emphatic 51–31 defeat of Yarmouth at Caister Road on 26 September. Even Billy Bales, home on leave from National Service, could not stem the tide as he scored eight points. The home riders had mechanical trouble in five heats, but on this form the Wolves would have won anyway. Harry Edwards was the star for Walthamstow, scoring a fine maximum and his team-mates all weighed in with good supporting scores.

In a challenge match at Third Division Rayleigh on the last day of September, the Wolves were easy 60–44 winners in an 18-heat match. Grant did well to top score with 14 and Harry Edwards would have scored more than 11 except for an engine failure in one ride. Newton fell twice and won his other four races in style.

One disappointment for the Supporters' Club was the lack of available facilities for the swimming section to get underway. The motor cycling and light cars section planned to maintain the interest of members throughout the winter by showing films of speedway and TT races at their meetings. A trip to Southend illuminations was organised for a party of supporters to enjoy on 30 September, presumably after the Rayleigh meeting.

October

Ashfield were easily accounted for in a league meeting at The Stow on 2 October. The 25-point winning margin was the result of a fine team performance, led by Windmill with a maximum. For the Giants, Ken Le Breton started with two wins, showing his liking for the circuit again, before crashing out of the match in his third race.

On 7 October, Walthamstow lost by 23 points at Coventry before triumphing by nine points in the return fixture at The Stow two days later. Les Hewitt again shone for Coventry with a maximum at Brandon. Harry Edwards and Grant posted the best scores of six points each for the Wolves. The Wolves provided only three race winners. The Coventry track was in poor condition and there were numerous falls. The *Coventry Evening Telegraph* report described the surface as 'mirror-like'. The 10th heat was disastrous for the visitors as Boyd collided with Newton. Boyd was excluded from the rerun, but neither rider took any further part in the match.

King with a maximum and Arch Windmill with nine points led the team in a better performance in the home meeting. May, now at reserve, continued to struggle and was a shadow of the rider of 1949.

Walthamstow travelled to Halifax in a rearranged fixture on 11 October and after another very disappointing performance were defeated by 26 points. The home side were missing their injured star Arthur Forrest, but still had three riders, Emms, Hughes and Allison, with maximums, together with Bill Crosland who was unbeaten by the opposition. In contrast, the Wolves provided a single heat winner, when Harry Edwards took the final heat.

The Wolves avenged their recent defeat at Southampton by winning the last league meeting of the season at The Stow by 15 points on 16 October. King signed off with a maximum and Grant dropped only one point to the visitors. There was just one point between the teams midway through the match before Walthamstow steadily increased their lead.

The Wolves provided the opposition for Third Division Leicester on 20 October in front of over 9,500 spectators and were soundly beaten 51–33. The home team gave reserve Les Beaumont extra rides and he eased to a maximum. Harry Edwards performed well and top scored for Walthamstow with 10 points. Grant crashed into the safety fence on the final lap of his first ride and was ruled out of the rest of the meeting. This was the eighth visit of a Second Division team to Blackbird Road in 1950 and the home team won every time. Local rivals Coventry Bees ended the Hunters' run of success with a two-point win the next week.

Walthamstow had a poor record at Cradley Heath and suffered another heavy defeat, by 28 points, on a league visit on 21 October. Boyd took no part in the meeting, having been injured at Leicester the evening before. Windmill took advantage of extra rides from reserve to top score with nine points. Grant was also ruled out through injury and was replaced by Bert Edwards. For the home team, Alan Hunt extended his fine record against the Wolves with a maximum.

With the team away at Newcastle on 23 October, the Walthamstow track staged the Third Division Riders' Championship meeting, for which top scorers of the various tracks had qualified. This meeting brought the season at The Stow to a close. Qualification for the meeting had been by way of points scored in second half races, in which the top four scorers from each side, including bonus points, took part. Aldershot fans considered Trevor Redmond's track knowledge would stand him in good stead and make him a favourite to take the title. They gave him and team-mate Basil Harris excellent support, with over 1,000 tickets sold at the Hampshire track and 25 coaches booked to transport them to the event. According to the *Aldershot News* there was a capacity crowd.

Ten of the 16 competitors won a race in a fairly even field. The title went to Oxford's Pat Clarke with a maximum 15 points. Second and third places went to Redmond and Ken Middleditch of Poole with 13 and 11 points respectively. Redmond was defeated first by Clarke, who led from the start in heat 11, then by Middleditch in his final race after the title was already out of reach. Although the Walthamstow management intended to continue their pursuit of Redmond, he had already been named on the Aldershot retained list for 1951 at the beginning of the month.

The Walthamstow season ended with a whimper as the team slumped to an 18-point defeat against lowly Newcastle at Brough Park. In a subdued display, only Grant with nine points and Harry Edwards with eight put up any resistance to the home riders. King won one race on his former home track, but failed to score in his other three.

Season's end

After being in a good position to challenge for league honours at the start of September, the team ended the season with the disappointing record of losing nine of the last 15 matches. Home track advantage was used to good effect, with only one home league defeat. However, after winning the first two away matches, there was only one further success on the road and that was not until late September.

Charlie May endured a disappointing season and it was no surprise when he was made available for transfer in the winter. He eventually joined Southampton in time for the new season. His average had dropped by over one and a half points per match from the previous season. He had slipped from second top rider down to reserve by the end of the year.

Jim Boyd was again the leading Wolves rider, even though nearly a point a match down on his 1949 average. He was still a match for most riders in the division, particularly at The Stow. Reg Reeves made great progress in his second season in the league and became the team's third heat leader. Harry Edwards shone very often, but was less consistent than Reeves and his average was only a marginal improvement on his first season. Arch Windmill developed into a reliable middle order rider, capable of big scores periodically. Benny King was not far behind Boyd in the league averages and showed a slight improvement on his scoring from the year before.

Of the newcomers, Jimmy Grant had the greatest impact, giving excellent support to the top riders. George Newton was spectacular, although far too inconsistent. Bert Edwards proved to be a reliable scorer when called upon at reserve.

As the season drew to a close, press reports focused on the decline in attendances around the country. Some of the reasons put forward to explain this were the high level of taxation which impacted on admission prices and the increasing cost of living. Poor weather throughout 1950 was claimed to be another major factor, with a high number of meetings postponed or staged in poor conditions. The tendency for many meetings to be easily won by the home side led to some calls for standardisation of tracks, which others said emphatically would be impossible. An aggregate bonus point for league matches was one idea put forward, although it was acknowledged that this would still not prevent runaway home wins. In an attempt to develop skills, the managers at Walthamstow and Halifax, John Deeley and Bruce Booth, suggested that their riders could visit each other's tracks in the winter for practice sessions. According to the *Stenner's Annual*, attendances at The Stow had shown no improvement on disappointing 1949 levels.

At the end of the season Bruce Gardiner set sail for home with his broken leg still in a plaster cast. It had mostly been a frustrating time in England for the young Australian. Fortunately, he recovered in time to ride again in the 1950–51 Australian season and performed well at Bathurst, New South Wales. In December, George Newton was transfer-listed by Walthamstow and would be on the move again, with Motherwell initially thought to be the likely destination. The final Supporters' Club gathering of 1950 was the Christmas Dance on 21 December at Walthamstow Assembly Hall, with Donald Peers in attendance.

By the end of December, plans were advanced for a Second Division of 18 or 19 teams, depending upon whether or not Norwich gained promotion to the top division. As in 1950, the season was intended to start with Northern and Southern Shield competitions. Tracks included in plans for the division at this stage were Ashfield, Coventry, Cradley Heath, Edinburgh, Fleetwood, Glasgow White City, Halifax, Hanley (Stoke), Leicester, Liverpool, Motherwell, Newcastle, Norwich, Oxford, Plymouth, Sheffield, Southampton, Walthamstow and Yarmouth.

Strong rumours circulated that at least two teams would be elevated to the First Division for the 1951 season, with the favourites being Norwich and Walthamstow. As champions of Division Two and with good attendances, it was natural that Norwich would be considered. Crowd levels at Walthamstow were referred to as being disappointing compared to other tracks in the division, except when First Division opponents visited. On those occasions the stadium was packed. It was strongly felt by the management that Walthamstow needed the bonus of numerous London derbies to bring spectator levels up. The Walthamstow management firmly believed that the existing team members would form the basis of a useful First Division outfit if supplemented by two or three star riders Mr Chandler had a history of spending money to boost the team strength when necessary and there was every reason to believe that he would do so again.

A newsletter was issued by the Speedway Control Board in late December. It said that it should not be thought that the Board was set against promotion of teams from one division to another. However, it went on to say that many factors had to be considered when a track applied for inclusion in a higher league. This included consideration of the current rider assets and means of strengthening the team if necessary, which would require the availability of both funds and suitable riders. On the basis that promotion should be expected to attract higher attendances, the capacity of the stadium concerned also needed to be sufficient. A third factor, which was said to be perhaps the most important of all, was the attractiveness of the team when racing their away meetings. Existing top division teams would not wish to host weak, unattractive opposition as attendances would plummet on those occasions. The Walthamstow management felt that provided a competitive team was assembled it was likely that the Wolves could be as attractive as most other teams in the league.

12. 1951: Falling short in the Shield

Promoters of the First Division tracks met on 4 January 1951 and agreed to make a number of recommendations to the SCB, including rejection of the applications from Norwich and Walthamstow to join the top league. On the starting area, the promoters were in favour of a tarmac surface, with track surfaces of shale, cinders or other approved material, an all-encompassing proposal.

Walthamstow were still keen to build a team strong enough to compete at the top level and made a substantial bid to Aldershot for the transfer of New Zealand star Trevor Redmond. According to the press, the offer had been accepted but progress was delayed as Redmond was not yet back from a visit to his home country. When Redmond did return, he decided to stay with the Hampshire team.

On Friday 19 January came news from the Board that the applications from Norwich and Walthamstow to join the First Division had been rejected. This was a huge disappointment for both clubs, although it turned out that for Norwich, admission to the top division was only a year away. The Walthamstow management was extremely disappointed, feeling that the benefits of local derbies which the First Division would have brought were crucial in terms of ensuring the track's future viability. The Board was broadly in agreement with the promoters on track surfaces and starting areas, although subsequently several materials were tested, including synthetic ones.

The winter training school at Rye House, which had previously been so productive in unearthing new talent, was severely hampered by continuing bad weather, with cancellations caused by a waterlogged track. In earlier years, the Walthamstow management had hired the Rye House circuit for use by the club's riders, but during the winter, agreement was instead reached with Norwich for use of the large Firs circuit. Intensive practice eventually took place there on 17 March, two days after a similar session at The Stow.

During February, discussions took place about changes to pay rates for the new season in an attempt to prevent tracks going out of business. Figures published by the SCB showed an upwards trend in the number of people watching speedway in Britain, from 6,623,587 in 1946, 9,238,660 in 1947, 10,694,361 in 1948, to 12,585,698 in 1949. However, it was claimed that attendances had fallen by about 20 percent in 1950. Details were leaked that the promoters wanted riders in the top league to consider a reduction in pay of 15 percent, with a smaller reduction in the Second Division and no change in the Third. Walthamstow manager John Deeley spoke to the *Speedway News* about the short-sightedness of certain First Division promoters intent on restricting the development of teams in the lower leagues. He felt that they preferred instead to cherry pick the better riders for their own benefit.

The Second Division promoters voted in February to admit four new tracks in 1951, Leicester, Liverpool and Oxford from the Third Division, together with Motherwell which had run open-licence meetings in 1950. At the same time, Plymouth were controversially omitted from the recommended composition of the Second Division due to its geographical location. The closure of Third Division Tamworth was not unexpected, but a change of heart saw St

Austell continue in the Third Division. Cardiff, Long Eaton and Wolverhampton entered the Third Division.

The recommendations were duly submitted and ratified by the SCB, along with proposals for the early season regional shield competitions to take the form of three leagues, split into North, Central and South. Walthamstow would be in the Southern Shield competition along with Coventry, Norwich, Oxford, Southampton and Yarmouth.

The reasoning of the SCB was severely criticised in some quarters, none more so than by Basil Storey in the *Speedway Gazette*. He highlighted one totally illogical decision made by the Board, to demote Plymouth to the Third Division, against the wishes of the club, purely on the basis of remote geographical location, when regionalisation on a north and south basis for teams outside the First Division might have been a more sensible option. The outcome for Plymouth was not good. Crowds in the first two months of the 1951 season were reported to have fallen by 50 percent compared to the previous year. Another proposal, which was not adopted, was to scrap the traditional second half events and increase the number of heats in team events to offset this.

Following the demotion of Plymouth, the Walthamstow management moved quickly to secure the services of Pete Lansdale, one of their top riders, who had averaged well over nine points in 1950 league matches. Motherwell contacted John Deeley about the availability of George Newton. The Walthamstow manager advised that a fee of £500 would secure his transfer. Newton lived in Todmorden in West Yorkshire, close to the border with Lancashire, so it was no surprise when he eventually joined Liverpool for the 1951 season.

In February, the arrangement for reciprocal practice facilities at each other's tracks was confirmed for Halifax and Walthamstow riders, with dates to be arranged in February and March. This was in addition to the similar agreement reached between Walthamstow and Norwich, with the opportunity taken up by most of the Wolves riders.

As the new season approached, there was deadlock in pay negotiations and promoters threatened that unless agreement could be reached then matches would not take place. After a meeting between First and Second Division promoters, it was agreed that the old pay rates would continue until 10 April, the date the budget was to be announced by the Chancellor of the Exchequer. Dependent upon whether there was any reduction in the Entertainment Tax rate, the promoters would then enter negotiations with the SRA to agree cuts if necessary. Compromise was eventually reached between the promoters and the riders.

One change instantly noticeable as the new season began was that the Walthamstow meeting programme was reduced from 20 pages to eight. This was due to a national paper shortage and rising costs of production. The paper shortage had continued after the war and economy measures in effect at the time included the re-use of envelopes by using economy gummed labels for posting.

For the new season, the cricket section of the Supporters' Club reached agreement to stage matches at Lloyd Park, close to the town centre, with their opening fixture arranged for 6 May. A repeat of the match against riders and staff was scheduled to take place at The Stow on 5 August. The darts team competed in the Chingford League. Jack Buck, the club secretary, was keen to expand club activities and boost membership. Items on sale for the

1951 season included scarves priced 11/-, leather flying helmets at 15/-, club ties 7/6, berets costing 5/-, rosettes 1/9, propelling pencils 2/- and photographs of riders at 6d each.

More supporters were urged to join the Flying Section of the club, with a weekly payment scheme offered for those wishing to travel by air to away fixtures. The first of these trips, again to Southampton, was on 30 March, leaving The Stow at 5pm. Although Jack Buck hoped that air travel would be possible to most away meetings, Southampton proved to be the only destination to come to fruition. Ahead of the new season, Walthamstow proudly announced that singer and Armed Forces sweetheart Petula Clark would be joining Supporters' Club President Donald Peers by taking the role of Vice President. Miss Clark was said to be a keen speedway follower.

March

Walthamstow manager John Deeley was keen to strengthen his squad of riders and showed an interest in Harringay's Sid Clark, who was signed for a fee of £400. This was a high fee for a rider who would initially ride in a reserve berth, but the Walthamstow management clearly saw a great deal of potential in him.

The season opened with the regional shield tournaments, again sponsored by Kemsley. After the Kemsley Shield matches, the 18 Second Division teams were to compete for the Division Two league title, with the winners to receive the Kemsley Cup.

Southampton were the opponents in the opening meeting of the new season on 26 March. Walthamstow won 51– 33 in the Southern Shield. Six of the riders who had completed the previous season were in the Walthamstow team, the only changes being the introduction of new signing Pete Lansdale in place of George Newton and the inclusion of Bert Edwards instead of Charlie May. Lansdale lived in nearby Romford and so was a local boy in speedway terms. Charlie May made an immediate return with his new club in this fixture and a heat win in his final ride made him joint top scorer for the Saints with seven points. The Wolves team members all scored well, and Lansdale might have been unbeaten on his debut, except for a fall in his second race when attempting to pass Les Wotton on the final bend. Harry Edwards made a good start to the season and was joint top scorer with nine points.

The big disappointment on the opening night was the atrocious weather, which made track conditions difficult. Speedway had been blighted by poor weather in 1950 and it was very unfortunate that the new season got off to a rain-affected start. Petula Clark presented the Easter Trophy to the winner, Bob Oakley, in the second half of the meeting. Music Hall comedian Arthur English was also named as a Vice President of the Supporters' Club. John Deeley told supporters in his programme notes that Trevor Redmond was due back in the country in a few days and would hopefully agree to joining Walthamstow.

Having scored a maximum 15 points a week earlier in Southampton's opening night to take the Charles Knott Trophy, Harry Edwards again performed well to lead the scores with 11 in the return Shield match on 30 March. This inspired the Wolves team to an impressive 50–34 success at Banister Court. Boyd, Lansdale and King added 27 points between them, giving the team a powerful top four. The Southampton management may well have regretted enabling Edwards, Lansdale, Boyd and King to enjoy practice on their track during the Trophy event the previous week.

In the second home meeting in the Shield, on 2 April, Norwich were well beaten 55–29. Of the two teams which had unsuccessfully sought promotion, the Londoners looked by far the stronger. On this occasion, the scoring was led by old favourites Boyd and Harry Edwards with maximums. This was the first time Edwards had scored a maximum since July 1949. Benny King was also in good form and dropped a single point to the opposition. Bob Leverenz provided the sole race win for the reigning league champions. Swedish riders Sune Karlsson of club side Getingarna and Lennart Carlstrom of Vargarna competed in the second half events, but neither made much impression. Karlsson went on to finish third in the Swedish Final later in the season, with Carlstrom in 10th place. Both were top riders in league racing in Sweden at that time and were part of touring team that appeared at Long Eaton, Motherwell and Stoke.

Awful weather greeted the team and more than 100 of their followers at Norwich on 7 April. On a wet track, the team's unbeaten run in the Southern Shield ended with a 28-point defeat. Walthamstow only won two races, both by Reeves who was top scorer with nine. New signing Lansdale had a disappointing match and scored a single point. Opinions of the relative strength of the two teams had to be revised after this change of fortunes, although both remained confident of challenging for honours. The Wolves' supporters enjoyed a post-meeting dance in the clubroom before making the long trek home, not arriving back in Walthamstow until 3am.

New signing Sid Clark made his debut at reserve against Yarmouth, who lost 50–34 in the next Southern Shield encounter two days later. Clark replaced Bert Edwards who was loaned to Aldershot, where he would undoubtedly benefit from more rides. The newcomer endeared himself to the home crowd by winning his first heat. King scored six points and was the only home rider not to win a race. Reeves top scored with nine points and his performance did much to ensure a comfortable victory. In his first ride, he skilfully team rode alongside his partner, Boyd, to keep their opponents at bay and then, after poor starts, he had to pass both visiting riders to win his next two rides. Harry Edwards dropped his only points to the opposition in his first race, falling when in the lead.

There was good and bad news the next day. A fifth win in six matches in the Shield came when Walthamstow stormed to a 56–28 success in the return match at Yarmouth. Reeves was joined by King in scoring maximum points and Harry Edwards was beaten only once. Lansdale had another disappointing away meeting, this time scoring two points and falling in his last race. The bad news was that rather than giving a reduction in the rate of Entertainment Tax, the Chancellor had decided to increase it, although full details were not immediately available.

The *Speedway Gazette* had an article by Basil Storey proposing that the announcement of race times should be discontinued. The suggestion was that by removing this element from the racing, it would be seen by the Chancellor of the Exchequer that speedway was not merely a test of speed, but rather a sport where individual and team-riding skill was of paramount importance. Ronnie Greene had previously stopped announcing times at Wimbledon in 1947 and 1948, but it was not an initiative that was followed by other tracks.

Walthamstow Wolves 1951: Archie Windmill, Benny King, Sid Clark, John Deeley (manager), Reg Reeves, Harry Edwards, Jimmy Grant, Pete Lansdale, Jim Boyd (on bike). (JSC)

Singer Petula Clark was popular with the Walthamstow fans. On the left she is with Pete Lansdale, on the right presenting a trophy to Reg Reeves. (Both JSC)

The Wolves' fine start to the season produced some additional bookings, the first of which was a challenge match at Aldershot on 14 April. The Wolves won 70–37. The home team was overwhelmed and the visitors provided 15 race winners in 18 heats. Trevor Redmond showed why Walthamstow were keen to acquire his services by winning three races and scoring 15 points. Aldershot were unlucky when Geoff Mardon, their other New Zealand star, crashed in his second ride and was ruled out of the rest of the match.

Newly promoted Oxford caused a huge upset when winning by six points at The Stow the following day. The home team suffered a major blow when Lansdale was injured in a fall in the third heat and was taken to hospital with facial lacerations. King was also brought down in the same incident, for which Bill Osborne was excluded from the rerun for causing the crash. Osborne scored eight points from his other three races to enjoy a successful return to his former track. Maybe he was trying a bit too hard to impress and his tactics annoyed the home fans throughout the match. King was also unable to ride in the rerun of the third heat, which meant that both reserves were used. Although he was able to take his other rides, King was handicapped by an ankle injury from the crash. The visitors led by four points going into the final heat, but the home side could field only one rider because the reserves had taken their full quota of rides and so had no chance to salvage a match point.

A large contingent of Walthamstow supporters followed their team in a challenge match at First Division New Cross on 18 April. The Wolves put on a fine show before losing by seven points. Thirty coach loads of supporters made the journey south of the Thames and hundreds more travelled independently. The Wolves team was boosted by the inclusion of transfer target Trevor Redmond, used as a guest to replace the injured Lansdale. Redmond showed his ability in top scoring for the team with 11 points, defeating home stars Cyril Roger and Eric French in the process.

Victory by 19 points against visiting Coventry on 23 April took the Wolves two points clear at the top of the Southern Shield table, although both Oxford and Norwich had raced two matches less. The match was won by heat 10. With Lansdale still absent because of injury, Alby Smith was given an opportunity at reserve. Trevor Redmond was invited to compete in a second half match race, in which he was beaten by Reeves. Part of the meeting was available to a wide audience as it was televised live on BBC from 7.30pm to 8.30pm.

The return of Lansdale from injury helped the Wolves overcome Coventry 43–40 at Brandon in the return fixture on the following Saturday. This win kept alive slim hopes of Southern Shield success. Coventry Bees were missing two riders due to injury and a team effort from Walthamstow saw them take the match points, led by Reeves with nine. After holding an eight-point lead at the halfway stage, the Wolves were pegged back as the Bees levelled the score in the ninth heat. A three-point lead was established before the last race, in which Landsdale and Reeves kept Wilf Plant behind them to win the match.

Boyd had recently experienced a series of mechanical problems, but he was on top form in the National Trophy Second Division First Round home leg against Southampton on 30 April, leading the team to a massive 46-point advantage by scoring a six-ride maximum. King, Lansdale and Reeves all achieved double figure scores, with Windmill winning both of his reserve rides. Former Walthamstow rider Charlie May was the only Saints rider to beat King.

The huge advantage gained made progress in this competition by beating Saints for the third year in a row almost certain.

In April, it came to the attention of Supporters' Club officials that away trips were also being arranged independently. This was a concern to Jack Buck as he was still working hard to reach a membership target figure of 6,000. His aim was to ensure that club trips and events would be well supported and costs per member kept at affordable levels.

May

At the beginning of May, the Sheffield promoter Frank Varey announced that his track was closing and the entire team was available for transfer. The reason for closure was the high rate of Entertainment Tax which was crippling the speedway operation. After a promising opening meeting attendance of around 8,000, subsequent meetings were said to have only attracted an average crowd of 4,000. This was not enough for the business to remain viable. Varey vowed to reopen the track if the rate of duty was reduced by the Chancellor of the Exchequer. Charlie New was available from Sheffield for a fee of £1,000 and Walthamstow immediately expressed an interest, although he moved to Coventry instead.

Fans around the country were urged to lobby their members of parliament about the unfair Entertainment Tax. Two of the MPs in the Walthamstow area were important figures in politics. The Rt. Hon. Winston Churchill, represented Wanstead and Woodford, and the Rt. Hon. Clement Attlee, the serving Prime Minister, represented Walthamstow West.

Hansard reports (HC Deb 01 May 1951 vol 487 cc125–6W) reveal that the Chancellor, Hugh Gaitskell, was questioned by several MPs in the House of Commons about why speedway racing was classified as a 'non-live' sport. This made it subject to the tax rating of approximately 48 percent, while football and boxing enjoyed the lower rate of 15 percent. The Chancellor replied by saying it was not correct to suppose that the higher rate of Entertainments Tax was intended to apply only to those forms of entertainment in which human beings play no direct part. He explained that the higher rate applied to horse racing and motor racing, as well as to cinemas and greyhound racing. In reviewing the position in the light of the representations made, he had reached same conclusion as his predecessors, that speedway racing was properly classed with the other forms of entertainment mentioned rather than with the entertainments which paid the lesser amount. This was an inadequate explanation and was incomprehensible to those involved in speedway.

In completing the double over the Wolves on 3 May, Oxford clinched the Southern Shield and ensured that the visitors finished in third place. Edwards, Reeves, Windmill and Clark totalled five points between them and the lack of strength in depth on this occasion cost Walthamstow dearly as they lost by 14 points. Lansdale shone for the visitors, winning his last three rides after failing to score first time out. Former Wolves rider Bill Osborne was joint top scorer for Oxford with nine points.

Walthamstow ensured an unlikely comeback by Southampton was not to happen in the second leg of the National Trophy tie on 4 May. An early six-point lead added to their first leg advantage and although the Saints eventually won the meeting, the Wolves triumphed by a comfortable 34 points on aggregate. Lansdale was top scorer with 13 points, with three heat wins. King scored 10 points and provided good support.

Reigning First Division champions Wembley, leaving out only 1949 World Champion Tommy Price, visited The Stow for a challenge match on 7 May. The home riders were in good form and won by six points. Bob Oakley scored an untroubled maximum for the Lions, but Freddie Williams, the current World Champion, was restricted to six points. Although the Lions provided the majority of heat winners, the home team all contributed good scores and King was their top man with 10 points.

Walthamstow and Hanley met in the Division Two Second Round of the National Trophy on 12 and 14 May, with the first leg in The Potteries. After falling eight points behind early on, the Wolves pulled the deficit back to two points at one stage before finally losing by 10 points. In another solid team performance, Grant was the only Wolves rider not to win a race. In scoring 81 points in the return leg, the Wolves team recorded its highest ever score to triumph by 130–85 on aggregate. The first leg deficit was wiped out after the fifth heat. The home side provided all 18 race winners and this time every team member recorded at least one heat win. King, Harry Edwards and Reeves were unbeaten by the opposition riders and Grant could have joined them but for a fall in his first ride.

On their previous visit to White City, the Wolves had come close to snatching a win but on 16 May they were comfortably beaten 49–35. Harry Edwards continued to show good form and in scoring 10 points, was beaten only by Glasgow maximum men Junior Bainbridge and Tommy Miller. King was the only other Wolves rider to win a race and there was insufficient support for the top two in this match.

Arthur Forrest, who scored maximum points, prevented a complete rout as Walthamstow overwhelmed Halifax by 30 points at The Stow in a league clash on 21 May. Forrest scored 12 of his team's 27 points as the home riders invariably led their opponents away from the start. A feature of the Walthamstow home performances at this stage of the season was the ability of all members of the team to win races. Sadly, on this occasion Boyd developed a high temperature and was forced to withdraw after two rides. The reserves took his last two rides and ably covered for his absence.

The motorcycle and light car supporters' section had a quiet start to the season, but was planning regular outings for the summer. The club began the year by holding its weekly meetings at the *Royston Arms* in Chingford, but switched to the stadium in mid-May. All other sections of the club followed suit and meetings took place on Friday evenings.

The Walthamstow team made a second trip to Ireland on 23 May. The previous visit, in 1950, had been to the Shelbourne Park track in Dublin. On this occasion the Wolves visited Chapelizod Stadium, situated north of the River Liffey on the edge of Phoenix Park, to the west of the city. The host team was riders brought over from England, together with three local novices. At various times during its short existence, the team was known as Chapelizod Lizods and Dublin Falcons, but in 1951 rode as the Dublin Eagles.

The meeting was affected by bad weather, something which blighted the 1951 season. After the ninth heat the Eagles held a narrow two-point lead before two consecutive 5–1 heat wins virtually secured a home win. The Wolves reduced the deficit, going down 44–40. Walthamstow provided only three heat winners, but packed the minor places, as the junior riders in the home team were out of their depth. Chapelizod were well-served by imported riders from the National League First Division, as Birmingham's Ron Mountford scored a maximum, supported by the Wembley duo of reigning World Champion Freddie Williams and his brother Eric, both with 11. Harry Edwards had the distinction of beating the champion in the final heat of the match. Alby Smith rode for Walthamstow in this meeting as Sid Clark was away making a guest appearance for non-league Ipswich.

Returning to The Stow for a league encounter against Yarmouth on 28 May, the Wolves continued their good home form and won easily 56–28. Boyd, who had not been fully fit in recent weeks, showed his best form to record a maximum. Lansdale also rode well and was beaten only by Fred Brand. Wembley's New Zealand star Bruce Abernethy livened up proceedings in the second half of the meeting. After beating Lansdale in a match race in 61.8 seconds, the fastest time of the meeting, he proceeded to win a heat and the final of the scratch race event.

Drawn away to Yarmouth in the first leg of the National Trophy Division Two Quarter Final on 29 May, the Wolves did well to restrict their opponents to a lead of six points. Walthamstow actually led by two points with four heats remaining, but two of these were won by Fred Brand to complete an 18-point maximum. Grant topped the scorers for the Wolves in a good all-round team performance.

At the end of May, John Deeley was still looking to strengthen his team in the quest for league success after the disappointment in the Southern Shield. His interest in Aldershot's Trevor Redmond had not waned, but Redmond still preferred to ply his trade in the Third Division and there he remained, although he did concede that Harringay was a First Division track which interested him.

From first year novice riders in 1949, Harry Edwards and Reeves had risen to first and third respectively in the Walthamstow averages by the end of the Southern Shield competition. At the same time the established star riders, Boyd, King and Lansdale, were still doing what was expected of them. With Windmill proving to be one of the most reliable reserves in the division, Walthamstow could go into the league competition confident of challenging for the title. The Southern Shield had again ended in disappointment after a fine start. Five of the first six matches had been won, but the home defeat against Oxford eventually cost the Wolves the title.

At the end of the month a *Speedway World* article warned that at least a further dozen tracks were facing the prospect of closure unless operating costs could be reduced. This would principally have to come about through a reduction in the money paid to riders. Losses of £200 per meeting were said to be common as attendance levels had plummeted.

June

A film with the title *There Is Another Sun,* featuring speedway racing sequences filmed at Walthamstow Stadium, was released in June. When subsequently released in the USA the following year, it carried the title *Wall of Death.* The film starred Maxwell Reed, Susan Shaw and Laurence Harvey. Arthur Mullard, a genial cockney giant, had a minor supporting role as a boxing booth contestant. The storyline involved Reed's unscrupulous character pulling off a robbery to finance his return to speedway. He was out of racing after causing a fatal accident through reckless riding and was instead earning a modest living as a wall of death rider on a travelling fair. Harvey played the part of a boxer who was blamed for the crime. Speedway journalist Eric Linden advised the makers on speedway sequences. Eric recalled the experience in *a Vintage Speedway Magazine* article, in which he also said he enjoyed the racing at the track. He felt that greater skill was required to win on the small Walthamstow circuit than on the bigger faster tracks such as West Ham, where he claimed the racing was less spectacular.

The good form of Harry Edwards was recognised with selection as reserve to represent Britain against Overseas at Leicester on 25 May. He joint top scored for his country against the same opposition with 13 points at Hanley on 2 June. This was followed by a call-up for England against Scotland at White City, Glasgow, on 13 June. In this match, he partnered Jack Parker and scored five points, with three bonus points for following Parker home.

The Walthamstow management expressed concerns regarding attendance levels and invited supporters to indicate whether a change of race night would be welcomed. Saturday afternoon racing was an option already contemplated, but this would have resulted in far too many clashes with the race days of other tracks and so was discounted. It was eventually decided to persevere with Monday as the designated race day.

Promoters had requested riders to consider a pay cut in view of falling attendances and high taxation of the sport, which had caused some tracks to close down and put many more in danger. A meeting of riders in early June resulted in a unanimous refusal to accept any lowering of prize money. An SRA spokesman told the press that costs had escalated, and the riders could not afford to compete for less money. The Association believed that the answer to speedway's problems was in the hands of the club managers. The riders' representatives felt the management needed to improve presentation and generally better promote their 'product'. Just sitting back and expecting spectators to fill the terraces as they had always done in the past was not a viable option.

Former Wolf Charlie May returned with Southampton on 4 June, but managed only six points as the home team took the league points with another big win, by 28 points. Good scores were recorded by all the home riders, as King recorded another maximum. The efforts by Walthamstow to sign Trevor Redmond continued when he was booked to appear with fellow New Zealander Geoff Mardon in two heats of a second half pairs contest. Home riders King and Boyd took the major places in the first heat, but Redmond won second time out to split the points. The result of this meeting was later removed from the records when Southampton withdrew from the league and the track closed.

A protest about dry conditions led to the meeting being halted after the second race to allow track work to alleviate dusty conditions during Walthamstow's visit to Motherwell on 8 June. Conditions were little better until further interruptions occurred for hosing and use of a water cart. The delays failed to halt the home team's progress towards a victory by 47–37. Harry Edwards was untroubled by the conditions and top-scored for the Wolves with 11 points. King had a disappointing meeting and failed to score, being excluded from one ride and being replaced in his final outing by the Wolves' reserve Clark.

The next evening a powerful performance by their top four riders, who amassed 43 points, ensured Edinburgh eased to a league victory over the Wolves at Old Meadowbank. Walthamstow provided only three race winners, although Lansdale led Jack Young for three laps in heat nine. King's nightmare visit to Scotland continued as he again failed to score from two races before being replaced by Clark. Young claimed another maximum as he continued his outstanding run of success. This was his 15th match of the season in league and Northern Shield competitions and he had won every race to date. Plans had been made for supporters to travel by train to the match, leaving Euston on an overnight service to reach the Scottish capital early on Saturday morning. The return journey would be by the service departing at midnight. A party rate of £3/5 was negotiated, dependent on at least 200 supporters booking the trip. The ticket price represented a huge discount from the normal figure of £5/7, but this was still a costly outing. Perhaps not surprisingly the target number was not reached and a single coachload made the journey by road instead, travelling through the night to arrive at breakfast time.

Yarmouth were easily defeated 73–35 in the second leg of the National Trophy tie on 11 June. The Bloaters had no answer to Jim Boyd who recorded an 18-point maximum, with King back to form and unbeaten by opposition riders. The first leg deficit had been wiped out after four heats, after which Walthamstow steadily increased their lead. Windmill was proving to be one of the best reserve riders in the division and was particularly reliable at The Stow. On this occasion he took four rides and scored nine points. The Wolves secured a Division Two semi-final place, where they were drawn to face Halifax.

Three days later the first Supporters' Club dance of the year took place at the *Royal Forest Hotel*. It was attended by several riders.

In a close fought match, with never more than four points separating the teams, Coventry just held on to beat the visiting Wolves 44–40 on 16 June in a Second Division match. In front of 14,500 fans, the scores were level at the end of the penultimate race. Then the home pair of Stan Williams and Charlie New, signed from Sheffield, beat Lansdale and Reeves to clinch the match. Lansdale led from the start in the deciding race, but the home pair passed either side of him on the first bend. Lansdale, Edwards and Windmill all scored nine points, but they lacked sufficient support.

Former Walthamstow rider Wilf Jay took second place ahead of Reeves in the opening heat and Harry Edwards was twice beaten into third place, by Alf Parker and Norman Hargreaves, as the Wolves beat Fleetwood 67–16 to achieve their record winning margin in league racing on 18 June. Every other heat went to the home team by the maximum 5–1 score except the ninth, which was 5–0 after both visiting riders failed to finish. Grant recorded his first maximum score for Walthamstow against woefully weak opposition. The highlight of the evening was a series of match races in which Jack Young of Edinburgh and Australia beat Wembley's England star Bob Oakley 2–1. Oakley won the first race and equalled the late Ken Le Breton's track record time of 60.6 seconds. Le Breton, the darling of Ashfield fans, had received fatal head injuries in a track crash in Australia earlier in the year.

For their second visit to Shelbourne Park in Dublin on 24 June, the Wolves put up a much better performance than the previous year, going down to a four-point defeat. On this occasion the host team comprised Dublin-based American riders rather than a team of

Wimbledon riders. Boyd showed his liking for the track and top-scored again with 11 points. Walthamstow led for most of the match and still held a one-point advantage going into the final race before disaster struck. In the deciding heat Lansdale fell, causing the race to be stopped. A re-run was ordered with Lansdale excluded. Harry Edwards led the race and a win would have ensured a match win for his team, but he fell and Manuel Trujillo was forced to lay his machine down to avoid running into him. Edwards was duly excluded from the race and a second re-run took place. This time the Shelbourne pair were unopposed and the 5–0 heat advantage gave the home side victory.

The Walthamstow management decided to stop announcing times during matches beginning with the visit of Motherwell in the league fixture on 25 June. The reason given was that 'certain experiments' were being carried out on the track. An exception would be made in the event of the track record being broken. Keith Gurtner was in maximum form for The Lanarkshire Eagles and his 12 points enabled his team to push the home side hard for most of the match. Walthamstow finally ensured victory by taking heats 11 and 12 with 5–1s in each race. Harry Edwards and King recorded double figure scores, although Reeves was out of luck and managed only two points. Alby Smith rode at reserve but was out of his depth.

Walthamstow ended June on a low note when losing a league encounter at Norwich 60–24. King was the sole race winner for the Wolves, recording his only points of the match in the process. None of the away team members showed their true capabilities on this occasion, as the strong Norwich team showed why they were favourites for the league title. By the end of the month Walthamstow occupied a mid-table position in the league, having won their four home matches, but been beaten in all five away matches.

Jack Buck appealed for more people to come forward and join the Supporters' Club, at the same time revealing that attendances at recent home meetings had been disappointingly low. He also announced that both the darts section and the motorcycle and light car section needed additional members. Walthamstow supporters managed to gather around 4,000 signatures for an Entertainment Tax Petition which was submitted by the speedway authorities to the Treasury.

13. 1951: Dark times for the sport

Southampton withdrew from the Second Division at the end of June and reports in the press claimed that Newcastle speedway was rumoured to be about to close, with Halifax also on the brink due to inadequate attendances. Southampton had been running at a loss with crowds down to 4,000. Jimmy Baxter, the promoter, explained that everyone associated with the track had taken a pay cut except the riders, who refused. Halifax and Newcastle eventually managed to see the season out before shutting down. Prior to the start of the Britain versus Overseas match at Coventry on 21 July, an announcement was made by Lt.-Col. R Vernon C Brook, chairman of the SCB, that the Board had been told that the rate of Entertainment Tax on speedway was to be reduced. No date for implementation was yet known and clearly the news was too late to save Sheffield and Southampton in 1951. In any event the information proved to be incorrect.

Walthamstow defeated Halifax on aggregate in the Division Two Semi-Final of the National Trophy at the beginning of July. It was fortunate for the Wolves that the first leg at The Stow had been a one-sided affair, as the 40-point winning margin was almost pulled back by their opponents in the return two days later on 4 July. The Wolves managed to cling on to win overall by a narrow margin of six points.

In the first leg, the visitors relied heavily on Arthur Forrest, Vic Emms and Jack Hughes. However, Forrest was carrying an injury sustained on test match duty and was below his usual standard, winning only two of his six rides. Hughes won his first two heats, but fell and picked up a leg injury third time out. After this he only scored two more points. Without this misfortune, it is likely that Halifax would have triumphed over the two legs. Lansdale was best for Walthamstow in the second leg, notching 12 hard-earned points. Boyd and Windmill both failed to register a point in the match. Reserve Sid Clark was given extra rides and his two heat wins in a total of eight points won the tie for the Wolves. Emms and Forrest both scored 16 points for Halifax.

The Leicester riders had difficulties in coming to terms with the small Walthamstow track and were easily beaten 59–25 in a league match on 9 July. All of the home riders did well, led by Harry Edwards and Lansdale with 11 each. Captain Boyd gave excellent support, scoring 10. A group of American riders were welcomed to The Stow to compete in the second half. Nick Nicolaides, Royal Carrol, Don Hawley and Johnnie Roccio had actually only travelled from Ireland as they were based at Shelbourne Park in Dublin for the season. The group also rode in a series of team meetings in the United Kingdom, usually described as an American Touring Team. Ronnie Greene, the Wimbledon promoter and Shelbourne manager, had brought the riders over to Ireland to give the Shelbourne supporters a team of their own to identify with rather than using Wimbledon riders on a regular basis.

The second half started with a match between the Wolves and the Americans over four heats. The visitors were outclassed and only an engine failure for Reeves prevented a whitewash. Hawley, Nicolaides and Roccio each claimed a second-place finish in the International Scratch Races. Hawley qualified for the final as fastest second in the heats and showed that he had got the measure of the track by winning from Windmill, King and Boyd.

Lansdale and Grant accompanied the Supporters Club's day cruise from Gravesend on 15 July, again aboard the *Royal Daffodil*. This time the cost was £2 for adults and 25/- for children up to age 14. The trip was also made available to non-members of the club, showing that it was struggling to attract support for the more expensive ventures.

Boyd took the winner's cheque for the third year in a row at the World Championship Qualifying Round at The Stow on 16 July. The final heat, in which Boyd met Birmingham's Ron Mountford, decided the outcome, with both riders on 11 points. Mountford reared at the start and although he chased hard for four laps, he could not catch his opponent. Hugh Geddes of Swindon had an unfortunate night, failing to score after leading in three of his races before being forced out with engine trouble. Boyd did not do enough to qualify for the next stage of the Championship because he collected only a single point in his other round at Leicester. Although only scoring nine points on his own track, Harry Edwards added 10 at Coventry to qualify for the Championship Round. He was drawn to ride at West Ham and Birmingham. He had done well to progress so far, but was out of his depth against the elite riders and failed to qualify for the World Final.

For the second consecutive season, Walthamstow were drawn against West Ham in the first round of the London Cup, with the matches on 23 and 24 July. In the home leg, the Wolves came very close to causing an upset against their First Division opponents before going down to a two-point defeat. The return was a one-sided affair, with the Hammers easy winners, 78–29. Walthamstow took the lead in the second heat in the first match and clung on to retain an eight-point advantage with four heats remaining. Three maximum heat wins then spared the Hammers' blushes, principally due to masterly displays by Aub Lawson and Wally Green, who both scored 16 points. The heroes for the Wolves were Boyd on 13 points and King with 11. In the return leg at Custom House, Lansdale was the Wolves' sole race winner, courtesy of a fall by home rider Arthur Atkinson when leading. Unlucky Sid Clark laid his machine down to avoid Atkinson and was unable to complete the race.

Managing director Charles Chandler provided full details in the match programme for the West Ham fixture on the new admission charges which would be implemented at Walthamstow from the following week. He explained that speedway attendances were down across the country, with Walthamstow being no exception. Mr Chandler speculated that the reasons might be a combination of diminishing interest in the sport in its present format and unaffordability, with the cost-of-living escalating.

In an attempt to boost attendances at The Stow, a range of reduced admission charges were implemented. On the popular side adult prices were down from 2/3 to 1/6 and children were to pay 6d instead of 1/-. Supporters' Club members continued to benefit from a discount of 3d. In the main stand, charges were reduced from 3/9 to 3/- for adults and from 1/9 to 1/- for children under 14 years of age. Supporters' Club members admission prices were reduced from 3/6 to 2/7. Even bigger reductions were implemented for the grandstand enclosure and ballroom, from 5/6 down to 3/- and reserved seats from 6/- to 4/9. These measures aimed at preventing a further decline in attendances were something of a gamble as the Entertainment Tax was set to rise further from 5 August. As the duty was levied on a scale according to admission prices, the management were looking to reduce the tax burden through this initiative. This was a brave move and did not prove to be successful. Jack Buck said that the reductions were made in the hope of keeping speedway going. In the course of the season, the tone of communications from the Supporters' Club secretary changed from the enthusiasm and optimism of the previous two years to constant pleas for more support and hints of closure.

Mr Chandler repeated his view that the London public expected to see First Division standards, with Walthamstow being held back in this regard. He also bemoaned the fact that by coming to the sport later than the established tracks, Walthamstow had been forced to adopt Monday as their race night. This was believed to be an obstacle to attracting more spectators. A final complaint by Mr Chandler concerned the promoters of Harringay and West Ham, the two nearest tracks. Both were said to have banned their riders from accepting bookings at Walthamstow. He claimed that the rival promotions feared local competition.

The Second Division Final of the National Trophy took place over two legs, with the first at Norwich on 28 July and the return at Walthamstow two days later. The away match formed part of a busy day for two Walthamstow fans, Miss I Chapple and Mr H Lewis. They got married at Leyton that morning and then travelled with fellow supporters by coach to the meeting. The Wolves had high hopes of success, but Norwich again showed their strength to triumph in both legs, winning 83–25 at home before running out winners by eight points at The Stow. Lansdale finished as second top scorer at Norwich with six points, courtesy of finishing third behind the Norwich pairings in each ride.

In the match at Walthamstow, Norwich's Australian star Bob Leverenz was in a class of his own. He raced to a maximum from six rides. Boyd and King both managed 12 points, but the home team could only provide seven winners in 18 heats. Norwich could even afford to lose Paddy Mills, one of their stars, with a dislocated shoulder after a fall in his second outing. With such strength in depth, it was easy to see why the Stars were already favourites to retain their Second Division title.

The Norwich meeting was the first one for which admission prices were reduced. Although no figures were given, John Deeley said in his programme notes for the postponed meeting against Oxford the following week that the attendance showed a marked improvement.

In mid-July, a meeting between representatives of promoters and riders found some common ground on the financial crisis affecting speedway. After exchanging views, each side took away proposals for further consideration. At the end of the month major concerns about falling attendances at Bristol and Cradley Heath were reported in the press.

August

A new, higher, rate of Entertainment Tax started on 1 August. Following the Walthamstow initiative, West Ham made similar reductions in admission charges immediately and a week later three Midlands tracks, Birmingham, Coventry and Cradley Heath followed suit, making smaller adjustments to admission prices. At Coventry some of the reduction was immediately clawed back by imposing a 50 percent increase in the price of the match programme, from 6d to 9d. Other tracks soon adopted this idea. Admission charges were subject to the levy of Entertainment Tax, but programme receipts were not.

Speedway suffered a second blow at the beginning of the month when rain severely affected the Bank Holiday programme. Eight meetings had to be postponed on Bank Holiday Monday. This was followed by another cancellation the next day, then seven more abandonments or postponements on the following Saturday. The home league engagement against Oxford on 6 August became the only post-war meeting to be rained off at Walthamstow, adding to one pre-war meeting against Wembley which was also lost.

Pre-war pioneer rider Lionel Wills expressed his views on how to address the problem of runaway victories and falling attendances in a letter to *Speedway News*. He suggested a change to less powerful machines of 350cc to create closer racing, a move which he believed would also reduce maintenance costs over the course of a season.

Reg Reeves missed the visit to Leicester on 3 August. He was replaced by Alby Smith. It is unlikely that Reeves could have prevented the 48–36 defeat. Lansdale recorded another disappointing away score of three points, but Boyd, King and Harry Edwards proved reliable as ever with 25 points between them. The outcome was decided in the first five heats when the home side raced into a 12-point lead, after which the teams were well matched.

By providing 11 heat winners, the Wolves eased to a 49–34 win in a league match at Hanley the next evening, once again showing a liking for the Sun Street track. The Wolves trailed by two points after five heats, then took the lead when both home riders failed to finish in heat six. After that, Walthamstow gradually extended their lead to 15 points with three races remaining. Lansdale had a better meeting with eight points and provided crucial support to Boyd, Edwards and King. Boyd was particularly impressive with a maximum.

Donald Peers agreed to captain the supporters' team in the cricket match on 5 August, with Leslie Clark, father of Petula, also appearing. The supporters triumphed on this occasion, thus gaining revenge for the previous year's defeat.

On 13 August, the Wolves had an easy win by 25 points over Newcastle, who were currently bottom of the league. Although Derick Close, the visitors' top rider, scored a maximum, the home riders were all in good form and returned solid scores throughout. Visiting rider Son Mitchell rode well, but had a frustrating final ride. The race had to be rerun after Lansdale suddenly pulled up with engine failure, causing Mitchell to fall. He then had trouble starting his machine and only just made it to the tapes in time for the restart. This time Mitchell fell twice on the final lap and being unable to restart his engine, began a long push home for a point, only to be excluded for having crossed the inner white line when he fell the first time. West Ham relented and allowed one of their riders to appear in second half events at the track. Howdy Byford competed in a Visitors' Scratch Race won by Alan Hunt of Birmingham, from Wimbledon's Ernie Roccio, with Birmingham's Ron Mountford fourth. Hunt also won the final of the Flying Twelve Scratch Race.

Lansdale and Harry Edwards received poor support as Walthamstow went down by 14 points at Liverpool on 20 August. Lansdale rode brilliantly to overtake the home pair in the opening heat after he had reared at the start. His winning time was only 0.8 seconds outside the track record. Edwards enjoyed a return to his home city and scored nine points, one less than Lansdale. Reeves and Boyd struggled on the big Stanley Stadium circuit and managed two points each. Former Plymouth star Peter Robinson was in good form for the home team and scored 11.

The Wolves were outclassed by fellow strugglers Fleetwood in an away league fixture on 22 August, losing 49–35. Having comprehensively beaten the Flyers at The Stow, the Wolves might have expected to at least push their opponents closer in the return match. However, Walthamstow provided only four race winners and would have had an even bigger defeat except for a series of machine problems for home riders. Lack of consistency cost the visitors dearly, reflected in the top scorers only managing six points. Wilf Jay enjoyed a good meeting against his former team, top scoring for Fleetwood with 11 points.

The league visit to Newcastle two days later was an opportunity to collect an away win against lowly opposition, but the result was a disappointing defeat, this time by 16 points. In another inconsistent performance, five members of the Walthamstow team won a heat. However, four of those riders also had a last place. Harry Edwards and King were best with seven points each.

Oxford had won at The Stow in the Southern Shield early in the season, but the home team made no mistake in the league encounter on 27 August. The Wolves stormed to an emphatic 58–25 win. The meeting was described as a 'local derby' even though the tracks were over 50 miles apart. The Oxford reserves top-scored for their team and surprisingly neither were given extra rides in place of out of touch team members. A series of rolling start match races took place in the second half. King did well to beat Bob Leverenz of Norwich and Australia in the first heat and Harry Saunders of Oxford overcame Boyd in the second. King went on to win the final, making up for a disappointing score in the league match, when he only scored six points.

Walthamstow proved far too strong for Wolverhampton Wasps in a challenge match on the Third Division team's track on the last day of August. The Wasps team included three guest riders, but was still outclassed. Lansdale and King showed a liking for the Monmore Green circuit and scored 11 points each. The 58–26 scoreline in favour of Walthamstow suggested there was a big difference in standards between the second and third divisions.

With the end of the season just a few weeks away, Walthamstow manager John Deeley was still negotiating to strengthen the team, focusing on either of Aldershot's New Zealanders, Trevor Redmond and Geoff Mardon, but his efforts came to nothing. He had also tried to sign Derick Close when he discovered that Newcastle were in financial difficulties and had decided to release the rider, but Close was granted his wish to move to Motherwell.

September

Meetings at The Stow throughout September were attended by officials of the Health and Architects Department of the local borough council. They were investigating complaints lodged by residents about noise nuisance from the stadium. With the three-year permission to stage speedway due to expire at the end of October, the officials' findings and any recommendations made could put the future of speedway at the stadium at risk. However, manager John Deeley was confident that permission to continue would be granted.

The home team mastered a track made treacherous by heavy rain far better than the visiting Coventry Bees on 3 September and took two league points with a 48–36 win. Reeves and Lansdale achieved double figure scores, but captain Boyd and King were ill at ease in the conditions and disappointed with only seven points between them. Walthamstow transfer target Trevor Redmond was booked to make an appearance in the second half of the match. Unfortunately, he was unable to appear as he was stranded in The Netherlands. With the mysterious track experiments having been completed, the management decided that race times would be announced again from this meeting onwards.

The early season Southern Shield success at Yarmouth could not be repeated in the league encounter the next day. Walthamstow lost by eight points. Boyd and Lansdale both scored 10 points, with the rest of the team again being inconsistent. Reeves, Windmill and Clark managed two points between them and this was a big factor in the Wolves defeat.

Walthamstow achieved their best result away to Cradley Heath with a 52–32 win in a league encounter on 7 September. The home team were experiencing difficulties and were in a poor run of results. Wolves adapted far better than their hosts to the rain-soaked track in which first away from the start invariably won. Lansdale was unbeaten by an opposing rider and Harry Edwards scored 11. The visitors were already 10 points ahead by the halfway stage and the result was never in doubt after that.

Progress in the cups had resulted in the need to rearrange fixtures and to catch up a double-header meeting was staged on 10 September. In the first match the Wolves secured the league points with a 63–21 win over Cradley Heath. Ashfield Giants were then beaten by 21 points to make it a profitable night for the home riders. In the first match the Wolves established a lead of 20 points by the end of the sixth race and the match was as good as won. All the home riders scored well. Boyd secured a maximum, supported by Edwards and Lansdale both with 10, Reeves and King totalled nine each.

Against Ashfield, the hard work was again done early in the match with a lead of 16 points gained by the halfway stage. Lansdale scored a maximum this time. Boyd won his first two rides, but then shed a chain and damaged his clutch. Two wins in one evening moved Walthamstow six places up the league table to fifth.

Immediately after the win over Ashfield, the riders made their way to King's Cross station to board the night train to Glasgow ready for the return match the next evening. Lansdale had another good meeting and top scored with 10, although the team were beaten 47–37. Clark was in the main body of the team for this match, with Reeves at reserve. Clark was off the pace, however, with Reeves taking his third and fourth rides.

Another big win was achieved against Hanley by 38 points on 17 September. Four of the home team achieved double figure scores, with King getting a maximum. The sequence of home wins needed to be backed up by successes on the road if a high finishing place was to be achieved in the league. However, the next match two days later resulted in another loss.

Giving a good performance at The Shay, Walthamstow lost by only two points to Halifax in a league match before 4,500 spectators. Lansdale and Harry Edwards, both with 10 points, again headed the scoring for the Wolves. The visiting riders consistently led from the tapes, but were too often unable to keep their opponents at bay on the big, highly banked track. Walthamstow trailed by two points going into the deciding final race and although Boyd and Grant briefly led, they could not keep out the home rider Al Allison.

Good relationships were formed with Edinburgh supporters during the visit there in June. A group from the home club met the Wolves fans and gave them a guided tour of the city.

Later in the season an Edinburgh branch of the Wolves Supporters' Club was formed, with 26 members. The Monarchs supporters reciprocated by opening a Walthamstow branch of their club, with a membership fee of 2/6. A party of Edinburgh fans were met by members of the Wolves Supporters' Club and given a tour of London on 20 September, the day of the World Championship Final at Wembley. The Monarchs supporters capped a great day out by witnessing their favourite, Jack Young, become the first Second Division rider to be crowned World Champion.

A second double-header was staged on 24 September and Walthamstow continued their surge up the league table by defeating Liverpool and Glasgow White City. Boyd was top scorer with 11 points in both matches. Liverpool provided little resistance as the home team supplied all but one race winner. George Newton only managed two points against his former team on his return to The Stow. Windmill fell and sustained a knee injury in his first race against Glasgow, forcing him to pull out of the meeting. The visitors might have come close to taking the match points if their top two of Tommy Miller and Junior Bainbridge had received better support, with both riders beaten just once.

On a track that was barely rideable due to heavy rain, the fast-starting Wolves riders had a massive advantage over the home riders and easily won by 14 points at Oxford in a league match on 27 September. Alby Smith was the only Walthamstow rider who failed to score and six of his team-mates won a heat. This victory provided some small consolation for the home defeat in the Southern Shield which meant that Oxford and not Walthamstow ended winning the competition.

A joint meeting between promoters and the SCB on 26 September included discussions about a proposed amalgamation of the Second and Third Divisions for 1952, with regionalisation being considered. Walthamstow was included in the proposed southern section. At the same time, losses for the season at Cradley Heath were estimated to be around £6,000 and doubts were already being expressed about the team appearing in 1952.

October

Champions-elect Norwich dented the hopes of a second-place finish for the Wolves by gaining a six-point win at The Stow on 1 October. Bob Leverenz, who had finished eighth in the 1951 World Championship Final, once again showed his great liking for the Walthamstow track by setting a new record time of 60.2 seconds in the opening race. He won three of his heats, but was relegated to third place by the home duo pf King and Lansdale in the seventh heat. The home team led the meeting by two points at this stage, but Grant, Harry Edwards and the reserve pair of Windmill and Alby Smith scored only six points between them. A more solid performance by the Norwich team saw them take the league points. The Wolves team could have gone close to a win except for three bouts of misfortune. Grant twice broke a chain causing him to stop when in scoring positions, then Windmill collided with a Norwich rider and was excluded from the rerun of heat 13.

Speedway came to an end at The Stow on 8 October 1951 with the visit of Edinburgh for a league encounter, which Walthamstow won 51–33. The spectators were not aware at the time that the sport would not continue at the track in 1952 and indeed they were being invited to renew Supporters Club membership for the next season. A programme of winter events for supporters was also arranged. Walthamstow eased to an 18-point win to finish the season in fifth place in the league. Reeves and King led the way, scoring 11 and 10 points respectively, both beaten only by Jack Young. For Edinburgh their recently crowned World Champion recorded a maximum. Young went on to retain his title the following year, after joining First Division West Ham.

Harry Edwards won the last event at the track, the final of The Wolves' Trophy. The trophy was presented to him by Petula Clark, the Supporters' Club vice president. Trevor Redmond continued to be in the Wolves' future plans and he was booked to take part in the second half scratch races. John Deeley said that Redmond had indicated a willingness to join the club in 1952. However, everything was dependent on decisions regarding the next season, including whether Walthamstow would be in the First Division. What proved to be the final race at the stadium was for mechanics, over three laps, won by Pete Lansdale's mechanic Ron Annall.

In his programme notes for the final meeting John Deeley reflected on the difficult time for speedway generally due to bad weather during the season, but also referred to attendances at Walthamstow not being as good as anticipated. He blamed this on the team being held back in what he described as a junior league and was sure crowds would improve if First Division racing was brought to The Stow. Describing the division as a junior league gave a hint that it could be the top league or nothing for the Wolves in 1952. Supporters were urged to continue to lobby politicians, with a General Election less than three weeks away. The point was made that retention of a greater proportion of the highly taxed receipts from the Wembley World Final would have been a means of reducing the losses made by a number of tracks during the season.

Season's end

Finishing fifth in a league of 16 teams should have been regarded as a satisfactory outcome, but it was still considered disappointing after the management felt they had assembled a team capable of challenging for the title. The only home league defeat was against the champions, Norwich, and even if this match had been won the team could still only have finished third, below Leicester Hunters. Clearly the Wolves' downfall was due to a lack of success on away circuits. In 20 away meetings in the league and Southern Shield only six were won.

Reeves had suffered a mid-season lapse in form which was later revealed to have been due to ill-health. He bravely carried on riding when suffering from throat ulcers for several weeks. Harry Edwards continued to make great progress, which saw him through to the Championship Round of the World Championship as well as earning international recognition. After a slow start, new signing Lansdale progressed to become the Wolves top points scorer in league matches. Boyd and King continued to be mainstays of the team, with Grant and Windmill providing reliable back-up. Clark and Alby Smith were inconsistent but showed good potential.

14. Farewell to Walthamstow Speedway

Despite falling attendances and heavy losses incurred, the Walthamstow management had suggested that the team could carry on in 1952 provided elevation to Division One was approved by the SCB. The agreement of the Division One promoters would be a pre-requisite for this to happen and they had consistently refused to allow this since 1949. However, in mid-October 1951, there were doubts expressed in some quarters that West Ham would continue and the prospects of Walthamstow replacing their local rivals would be bright in that event.

A statement was released by West Ham Stadium Limited to the effect that the agreement with Speedway Stadiums (1946) Limited to operate speedway would not be renewed. However, this did not rule out the possibility of the sport continuing at Custom House under the direction of a different company. West Ham Stadium Limited, of which Mrs Tippy Atkinson and Stan Greatrex were principal directors, had already gone into liquidation.

Walthamstow manager John Deeley released details of the track's retained list of riders for the 1952 season towards the end of November. Jim Boyd was not included. Also missing from the list was Arch Windmill. Mr Deeley had meanwhile contacted the SCB with offers to secure the services of three West Ham riders in the event of the sport not continuing at Custom House. The riders concerned were Howdy Byford, Malcolm Craven and Wally Green. Green had finished third in the 1950 World Championship Final.

As progress was made towards a possible new pay deal between promoters and riders, money was shown to still be available in the sport when five clubs were said to be bidding to acquire the services of World Champion Jack Young from Edinburgh. Walthamstow was rumoured to be one of the tracks concerned, with a fee of £2,500 alleged to have been offered. Ironically, when West Ham secured new owners shortly afterwards and continued in the First Division, that proved to be Young's destination.

At the end of December, it was clear that the future of Walthamstow as a speedway centre was entirely dependent upon the track being admitted to the First Division. The club was able to boast the use of fine stadium facilities and a good racing track, backed by the ability to build a first-class team through existing retained riders and via the transfer market. Although losses had been incurred in the three post-war seasons to date, it was argued this was due to the remoteness of the track from rival teams in the Second Division, with very little travelling support to boost attendances. It was felt that this situation would change completely in the First Division, with a high number of local derbies leading to profitability. Walthamstow supporters pointed out that their London rivals would enjoy the benefits through their own turnstiles, bearing in mind that for a cup tie at West Ham there had been 4,000 travelling fans and 3,000 had followed the team to New Cross.

By mid-January it became evident that there would be room for either West Ham or Walthamstow in the First Division, but not both. The elevation of Norwich, however, had been confirmed. At this stage it also appeared certain that Fleetwood, Halifax and Newcastle were lost to league racing.

John Deeley with Aldershot's Trevor Redmond. Walthamstow tried to sign the New Zealander several times, but he stayed with Aldershot and subsequently joined the Wembley Lions. (JSC)

Left: Charles Chandler, a key member of the Chandler family who owned Walthamstow Stadium. (JSC)

On 17 January 1952 the SCB refused Walthamstow's application to join the First Division. Promoter Charles Chandler immediately announced that losses amounting to £10,000 had been incurred over the three years of operation and could not be sustained, with the speedway to close as a result. He admitted that the gamble of reducing admission prices in the hope of attracting larger attendances towards the end of the previous season had backfired. Spectator numbers had actually declined further. Mr Chandler subsequently applied to the Board for a licence to stage occasional open meetings, but this was refused on 28 February. The decision to close was then finally confirmed.

The budget proposals by the Chancellor of the Exchequer in March 1952 brought changes too late to save some tracks. The changes included increasing the tax on sports such as football and reducing it on speedway, so that all forms of entertainment were taxed at the same rate of approximately 25 percent. Reductions in admission charges were possible as a result and riders' pay rates were also restored to 1950 levels. Notwithstanding the change, Long Eaton closed in mid-season and Cradley Heath shut at the end of the year.

In March, the Walthamstow riders were made available for transfer as Mr Chandler sought to recoup some of his substantial investment. Harry Edwards was the first to leave, joining First Division Belle Vue for a fee of £1,000. He had cost Walthamstow nothing when he joined direct from a training school in 1949 to become one of the club's success stories. He went on to enjoy a long career, performing steadily in the top league before later dropping down to the Provincial League in 1961.

Next to depart was Pete Lansdale who returned to Plymouth, also for a fee of £1,000. It had been a brief stay at Walthamstow, but one in which he rose to the top of the team's league averages. Although he had been a late starter, he went on to have a lengthy and successful career at second tier level.

Benny King and Jimmy Grant both linked up with Southern League Wolverhampton in April for a combined fee of just under £1,000. After enjoying his best season with Wolverhampton in 1952, King's form dipped the following year, after which he was lost to the sport. Grant retired after two successful seasons, the second with Southern League Ipswich. Jim Boyd moved to Second Division Oxford and after an indifferent first year he regained his best form in their 1953 Southern League season before retiring.

Reg Reeves, who like Edwards had joined the Wolves as a novice straight from training school, joined First Division West Ham before being loaned to Second Division Yarmouth, who also had an option to purchase included in the arrangement. His disappointing stay with West Ham was fairly brief, but Reg then went on to enjoy considerable success in the Provincial League after coming out of retirement in 1960.

Arch Windmill dropped down to the Southern League by joining Aldershot, but he failed to maintain the form he had shown with the Wolves and retired at the end of 1952. Sid Clark and Alby Smith also moved into the Southern League by joining Ipswich. Clark enjoyed two successful seasons before retiring during 1954. Smith continued to make progress after moving on to Rayleigh, but struggled when the Southern League and Division Two combined in 1954, retiring at the end of the season.

Although John Deeley received an approach in April 1952 to run Wolverhampton speedway, which had recently been acquired by the Poole owner Len Matchan, he declined the offer. Deeley eventually became General Manager and Clerk of the Course at Oxford in 1953. When Arthur Simcock left his managerial position with Wolverhampton in June 1953 he was replaced by Les Gregory, who was also the Stoke manager. As well as continuing with Oxford, Deeley this time agreed to take on a role with Wolverhampton, particularly covering for Gregory when he was unavailable due to his Stoke commitments. Charles Chandler kept his interest in Walthamstow Stadium until his death in 1976, following which the operation continued to be run by the family, several members of which were directors.

The Walthamstow Speedway Supporters' Club had been very active over the three post-war years of operation, with activities including weekly dances after matches, clubs for cricket, darts, cycling, bowls, swimming, angling, motorcycles and light cars. Also arranged were annual boat trips in the English Channel, winter dances and a visit to Southend illuminations. Jack Buck, the Supporters' Club secretary, had worked tirelessly to enrol members and had set a target figure of 6,000, which was never met. However, of those supporters who did regularly attend at The Stow, whether members or not, it is likely that some would have continued to follow the sport at nearby Harringay or West Ham. With speedway attendances generally continuing to fall though, it is highly likely that are a high proportion of Wolves followers were quickly lost to the sport. Not only had they lost their speedway team, but many of them had also been deprived of the wide-ranging social activities linked to the club.

Speedway was to plunge further into the doldrums as the decade progressed. Three divisions of the National League, with 33 member teams, had operated in 1949. In 1950 there were 34 teams, then 36 in 1951 when Sheffield pulled out after competing in the Central Shield. Swindon took over the Hull fixtures in the latter part of the 1949 season and Southampton withdrew in the course of 1951. A change for 1952 saw the Southern League created in place of Division Three, with the number of teams in the leagues dropping to 32 after Long Eaton folded in July. The decline in numbers gathered pace, down to 26 in 1953 after each league lost a team after the season started, then just 19 in 1954 after four tracks failed to last the distance and only two professional leagues were left. Two more league tracks closed during 1955 as the number dropped to 16, before a further fall to 14 the following year. Only one league of 11 teams survived for 1957, followed by 10 in 1958 and as the sport hit rock bottom there were nine left in 1959.

With hindsight, Walthamstow returned to the sport just as the post-war boom was levelling out in 1949. Speedway had ongoing financial difficulties due to the level of Entertainment Tax and then endured particularly poor weather during the summers of 1950 and 1951. The sport subsequently also had to contend with social change, including greater mobility of the population as the end of fuel rationing permitted people to travel further afield for leisure activities, together with the impact of television. There were only around 20,000 television sets in Britain prior to the start of the Second World War. Televisions became more affordable after the War as the technology became cheaper, with transmission also becoming available to wider areas of the country from 1949. In 1953, the FA Cup Final involving Stanley Matthews, followed by the Coronation of Queen Elizabeth II saw an upsurge in purchase or hire of television sets. By the end of the 1950s around 75 percent of homes in Britain had a television set and people who had flocked to local outdoor sporting attractions in the immediate post-war years now had an alternative form of entertainment at comparatively modest cost.

The Walthamstow management admitted that three years of contesting speedway at the Second Division level had led to losses in the region of £10,000. Promotion to the First Division may have led to a short-term increase in attendances, but operating costs would have also increased in terms of prize money and the essential strengthening of the team. The First Division of the National League started 1949 with eight teams, five of which were in London: Harringay, New Cross, Wembley, West Ham and Wimbledon. The management at Walthamstow made it clear from the outset that First Division status was their aim and they believed that elevation was resisted by promoters of some of the other London tracks because of fears it would adversely affect their weekly attendance levels. Only nearest neighbours Harringay and West Ham would have potentially been affected in this way. The contrary Walthamstow view was that local derbies would benefit their neighbours with large crowds and attendance levels would not be otherwise adversely impacted in any way.

The First Division promoters and the SCB approved the elevation from the second tier of Birmingham in 1949, Bristol in 1950 and Norwich in 1952. In each case, not only did the tracks concerned have a good level of support, but they had experienced success in the lower division. Bristol were champions in 1948 and 1949, with Norwich taking the title in 1950 and 1951. Birmingham were runners-up to Bristol in 1948, after which it might have been expected that both would have been promoted. It is highly probable that the promoters and the Control Board did not want to elevate Walthamstow without first being convinced of sound management and sustained track success. It is difficult to see how Walthamstow could have survived the downturn in the fortunes of the sport from 1952 onwards as a Second Division track, given that the operation made a substantial loss during 1949 to 1951.

If Walthamstow had been promoted to the First Division for the 1952 season, it is likely that closure would only have been delayed for a season or two. The reduction in Entertainment Tax and the resultant lower admission prices gave the sport a short-term boost. However, as attendances fell over the next few years and a number of venues were forced to close, London and the First Division was not immune. The first team in the capital to close was New Cross in June 1953, Harringay quit after the 1954 season and West Ham only survived a year longer. The Walthamstow ideal of a league centred on London and local derbies was gone in no time at all and when Wembley also closed it left Wimbledon as the only track in the capital for 1957. It can be argued that the wisdom of the First Division promoters and the members of the SCB prevented the Walthamstow management from incurring even greater losses than those prevailing at the time of closure.

Speedway was never to return to The Stow, although between 1962 and 1974 it hosted stock car, hot rod, banger and midget car racing. It was remarkable that the cars continued to race at the stadium for so many years without a concerted effort by residents in the immediate area to halt them on noise grounds. Greyhound racing continued to be staged successfully for many years until a decline in popularity led to final closure in 2008 ahead of redevelopment of the site, primarily for residential use.

In April 1957 several newspapers reported that, following abolition of Entertainment Tax, applications had been submitted to the SCB to reopen tracks at Walthamstow, New Cross, Yarmouth and Liverpool. The latter two were duly granted open licences and New Cross eventually returned in 1959. Aldershot and Exeter also reopened in 1957, but sadly there was no return of speedway to Walthamstow. Part of the iconic stadium lived on for a while, as it was reported that Len Silver acquired 1,100 seats when The Stow closed in 2008 to install at his Rye House speedway track.

A fine stadium and a good racing track had served speedway well for all too short a time. The brief existence in 1934 could have been built upon, but for the difficulties brought about by the noise-related complaints and the subsequent court judgement, which would have required the use of silencers to allow the bikes to continue at that time. The reintroduction of the sport unfortunately missed the immediate post-war boom when profitability would have been assured for a while. Closure was perhaps inevitable, with the management probably wise not to proceed beyond 1951.

Walthamstow had been allowed to stage speedway racing using machines without silencers for three years in the post-war period. At the same time, spectators had been strictly prohibited from using rattles and other noise instruments so as not to cause a nuisance to residents. Now the Wolves had been silenced completely.

15. Farewell to Walthamstow Stadium

Having started out as an athletics track on former grazing land, the site became used as a rubbish tip until becoming home to the Walthamstow Grange amateur football club in 1919. After the football club folded, the site was further developed by a greyhound racing company in 1931. The greyhound track, known as Crooked Billet, was unlicenced. The Art Deco parapet entrance, dating from 1932, became a landmark feature, along with the clock tower and totalisator board designed and built by Thomas & Edge Limited of Woolwich.

William Chandler purchased the site in 1933 and early work to create a stadium included the provision of covered accommodation along both straights and construction of club facilities on the first and second bends. The stadium remained in the ownership of the Chandler family until being sold for redevelopment in 2008.

After the death of William Chandler in 1946, his eldest son Charles took on the role of general manager and another son, Percy, became catering manager. Two other sons, Victor and Jack, took over the betting business, later to be branded as BetVictor. A fifth son, Ronnie, trained greyhounds. In addition to five sons, William also had three daughters. When Charles died in 1976, the stadium continued to be owned and operated by the family, with the company directors all being grandchildren of William Chandler. They were Charles Henry, Jack Alan, William George, Philip Henry, Robert Douglas, Vicki and Annie. Charlie Chan's nightclub ran beneath the totalisator board at the stadium from 1984 to 2007 and was managed by Philip Henry Chandler.

From 1933, racing was staged under National Greyhound Racing Club rules, growing to become a leading venue for the sport. Spectators enjoyed fine viewing accommodation and diners were catered for in plush glass-fronted restaurants. Speedway had its two brief spells of operation at the track and stock car racing lasted for 12 years after being introduced in 1962. The iconic stadium featured in films and television programmes, including the film *Snatch*, starring Brad Pitt and Vinnie Jones, and BBC Television's *New Tricks*. The booklet accompanying the *Blur* album *Parklife* includes photographs of band members at The Stow.

In the 1990s, the stadium crowd capacity was reduced to 5,000 to comply with new safety regulations. The Stow was still at the forefront of the greyhound racing world, however, and continued to host prestigious events. Over the next decade, spectator numbers fell. The nightclub closed in 2007 and the last greyhound race was run on 16 August 2008. A sale was negotiated by the directors of the company, with the site set to be redeveloped for residential use. Substantial trading losses were said to have occurred over the previous three years, leading to the decision to close. This mirrored the circumstances which led to the cessation of speedway racing at the venue in 1951.

The purchasers of the stadium site were London and Quadrant Housing Trust, a major social housing developer and landlord. Having acquired the site during a property boom, it was reported in 2012 that the company was set to make a huge loss on the development of 294 homes, which was to include maisonettes, apartments and houses. A nursery, sports facilities and a café were also included in the redevelopment scheme. Construction of the new dwellings was not completed on the site until 2017, but there were subsequently huge issues with defects which required a range of repairs to be carried out. The defects were identified by Vicky Savage, L&Q's group director of development and sales, as including inadequate cladding and cavity barriers within internal and external walls, incorrectly installed windows and doors, alongside problems with the roof, ground drainage issues and cracking in paving slabs in the external areas. The highest priority repairs were said to relate to cladding and fire safety issues.

An unsuccessful campaign to save the stadium had been supported by local Members of Parliament, members of the greyhound racing community and the 'Save Our Stow' group. Although the stadium is no more, there is one saving grace in that the refurbished iconic art deco structure at the front of the site was saved and incorporated into the redevelopment. It will serve as a permanent reminder of the sporting activities which took place at the venue, including providing thrills and spills for thousands of speedway fans for two brief periods between 1934 and 1951.

16. The Walthamstow riders

The riders in this section all rode for Walthamstow in 1934 or between 1949 and 1951. They are arranged in alphabetical order for those eras.

In the riders' statistics, CMA is the calculated match average, used for comparison purposes to show the scoring of each rider assuming they had taken four rides per meeting. It is arrived at by dividing the total number of points scored by the number of rides taken and multiplying the result by four. FM is the number of full maximums and PM is the number of paid maximums, i.e. including bonus points for which the rider is paid, although they are not included in the match scores. NL - National League, NL2 - National League Division Two, NT - National Trophy, ACU - A.C.U. Cup, LC - London Cup, SS - Southern Shield.

The data gathered by Matt Jackson and Hugh Vass has been edited by the author to cover the time when the riders raced for Walthamstow.

Riders in 1934

BIBBY, John Thomas (Jack)
Born: 24 September 1910, Harrietville, Victoria, Australia
Died: 2 October 1992

One of the tallest riders of his era, Australian Jack began riding in the late 1920s and came to Britain in 1934 on the recommendation of pre-war superstar Vic Huxley, after finishing third in the 1933 Australian Championship. He represented several clubs including Walthamstow, Lea Bridge, Plymouth and Bristol in the pre-war years and won his first test cap on 19 December 1936 against the USA at Melbourne.

After serving with the fire brigade in London throughout the War, Jack was signed by Sheffield and became an integral member of the 'Tigers' side, playing a superb supporting role in his four years at Owlerton – a spell which saw him score almost 700 points for the club. His best season came in 1947 when he averaged over eight points per match and recorded a succession of high scores including five maximums.

He missed the 1950 British season after breaking his leg riding for Australia against England in the Melbourne test match, but returned to action the following year, having short and unproductive spells at Ashfield and Cardiff, where his stint was ended after suffering an ankle injury. Jack Bibby settled in Cardiff after retiring from racing.

Walthamstow Statistics

Competition	Matches	Rides	Points	Bonus	Total	CMA	FM	PM
NL	5	13	9	2	11	3.38	0	0
LC	1	4	1	0	1	1.00	0	0
ACU	1	3	3	0	3	4.00	0	0
Total	7	20	13	2	15	3.00	0	0

International Honours: Australia, 4 caps – 9 points.

BLAIN, Eric Williams
Born: 29 August 1905, Frodsham, Runcorn, Cheshire, England
Died: 12 May 1987

Beginning with Liverpool in 1929, Eric also rode for Sheffield, Crystal Palace, Lea Bridge, Walthamstow, Belle Vue and Leicester Stadium. His most successful seasons were with Sheffield in 1931 and following his return to Liverpool in 1936. During the War he worked for the Air Ministry, constructing landing strips for aircraft in Ceylon. He returned briefly to the track after the War to ride in open meetings at Glasgow and Wigan in 1947. In his retirement he lived in Bartington in Cheshire.

Walthamstow Statistics

Competition	Matches	Rides	Points	Bonus	Total	CMA	FM	PM
NL	8	23	23	1	24	4.17	0	0
LC	2	12	18	3	21	7.00	0	0
ACU	1	6	4	0	4	2.67	0	0
Total	**11**	**41**	**45**	**4**	**49**	**4.78**	**0**	**0**

BURTON, Cyril Frederick (Squib)
Born: 16 January 1908, Cossington, Leicestershire, England
Died: 11 June 1990

Squib Burton began his speedway career in 1928 when he first appeared at Coventry, before moving on to Leicester. In a lengthy career, he also represented Rochdale, Manchester White City, Sheffield, Lea Bridge, Walthamstow and Hackney. Squib represented England in four of the first five tests against Australia in 1930. His high scoring exploits were halted when he suffered serious injuries in a crash in the England versus Australia test match at Leicester Super in 1931. He made a comeback only to break his leg at Wimbledon the following year, following which he never regained his best form. After the war he managed Leicester from 1950 until new promoters took over in 1962.

Walthamstow Statistics

Competition	Matches	Rides	Points	Bonus	Total	CMA	FM	PM
NL	10	28	37	2	39	5.57	0	0
LC	2	12	14	0	14	4.67	0	0
ACU	1	5	3	0	3	2.40	0	0
Total	**13**	**45**	**54**	**2**	**56**	**4.98**	**0**	**0**

International Honours: England, 7 caps – 48 points.

CASE, Roy George Arthur (Dick)
Born: 7 June 1909, Toowoomba, Queensland, Australia
Died: 24 December 1987

Dick Case represented Wimbledon, Coventry, Lea Bridge, Walthamstow, Hackney and Wembley between 1930 and 1939. He rode for Australia in all of the tests in the first series against England in 1930 and was still representing his country seven years later. He finished third in the 1932 Star Riders' Championship and sixth in the inaugural World Individual Championship Final in 1936. After retiring from racing, he ran the training school at Rye House which produced post-war Walthamstow riders Harry Edwards and Reg Reeves. Dick was also the proprietor of the public house adjacent to the Hertfordshire track.

Walthamstow Statistics

Competition	Matches	Rides	Points	Bonus	Total	CMA	FM	PM
NL	9	26	56	1	57	8.77	0	0
LC	2	12	24	0	24	8.00	0	0
ACU	1	6	14	0	14	9.33	0	0
Total	12	44	94	1	95	8.64	0	0

International Honours: Australia, 42 caps – 295 points.

HAIGH, Herbert (Dusty)
Born: 20 January 1906, Huddersfield, West Yorkshire, England
Died: 15 May 1936

After beginning his speedway career in 1928, when he appeared at numerous northern tracks, Dusty went on to represent Halifax, Belle Vue, Sheffield, Lea Bridge, Walthamstow and Hackney. He also took part in a tour to Argentina in 1930. His best year was with Sheffield in 1931. Although his scoring dipped during the next few seasons, he was back to his very best before he was killed in a track crash at Hackney in 1936. Dusty represented his country in two test series in Australia, in 1934–35 and 1935–36, having also ridden in home tests against the same opponents in 1931 and 1932. He was a fine athlete and a club cricketer, as well as having become a member of the Hackney Royals baseball team.

Walthamstow Statistics

Competition	Matches	Rides	Points	Bonus	Total	CMA	FM	PM
NL	10	29	31	4	35	4.83	0	0
LC	2	12	5	2	7	2.33	0	0
ACU	1	6	5	1	6	4.00	0	0
Total	13	47	41	7	48	4.09	0	0

International Honours: England, 14 caps – 69 points.

HULL, Walter Norbury (Wally)
Born: 2 March 1907, Hale, Greater Manchester, England
Died: 10 March 1985

Walter's speedway career dates back to 1928 when he appeared at the Audenshaw trotting track in his hometown of Manchester. As well as representing Wimbledon, Lea Bridge, Walthamstow and Sheffield in the pre-war years, he was also a member of the dominant Belle Vue team in that era. He rode for England in the second test match against Australia in 1930. He made his only two international appearances that year, but remained a reliable and popular club man until the outbreak of War.

After missing the 1946 season, Walter decided to return to the saddle in 1947 at the age of 40, and rejoined Belle Vue where he provided consistent scoring in the lower order of the side. He reserved his best performances for his home Hyde Road circuit. His showings in 1948 were particularly impressive despite a broken collarbone and shoulder blade during the season. He bowed out of the sport on a high note with a creditable 5.82 average and a National Trophy winner's medal. He was appointed as team manager at Sheffield in 1950 under the promotion of his former Belle Vue boss, Alice Hart.

Walthamstow Statistics

Competition	Matches	Rides	Points	Bonus	Total	CMA	FM	PM
NL	7	20	18	4	22	4.40	0	0
LC	2	4	2	2	4	4.00	0	0
ACU	1	6	4	1	5	3.33	0	0
Total	**10**	**30**	**28**	**7**	**31**	**4.13**	**0**	**0**

International Honours: England – 2 caps, 11 points.
Team Honours: Northern League Championship winner 1931, National League Championship winner 1935, 1936, National Trophy winner 1935, 1936, 1937, 1947.

LANGTON, Joseph Steven (Steve)
Born: 3 September 1909, Toowoomba, Queensland, Australia
Died: 20 March 1987

Steve rode for a succession of clubs in the pre-war era, failing to settle at any one track after coming to England in 1930. He had started his career two years earlier at Brisbane and spent most of the 1930s riding in the UK, surviving a serious crash at Hackney in 1937 to continue his career. In the pre-war years, he represented Southampton, Clapton, Lea Bridge, Walthamstow, Hall Green (Birmingham) and Nottingham.

After serving with the Australian Army in the Solomon Islands, Steve returned to England in 1947 and became captain of Third Division Tamworth where he headed a team with a heavy Australian influence. He used his experience to become one of the leading riders in the league.

As Steve approached 40 and the new post-war talent of the Third Division began to emerge, his scoring inevitably dipped, but he remained an influential figure in the Staffordshire side for three seasons. He ended his British career with a season in the Second Division with Southampton in 1950, 20 years since he had first ridden for the club, and posted a solid average of almost 6.5 points per match. Although Steve's international career was unremarkable in that he failed to score from two appearances for Australia, it is worth mentioning that the two outings came 16 years apart – making his debut in 1936 and his second and final appearance in 1952.

Steve Langton's only appearance for Walthamstow came in a challenge match against West Ham.

International Honours: Australia, 2 caps - 0 points.

MOORE, Walter (Chun)
Born: 5 July 1911, Kidsgrove, Staffordshire, England
Died: 8 June 1981

Starting with Stoke in 1929, Chun Moore also represented Belle Vue, Sheffield, Manchester, Lea Bridge, Walthamstow, Cardiff, Nottingham, Belle Vue and Norwich in a career that lasted until 1938. He struggled for points in the top league, but enjoyed more success at Provincial League level with Nottingham in 1936. Chun represented a team labelled 'London' when riding in Australia in 1932–33.

Walthamstow Statistics

Competition	Matches	Rides	Points	Bonus	Total	CMA	FM	PM
NL	10	28	20	4	24	3.43	0	0
LC	2	12	12	1	13	4.33	0	0
ACU	1	3	4	0	4	5.33	0	0
Total	**13**	**43**	**36**	**5**	**41**	**3.81**	**0**	**0**

STANLEY, Reginald Eric (Reg)
Born: 18 August 1909, Tottenham, London, England
Died: 20 December 1999

Reg Stanley had his first rides at Harringay in the 1928 pioneer season, then made regular appearances at High Beech the following year, before finishing the season riding at Lea Bridge. During the 1930s he saw service with Lea Bridge, Norwich, Wimbledon, Plymouth, Walthamstow and finally made a few appearances for Hackney in 1935. His most successful season was for Lea Bridge in the Southern League in 1930, but his scores never consistently reached the same heights in subsequent years.

Walthamstow Statistics

Competition	Matches	Rides	Points	Bonus	Total	CMA	FM	PM
NL	1	3	3	1	4	5.33	0	0

THOMAS, William Clemishaw (Clem)
Born: 19 October 1912, Healesville, Victoria, Australia
Died: 27 May 1971

Clem Thomas spent two seasons racing in England. He arrived from Australia in 1934 to join Lea Bridge and moved with the team to Walthamstow and then Hackney, where he made steady progress in 1935 before returning home. Although he originally announced his retirement in 1936, Clem made a comeback a year later and also appeared post-war at the Melbourne track, in 1947.

Walthamstow Statistics

Competition	Matches	Rides	Points	Bonus	Total	CMA	FM	PM
NL	5	8	7	0	7	3.50	0	0
LC	1	4	3	3	6	6.00	0	0
ACU	1	1	0	0	0	0.00	0	0
Total	**7**	**12**	**10**	**3**	**13**	**4.33**	**0**	**0**

TRACEY, Frederick Alfred Victor (Fred)
Born: 11 March 1909, Melbourne, Victoria, Australia
Died: September 1990

Fred Tracey joined Lea Bridge in 1934, having enjoyed some track success in Australia, including winning the Victoria State Championship- in 1932. He moved to Walthamstow when the team relocated there part-way through the season, but was selected only once, in a challenge match against West Ham. He was not called upon to ride in the match, but was selected to represent the Walthamstow Cubs in four junior challenge matches. Having been unable to secure a regular team place with Walthamstow, Fred was undecided about making a return to Britain in 1935. However, on hearing that the London track had closed, he opted to stay in Australia. He continued riding and finished runner-up to Bill Rogers in the 1940 Victoria State Championship. After the War, Fred appeared in meetings at Sydney, Wangaratta in Victoria and Kirjon, Victoria.

Fred had reached the veteran stage of his career by the time he made a post-war return to Britain in 1948. He joined Coventry and suffered a hand injury in his first meeting, but he carried on racing regardless in a desperate struggle for points. After continuing for several more meetings, it was discovered that the hand was actually broken and, with little prospect of the injury healing quickly, he set sail for his homeland in mid-season.

In 1951 Fred took over and promoted at the Kirjon speedway track in the Maribyrnong suburb of Melbourne, in partnership with his wife Beryl, renaming it *Tracey's Speedway*. The Kirjon track had not staged meetings during the 1950–51 season, the previous promoters having lost money. The Tracey's venture proved highly successful, with an opening-night crowd of 6,000, although its operation was subject to strict restrictions, particularly regarding noise and meeting times. The track eventually closed on 11 April 1964 after the local authority received a high number of complaints about noise and other nuisance from the venue, which was situated in a densely populated district. Ironically, this mirrored the pre-war demise of Walthamstow.

Riders from 1949 to 1951

ARGALL, Edward William (Ted)
Born: 20 January 1921, Melbourne, Victoria, Australia
Died: 30 January 1979

Having started his speedway career in Melbourne in November 1946, Ted arrived in Britain in 1949 with a good reputation after impressing on the Sydney tracks the previous winter. He was initially earmarked for Coventry, but at the last moment he was allocated to Walthamstow after the two clubs agreed a swap deal. Les Hewitt took his place at Brandon.

Walthamstow were new to the Second Division that year and Ted was named in their side for the opening matches of the league season. He made a slow start, recording a top score of just four, paid five, at home to Newcastle in April and crashed at Sheffield at the end of the same month. He sustained a broken leg which ruled him out for the rest of the year. A move into Division Three to join Rayleigh in 1950 saw no change in his fortunes and he was given only six outings at the Essex club before being transferred to West Ham to race in their junior league side. Ted returned home to Australia at the end of the season, never having found fame in Britain.

Walthamstow statistics

Year	Competition	Matches	Rides	Points	Bonus	Total	CMA	FM	PM
1949	NL2	12	34	15	7	22	2.59	0	0

BOYD, James David (Jim)
Born: 11 October 1913, Maidenhead, Berkshire, England
Died: 26 June 1972

Originally a grass track rider, Jim tried speedway at Rye House and Dagenham before the war and impressed enough to be offered a contract by Harringay. He was sent to Southampton to gain experience and proved to be a popular member of the side at Bannister Court until racing was suspended when war was declared in September 1939.

When league racing resumed in 1946, he was chosen by Belle Vue from the pool of available riders and spent three and a half seasons at Hyde Road, proving to be a reliable performer in the middle order of the side. He helped the 'Aces' to consecutive National Trophy triumphs in 1946 and 1947. After struggling for form early in 1949, he figured in a mid-season move to Second Division Walthamstow – initially on loan – and averaged over nine points per match in 36 outings in East London that season.

The move was eventually made permanent and he established himself as one of Division Two's top men, especially at Walthamstow where he was a match for the best. He was not retained by the club in 1952 and moved to Oxford where his form became patchy, although he was the perfect man to lead the side the following year when the 'Cheetahs' operated in the Southern League. This gave the vastly experienced Jim an ideal chance to end his career on a high note, being amongst the top half dozen in the section.

Walthamstow statistics

Year	Competition	Matches	Rides	Points	Bonus	Total	CMA	FM	PM
1949	NL2	30	120	255	19	274	9.13	3	2
1949	NT	6	34	68	5	73	8.59	1	0
1949	LC	2	12	21	4	25	8.33	0	0
1950	NL2	24	93	182	14	196	8.43	4	0
1950	SS	12	48	112	3	115	9.58	2	1
1950	NT	6	35	73	7	80	9.14	0	1
1950	LC	2	12	20	1	21	7.00	0	0
1951	NL2	30	116	228	12	240	8.28	3	2
1951	SS	10	40	72	12	84	8.40	1	0
1951	NT	10	52	89	6	95	7.31	2	0
1951	LC	2	12	19	1	20	6.67	0	0
	Total	134	574	1140	83	1223	8.52	16	6

Team Honours: National Trophy winner 1946, 1947.
International Honours: Britain (Division 2), 1 cap - 11 points.

BULL, Harold Andrew
Born: 7 August 1924, Newcastle, New South Wales, Australia
Died: 20 December 1990

A cousin of the famous Duggan brothers, Harold impressed on the Sydney tracks in the winter of 1948–49 using the pseudonym of Frank Richards.

Assuming his true title, he joined Second Division new boys Walthamstow on arriving in Britain in 1949 and spent most of the season in second half races after failing to impress in the early league matches. Harold moved to St Austell the following year and, although he was inconsistent, he often performed well at Third Division level and scored over 700 points in his four seasons as a 'Gull'.

When the Cornish side closed their doors at the end of 1953, Harold stayed in the south-west with Plymouth, but quit British speedway when the Devon side withdrew from the league early in the 1954 league campaign.

Walthamstow statistics

Year	Competition	Matches	Rides	Points	Bonus	Total	CMA	FM	PM
1949	NL2	6	9	9	4	13	5.78	0	0

CLARK, Sidney George (Sid)
Born: 28 August 1924, Stepney, London, England
Died: 28 June 2010

Signed by Harringay after showing promising form at the Rye House training school, Sid was initially loaned to Third Division Poole to gain experience. He was a great success at

Wimborne Road, recording several double figure scores and notching a paid maximum in only his second official match.

These performances earned Sid the chance to stake his claim for a regular spot with his parent club in 1949. However, despite a paid 11-point haul on his First Division debut, he failed to make the grade in the top tier and averaged less than a point per ride in his two years with the 'Racers'.

A spell with Walthamstow in the Second Division was also unproductive, but he was asked to help out the newly formed Ipswich Witches as they embarked on a series of non-league meetings in 1951. He became a big favourite at Foxhall Heath and signed for the club on their entry into the Southern League the following year. He was appointed captain, recapturing the form he had shown early in his career, and was number one at the Suffolk club for two successive seasons, scoring over 550 points in the process. However, a poor run of form in 1954 when the Southern League was amalgamated with the National League Second Division saw him quit the sport.

Walthamstow statistics

Year	Competition	Matches	Rides	Points	Bonus	Total	CMA	FM	PM
1951	NL2	20	48	39	14	53	4.42	0	0
1951	SS	7	16	10	4	14	3.50	0	0
1951	NT	9	26	30	4	34	5.23	0	0
1951	LC	2	5	5	1	6	4.80	0	0
	Total	38	95	84	23	107	4.51	0	0

EDWARDS, Henry (Harry)

Born: 30 August 1918, Liverpool, Merseyside, England
Died: Mid–1980s

Ginger haired Harry was a terrier like rider who was never beaten until the chequered flag dropped, making him a popular performer at all the tracks to which he was connected. He had spent four years in a Japanese Prisoner of War camp during the Second World War and took time to recover on his return home as he was suffering from malnutrition.

He started his speedway career at the *Speedway World* Training School at Rye House in 1948 and was snapped up by Walthamstow as the East London club tried to build a side for their first season in post-war league racing. He was a great favourite with the Wolves. He made exceptional progress to record an average of over six points per match in his first year in the sport. After a year of consolidation, he made further strides in 1951 and, when Walthamstow withdrew from racing after being denied entry to the First Division, Harry signed for Belle Vue.

He justified the four-figure fee paid for his services with a solid season in the top flight and later joined Norwich where he spent the best part of six years. He claimed a National Trophy winners medal in 1955 as the Stars beat Wembley over two legs in the Final and scored over 600 points in official fixtures for the Norfolk club. After being released by the Stars, Harry moved into the Provincial League with spells at Rayleigh, Leicester and

Wolverhampton and proved himself a capable performer at that level of racing. He finally retired in 1964 at the age of 46. Harry died at sea off Dubai in the mid-1980s.

Walthamstow statistics

Year	Competition	Matches	Rides	Points	Bonus	Total	CMA	FM	PM
1949	NL2	43	147	213	26	239	6.50	1	0
1949	NT	6	20	23	3	26	5.20	0	0
1949	LC	2	6	8	0	8	5.33	0	0
1950	NL2	28	111	157	29	186	6.70	1	0
1950	SS	11	44	68	10	78	7.09	0	0
1950	NT	6	30	28	5	33	4.40	0	0
1950	LC	2	8	5	1	6	3.00	0	0
1951	NL2	30	118	224	20	244	8.27	0	0
1951	SS	10	40	85	3	88	8.80	1	0
1951	NT	10	49	70	9	79	6.45	0	1
1951	LC	2	11	13	1	14	5.09	0	0
	Total	**150**	**584**	**894**	**107**	**1001**	**6.86**	**3**	**1**

Team Honours: National Trophy winner 1955.
International Honours: England, 1 cap – 5 points, Britain (Division 2), 2 caps - 14 points.

EDWARDS, Richard Herbert (Bert)
Born: 8 February 1917, Liverpool, Merseyside, England
Died: 13 June 2008

A universally popular rider, Bert was the elder brother of Harry Edwards and followed Harry into the sport at Walthamstow in 1950 after previously competing in grass track events. He showed flashes of promise but was by no means a regular at The Stow and he was loaned to Division Three side Aldershot in 1951. Bert became a star at his new home and scored a paid maximum for the Shots in only his third match, quickly mastering the tricky Tongham track. He ended that season with an average of over eight points per match and started the 1952 campaign with the same club.

However, Aldershot were struggling financially and, when they could not raise the money for the transfer fee, Bert's contract was purchased by their Southern League rivals Cardiff in June. Again, Bert was forced to move on during the following season as Cardiff closed down due to poor crowds and he settled at Ipswich where he spent the rest of his career/ He became one of the most popular riders ever to race for the Foxhall Heath club. A step up in class when the Witches joined the Second Division in 1954 made little difference to his scoring and he formed a fine spearhead with Junior Bainbridge and Dick Campbell as the side finished in a respectable mid table position in front of some of the biggest crowds in the league.

Bert took over as number one in 1955 and by the 1956 season he was one of the best English riders, with international selection for the home fixtures against Australasia and Sweden, as well as the return series against the Swedes. He had also put himself in a fine position with regards to qualification for the World Final but, riding at the peak of his form, he crashed in a test match at Poole on the eve of his second and vital qualifying round and had to make an early withdrawal from the competition. Not only did this cost Bert an almost certain place in the Wembley big night, he had injuries – including a damaged shoulder – from which he never fully recovered. He bravely tried to return to his former glories in 1957 but was nowhere near the same rider and finally bowed out of the sport after slipping back into second half rides at Ipswich in 1958. Bert's combination of cheery personality and never-say-die riding style ensured his reputation as one of Britain's most well-liked riders.

Walthamstow statistics

Year	Competition	Matches	Rides	Points	Bonus	Total	CMA	FM	PM
1950	NL2	12	27	19	5	24	3.56	0	0
1950	SS	2	4	4	2	6	6.00	0	0
1950	NT	6	12	15	3	18	6.00	0	0
	Total	**20**	**43**	**38**	**10**	**48**	**4.47**	**0**	**0**

International Honours: England international – 7 caps, 33 points.

GARDINER, Bruce
Born: 28 August 1927, Windsor, New South Wales, Australia
Died: 15 September 2018

When Bruce signed for Walthamstow in 1950, the Wolves looked like they were on to a winner as they had captured the New South Wales Junior Champion of the previous winter. However, when he arrived in England, Bruce was well off the pace and could not break into the side until George Newton had to miss a match. He then got his chance to show what he could do in the home meeting against Edinburgh in July. He failed to score from two rides and returned to second half racing until he was injured in a crash at Rye House, spending much of rest of the campaign with his leg in plaster. He returned home to Australia at the end of the season with the trip to the UK having turned into a nightmare.

Walthamstow statistics

Year	Competition	Matches	Rides	Points	Bonus	Total	CMA	FM	PM
1950	NL2	1	2	0	0	0	0.00	0	0

GEARY, Leonard Edgar (Dick)
Born: 19 March 1917, St. Albans, Hertfordshire, England
Died: 29 September 1976

Son of former rider Len Geary and the brother-in-law of Cyril and Percy Brine, Dick was a junior in the pre-war era and was first associated with West Ham. He rejoined the Hammers in 1946, but found points hard to come by in the top flight and was soon on his way to Sheffield where he settled into a useful middle order role.

Dick started the following season in fine form at Owlerton but was loaned to Second Division new boys, Wigan. They were desperately short of top end strength as they tried to build a team capable of holding their own in the Second Division. He became a quality performer at the Poolstock Stadium and recorded a succession of double figure scores for the Lancashire side. He firmly established himself as the club's number one rider and qualified for the Division One rounds of the British Speedway Championship.

His good form continued the following year as the club moved en bloc to Fleetwood and he was named as the first challenger for the Second Division Match Race Championship. He lost out over two legs to Bristol's Fred Tuck. He broke his arm at the end of the 1948 season, but was expected to make a full recovery, with new boys Walthamstow paying £1,000 for his signature.

However, the arm bothered him throughout the year and the Wolves got little return on their investment. His average dipped to just over five points per match. He moved back to Fleetwood in May 1950, just prior to the start of league fixtures, but again struggled and quit when he broke his arm again at the end of August. A proposed comeback for Dick to ride for Aldershot in 1952 did not materialise.

Walthamstow statistics

Year	Competition	Matches	Rides	Points	Bonus	Total	CMA	FM	PM
1949	NL2	40	148	166	29	195	5.27	0	0
1949	NT	6	23	25	2	27	4.70	0	0
1949	LC	2	10	12	1	13	5.20	0	0
1950	SS	9	23	24	6	30	5.22	0	0
	Total	57	204	227	38	265	5.20	0	0

GRANT, James Dammarell (Jimmy)
Born: 10 December 1916, York, North Yorkshire, England.
Died: 4 February 1973.

After some impressive training school performances in the winter of 1947–48, Jimmy was targeted by Plymouth but had watched Harringay from the terraces that season and jumped at the chance of representing the Racers in the top flight. It was a brave move by both rider and club as Jimmy was an out and out novice, but he turned in some impressive displays including eight, paid nine, on his home debut against Wembley on 9 April.

He held down his team place throughout the season to record an average of just less than five points per match in what was undoubtedly a successful first term. It was a disappointment, therefore, when he was unable to build on that first season. He eventually lost his place at Green Lanes early in 1950. He moved to Walthamstow and spent two years at The Stow, showing glimpses of his ability without fulfilling the promise he had revealed in that initial year. Jimmy filled a heat leader role with Wolverhampton in 1952 and retired after a spell at Ipswich the following season.

Walthamstow statistics

Year	Competition	Matches	Rides	Points	Bonus	Total	CMA	FM	PM
1950	NL2	23	83	127	20	147	7.08	0	2
1950	LC	2	7	9	4	13	7.43	0	0
1951	NL2	30	105	146	30	176	6.70	1	0
1951	SS	10	39	50	8	58	5.95	0	0
1951	NT	10	49	56	17	73	5.96	0	0
1951	LC	2	10	5	0	5	2.00	0	0
	Total	77	293	393	79	472	6.44	0	0

International Honours: Britain (Division 2), 1 cap – 11 points.

JAY, Wilfred (Wilf)
Born: 28 June 1913, Rotherham, South Yorkshire, England.
Died: 28 June 1973.

Wilf was an accomplished grass track rider before starting his speedway career with practice sessions at Belle Vue in 1936. He was taken under the wing of the Norwich promoter Max Grosskreutz and signed for the Stars in 1937, remaining with the Norfolk club when racing resumed after the war.

Wilf became one of the leading riders in the Second Division in the immediate post-war years and achieved a fine nine-point average with the Stars in 1946. He then moved to Newcastle the following season. His spell at Brough Park confirmed his position as one of the biggest attractions in the Second Division and he held the Second Division Match Race title in June 1948 before a broken leg forced him to give up the honour.

After two successful years at Newcastle, Wilf was targeted by the new promotion at Walthamstow and joined the Wolves for a fee of £1,000. However, he failed to settle with the East Londoners and by mid-season was back with the Diamonds after an exchange deal with Benny King was arranged. After becoming somewhat stale at Brough Park, Wilf's career took on a brief new lease of life with an excellent season at Fleetwood in 1951.

However, a move into the top flight with Wimbledon was a mistake and his career was all but over. Wilf retired from regular racing following a spell with Edinburgh in 1953, but did return for one match 11 years later, when he helped out Sheffield in a meeting against Long Eaton in 1964. He joined his sons Alan and Derek in the Tigers side, at the remarkable age of 51.

Walthamstow statistics

Year	Competition	Matches	Rides	Points	Bonus	Total	CMA	FM	PM
1949	NL2	19	76	148	6	154	8.11	2	0
1949	NT	2	11	17	2	19	6.91	0	0
	Total	21	87	165	8	173	7.95	2	0

Individual Honours: Division Two Match Race champion June 1948.

KING, Benjamin John (Benny)
Born: 26 July 1920, Forest Gate, Poplar, London, England.
Died: 21 June 1974.

Benny saved up for a shared bike before the War with his great friend Dave Anderson and the pair were taken on by New Cross as juniors. They both had to wait until the conflict had ended before they were able to start a proper career on the cinders. Benny was signed by West Ham where he broke into the side at the end of May 1946.

By the end of the season, he was a regular in the Hammers team and showed a slight improvement the following year, lifting his average to above four points per match. In 1948, he signed for Middlesbrough as part of the deal which saw Fred Curtis move to Custom House, but was back with West Ham at the start of the following year. A short spell with Newcastle followed before he figured in another exchange deal – this time with Wilf Jay – which took him to Walthamstow, where he was to spend the most successful years of his speedway career.

Finally establishing himself as a heat leader in the Second Division, Benny was superb on his home track and remained in East London until Walthamstow closed, before ending his racing days with spells at Wolverhampton and Oxford.

Walthamstow statistics

Year	Competition	Matches	Rides	Points	Bonus	Total	CMA	FM	PM
1949	NL2	25	100	171	17	188	7.52	1	1
1949	NT	4	23	33	3	36	6.26	0	0
1949	LC	2	11	20	0	20	7.27	0	0
1950	NL2	28	103	193	10	203	7.88	6	1
1950	SS	12	48	89	11	100	8.33	1	0
1950	NT	6	33	53	3	56	6.79	0	0
1950	LC	2	9	12	1	13	5.78	0	0
1951	NL2	30	117	205	24	229	7.83	2	0
1951	SS	10	39	74	7	81	8.31	1	0
1951	NT	10	59	110	8	118	8.00	0	2
1951	LC	2	11	15	2	17	6.18	0	0
	Total	131	553	975	86	1061	7.67	11	4

International Honours: Britain (Division 2), 1 cap – 11 points.

LANSDALE, Harry Douglas (Pete)
Born: 26 December 1912, Marylebone, London, England.
Died: 13 September 1989.

Despite being an experienced motorcyclist, Pete did not start his speedway career until taking part in the Rye House training school after the War. He made his debut for Southampton in 1947, at the age of 34. Although he was a comparatively late starter, Pete managed 17 years in the sport and was still scoring well for Exeter at the grand age of 50. During his riding days he was recognised as one of the finest lower division riders of the era. He was a legend at Plymouth where he broke the club records for both appearances made and points scored in six years with the Pennycross club.

He joined the Devils in 1948 and quickly became a great crowd favourite. His best season came the following year when he managed to finish third in the Third Division averages behind Vic Emms and Billy Bales. He achieved figures of over nine points per match in 1950 even though the club had been promoted to the Second Division. He moved to Walthamstow when the Devils were forcibly moved back into the Third Division for geographical reasons. Despite finishing the season as number one at The Stow, he decided to return to Pennycross after just one year in London, even though his move meant him dropping down a division.

After the doors were closed at Plymouth during 1954, Pete moved to Rayleigh and stayed at the Weir Stadium until 1957 when he retired from the sport. However, when Provincial League speedway returned to the Essex venue in 1960, Pete made a comeback to help the club win the league. He later spent three years at Exeter before finally deciding to quit at the end of the 1963 season. After his racing days were over, Pete assisted the Wally Mawdsley promotion in the administrative side of the sport at various league tracks.

Walthamstow statistics

Year	Competition	Matches	Rides	Points	Bonus	Total	CMA	FM	PM
1951	NL2	30	120	245	26	271	9.03	1	5
1951	SS	9	32	52	6	58	7.25	0	0
1951	NT	10	52	86	5	91	7.00	0	0
1951	LC	2	10	12	2	14	5.60	0	0
	Total	**51**	**214**	**395**	**39**	**434**	**8.11**	**1**	**5**

International Honours: England, 1 cap – 9 points.
Team Honours: Provincial League Championship winner 1960, Provincial League Knock Out Cup winner 1962.

MAY, Charles Edward (Charlie)
Born: 18 October 1917, Park Gate, Southampton, Hampshire, England.
Died: 29 May 1998

Charlie started and finished his 20-year speedway career with his hometown club, Southampton, after having started out as a junior at Banister Court in 1937.

He did not have much success before the War but, after practising at Rye House, he was signed by the Wembley Lions for the 1946 season. He added useful points from reserve at the Empire Stadium and claimed two consecutive league winner's medals with the club. However, he moved down a division to join Birmingham in 1948 for a £400 fee.

In the lower leagues, Charlie was a fine performer, particularly in his first season with Walthamstow when he was a heat leader. Later at Cardiff he was the mainstay of the Welsh side's line-up. When the Penarth Road track closed in 1953, Charlie had half a season with

Exeter before returning to Southampton in 1954. This was his third spell with the club and he remained with the Saints until his retirement in 1956.

Walthamstow statistics

Year	Competition	Matches	Rides	Points	Bonus	Total	CMA	FM	PM
1949	NL2	43	165	317	16	333	8.07	2	2
1949	NT	6	33	80	3	83	10.06	0	2
1949	LC	2	10	19	0	19	7.60	0	0
1950	NL2	24	73	93	20	113	6.19	0	0
1950	SS	12	40	62	9	71	7.10	0	1
1950	NT	6	31	50	7	57	7.35	0	1
1950	LC	2	6	11	0	11	7.33	0	0
	Total	95	358	632	55	687	7.68	2	6

Team Honours: National League Championship winner 1946, National League Division One Championship winner 1947.

NEWTON, George William
Born: 27 January 1913, Ash Vale, Hampshire, England.
Died: 5 October 1984.

George was one of the most popular riders of his generation and displayed a huge amount of courage to continue his speedway career against all medical odds. He was an overnight sensation at the beginning of his career as a teenager in 1932 at Crystal Palace, He equalled the West Ham track record shortly after embarking on the cinders. However, he suffered an injury hit spell where he seemed to make little progress, before he re-emerged as an England international in 1936 while with New Cross.

From there, he developed into one of the country's finest riders of the late 1930s, reaching three successive World Finals. He was a master of the New Cross circuit where he held the track record prior to the War. Illness took its toll and he retired just before the conflict, spending 10 years out of the saddle before unbelievably returning to New Cross in 1948.

Despite being blighted by internal trouble and the extreme handicap of racing with no ribs on one side of his body, George put in some stirring performances and played a role in helping New Cross to break Wembley's domination of the sport. A major operation in July saw many predicting the end of the diminutive racer's career. However, he returned to the sport he loved with Fleetwood at the start of 1949.

He had a fine season in Lancashire, scoring eight maximums and averaging a shade less than eight points per match. He started the 1950 season still at Highbury Avenue, but moved to Walthamstow in May for £700 before the league fixtures began. He had further spells at Liverpool and St Austell before retiring at the age of 39. At each venue George was hugely popular and was one of the last leg trailers of the post-war era.

Walthamstow statistics

Year	Competition	Matches	Rides	Points	Bonus	Total	CMA	FM	PM
1950	NL2	27	97	107	12	119	4.91	0	0
1950	SS	3	12	14	2	16	5.33	0	0
1950	NT	6	24	21	3	24	4.00	0	0
1950	LC	2	10	15	2	17	6.80	0	0
	Total	38	143	157	19	176	4.92	0	0

Individual Honours: World finalist 1936 (9th), 1937 (9th), 1938 (14th).
International Honours: England – 12 caps, 82 points, Britain (Division 2) – 1 cap, 3 points.
Team Honours: National League Division One Championship winner 1938, 1948.

OSBORNE, William Ernest (Bill)
Born: 26 March 1921, Shoreditch, London, England.
Died: 2 February 2004.

Bill first rode at Rye House after the War and was signed by Bradford in 1946. He made three appearances for the club that season. He won a regular place in the side in 1947 and was starting to find his feet when he crashed at West Ham in July, He badly broke his arm which necessitated him having to ride with specially adapted handlebars for the rest of his career.

Bill returned to the Bradford line-up at the start of the following season but, after three pointless meetings, was dropped and allowed to go out on loan to Hastings in the Third Division. After taking time to settle at the Pilot Field track, he showed some sensational form and in a mid-season purple patch recorded four successive maximums. This earned him a recall to Bradford before the end of the season and the benefit of his time with the Saxons was shown as he scored in every remaining match.

Bill was signed by big-spending newcomers Walthamstow for £250 in 1949, but spent just one season with the East Londoners before moving on to Oxford where he showed some of the best form of his career. Despite an early season broken leg, his first year at Cowley saw him score over seven points per match as the club won the Third Division title. He topped the Cheetahs averages in 1952, raising his average to 7.35 despite the step up in quality to Second Division level. This proved to be the high spot of Bill's career and he retired in 1954 after breaking his leg at Leicester. A comeback in the Provincial League in the early 1960s at Edinburgh and Leicester brought little success.

Walthamstow statistics

Year	Competition	Matches	Rides	Points	Bonus	Total	CMA	FM	PM
1949	NL2	44	128	153½	19	172½	5.39	0	0
1949	NT	6	25	28	4	32	5.12	0	0
1949	LC	2	7	9	1	10	5.71	0	0
	Total	52	160	190½	24	214½	5.36	0	0

Team Honours: National League Division Three Championship winner 1950.

REEVES, Reginald (Reg)
Born: 6 August 1923, West Ham, London, England.
Died: 19 September 1992.

A tough East Londoner, Reg began his career as a novice with Walthamstow, just a few miles from his home, and made remarkable progress to record an average of over six points per match in the Second Division in 1949. This was an outstanding achievement for a first season rider. He made similar progress the following year in adding a further two points per match to his average and reaching heat leader status at The Stow. He looked a safe bet for future international recognition at that stage of his career, but went backwards slightly in 1951 and was forced to move when Walthamstow closed. Reg moved closer to home on joining West Ham, but the transfer was not a success. He then moved back to the second tier, settling at Yarmouth after an unsuccessful trial at Coventry. Eventually he became accustomed to the Caister Road track and regained his heat leader status in his second year at the club. A prolific mid-season spell saw him score four successive full maximums in 1953.

When Yarmouth closed, Reg had a couple of very good seasons with East Anglian neighbours Ipswich, but the diminishing number of clubs saw him drift out of the sport for several years. When Provincial League racing was introduced in 1960, he was tempted back into the saddle and he joined Rayleigh. He proved to be one of the best riders in the league in helping the 'Rockets' to the title. His leadership proved invaluable as over half his league and cup matches that year ended in a maximum return. He was the main reason for the club narrowly beating Poole to the championship. Although he made less appearances in 1961, his average increased to a remarkable 11.35, dropping just nine points in 13 league and cup matches but, as he was approaching 40, this proved to be his last regular league season – he appeared briefly for New Cross and Hackney in later years.

Walthamstow statistics

Year	Competition	Matches	Rides	Points	Bonus	Total	CMA	FM	PM
1949	NL2	44	169	226	44	270	6.39	0	2
1949	NT	6	27	27	8	35	5.57	0	0
1949	LC	2	9	9	2	11	4.89	0	0
1950	NL2	28	108	183	31	214	7.93	0	2
1950	SS	12	47	81	6	87	7.40	0	0
1950	NT	6	31	66	5	71	9.16	0	0
1950	LC	2	11	19	3	22	8.00	0	0
1951	NL2	29	106	176	30	206	7.77	0	2
1951	SS	10	40	74	8	82	8.20	0	0
1951	NT	10	41	68	9	77	7.51	0	1
1951	LC	2	6	5	0	5	3.33	0	0
	Total	**151**	**595**	**934**	**146**	**1080**	**7.26**	**0**	**0**

Team Honours: Provincial League Championship winner 1960.
Individual Honours: Provincial League Riders Championship winner 1961.
International Honours: Britain (Division 2), 2 caps – 19 points.

SHEPHERD, Terence Ernest (Dick)
Born: 21 February 1920, Wellingborough, Northamptonshire, England.
Died: 18 September 2007.

Plagued by injury for much of his speedway career, Dick was one of the unluckiest riders of his era. He had been a fan at Leicester in the 1930s and took up the sport after the War with outings at the Tiger Stevenson training school. He was considered good enough to be given league outings by Plymouth in the initial year of the Third Division in 1947. However, after a single ride for the Devils against Eastbourne in July, he injured his spine. Not only was he out for the rest of the season, he was troubled with his back throughout his career and even became a stage manager to a flying ballet, finding that the work strengthened his back.

It was with Hull that Dick made his mark, making super progress and recording six maximums in what was effectively his debut season. These performances persuaded the new promotion at Walthamstow to sign him in 1949 for a £150 fee. However, after a paid maximum in the opening league match of the season, the injury bug struck again and he suffered serious head injuries shortly afterwards. This put him out for the rest of the year. He made an abortive comeback in 1950 followed by an unsuccessful stint with New Cross, before rebuilding his career in the Southern League with Ipswich. In his two seasons at Foxhall Heath, Dick was a popular member of the side on the well-stocked terraces and announced his retirement when he was released by the Witches at the end of 1953.

Walthamstow statistics

Year	Competition	Matches	Rides	Points	Bonus	Total	CMA	FM	PM
1949	NL2	4	15	21	4	25	6.67	0	1
1950	SS	9	33	34	7	41	4.97	0	0
	Total	13	48	55	11	66	5.50	0	1

SMITH, Albert Edward (Alby)
Born: 27 September 1930, Forest Gate, London, England.
Died: 13 October 2014.

An East Londoner from Forest Gate, Alby first rode for Walthamstow in 1951 and spent the season as the ninth man in the side. He stood in when any of the regular team members were injured. When Walthamstow closed, Alby moved to Southern League newcomers, Ipswich. Despite some decent performances, including a 10-point score against Cardiff at Foxhall Heath, he generally struggled on tracks he was seeing for the first time. He was eventually transferred to Rayleigh in a late season move. He supplied some useful points from reserve as the Rockets took the Southern League title. He repeated this the following year when he was an ever present in the championship winning side. When the bottom two leagues combined in 1954, Alby found the increased competition a struggle to cope with and dropped out of the sport before the end of the season. He made an unsuccessful comeback at Plymouth in 1962 and rode several times at the non-league Weymouth track. He is also thought to have been a boxing promoter in the late 1950s and early 1960s.

Walthamstow statistics

Year	Competition	Matches	Rides	Points	Bonus	Total	CMA	FM	PM
1951	NL2	12	26	18	4	22	3.38	0	0
1951	SS	1	2	1	0	1	2.00	0	0
1951	NT	2	6	7	1	8	5.33	0	0
	Total	15	34	26	5	31	3.65	0	0

Team Honours: Southern League Championship winner 1952, 1953.

WINDMILL, Albert Archibald (Arch)

Born: 5 June 1915, Bushey Heath, Hertfordshire, England.
Died: 5 March 2007.

A grass track rider in his teens, Arch took up speedway in 1936 and rode for Hackney until 1939, partnering the famous American star Cordy Milne during his spell at Waterden Road.

After serving with the RAF in the War, the long-legged rider joined Wimbledon and spent three seasons there, usually at reserve or a second-string. He was a force to be reckoned with at times at Plough Lane while frequently struggling on away tracks. He is remembered for his remarkable paid maximum at Wembley in a league match for the Dons on 8 May 1947 when his efforts enabled Wimbledon to win 42–41. After leaving Plough Lane, Arch joined Walthamstow in 1949 and spent three years with the East London side, having his best campaign in 1950 when he scored two full maximums and recorded a 7.44 average. Signed by non-league Wigan in 1952, he moved to Aldershot when the Lancastrians were refused admittance to the league, although he did ride in challenge matches for the club.

Walthamstow statistics

Year	Competition	Matches	Rides	Points	Bonus	Total	CMA	FM	PM
1949	NL2	40	122	147	32	179	5.87	0	0
1949	NT	6	20	22	5	27	5.40	0	0
1949	LC	2	6	6	2	8	5.33	0	0
1950	NL2	28	87	151	10	161	7.40	2	0
1950	SS	12	33	42	10	52	6.30	0	0
1950	NT	6	20	33	5	38	7.60	0	0
1950	LC	2	9	13	2	15	6.67	0	0
1951	NL2	29	85	114	26	140	6.59	0	0
1951	SS	10	24	37	5	42	7.00	0	0
1951	NT	9	26	49	5	54	8.31	0	0
1951	LC	2	7	8	1	9	5.14	0	0
	Total	146	439	622	103	725	6.61	2	0

Team Honours: National League Division Two Championship winner 1938.

Managers

DEELEY John Edwin Cross
Born: 2 August 1908, Newland, Malvern, Worcestershire, England.
Died: 7 March 1969, Redbridge, Essex, England.

John Deeley was employed at the BSA works in Greet, Birmingham in 1928, where leading rider Jack Parker tested dirt-track machines. He rode in the pre-war era for Coventry, Hall Green (Birmingham), Leicester, Lea Bridge, Sheffield and Cardiff, before moving into management with Walthamstow. He also rode in South Africa in 1930–31. John moved on to management roles with Oxford and Wolverhampton after the London track closed.

LLOYD, Walter Richard (Wally)
Born: 6 February 1910, Birmingham, England.
Died: 11 February 1989.

Wally Lloyd began his speedway career in 1928 at Hall Green, Birmingham before moving across the city to the Perry Barr track. In the pre-war years he subsequently rode for Crystal Palace, Lea Bridge, Southampton, Clapton, Hackney Wick, Wembley and Wimbledon. After the War, Wally rode for Belle Vue before retiring and becoming manager at Walthamstow. After one season he came out of retirement and took a role as rider-coach at the new Dunmore track in Belfast, Northern Ireland. Lloyd represented England before and after the war. He also briefly rode and promoted in South Africa.

Appendix 1: Results and scorers

NL - National League, NL2 - National League Division Two, NT - National Trophy, ACU - A.C.U. Cup, LC - London Cup, SS - Southern Shield, Ch - Challenge.

Walthamstow 1934

Wednesday 8 August 1934 New Cross London
New Cross 36 Walthamstow 17 (NL)

New Cross	Walthamstow
Ron Johnson 7+2	Dick Case 7
Nobby Key 6	Jack Bibby 1+1
Tom Farndon 9	Dusty Haigh 1
Stan Greatrex 3+1	Chun Moore 1
Joe Francis 6	Squib Burton 1
George Newton 5+2	Eric Blain 5
	Clem Thomas 1

Tuesday 14 August 1934 West Ham London
West Ham 36 Walthamstow 17 (NL)

West Ham	Walthamstow
Tiger Stevenson 6	Dick Case 2
Jack Dixon 6+2	Jack Bibby 1
Tommy Croombs 7+1	Chun Moore 2
Arthur Atkinson 5+1	Dusty Haigh 3
Bluey Wilkinson 9	Squib Burton 6
Eric Gregory 3+1	Eric Blain 0
	Clem Thomas 3

Thursday 16 August 1934 Walthamstow London
Walthamstow 29 Wimbledon 25 (NL)

Walthamstow	Wimbledon
Dick Case 8	Claude Rye 5
Jack Bibby 2+1	Wally Little 4+1
Chun Moore 4+1	Gus Kuhn 8
Squib Burton 6	Alf Sawford 4+2
Dusty Haigh 6	Wal Phillips 0
Eric Blain 3	Geoff Pymar 3
	Fred Leavis 1

Thursday 23 August 1934 Walthamstow London
Walthamstow 39 West Ham 65 (Ch)

Walthamstow	West Ham
Squib Burton 5	Arthur Atkinson 15
Steve Langton 3+1	Rol Stobbart 5
Chun Moore 10	Jack Dixon 15+1
Eric Blain 4	Stan Dell 8+2
Jack Bibby 2	Eric Gregory 14
Reg Stanley 7	Wal Morton 8+2
Wally Hull 8	Ken Brett 1
Fred Tracey	

Wednesday 29 August 1934 New Cross London
New Cross 69 Walthamstow 38 (LC)

New Cross	Walthamstow
Ron Johnson 17+1	Dick Case 11
Joe Francis 6	Wally Hull 1+1
Tom Farndon 18	Eric Blain 6+3
George Newton 5+2	Squib Burton 7
Stan Greatrex 18	Chun Moore 7
Nobby Key 5+2	Dusty Haigh 3+1
	Clem Thomas 3+3

Thursday 30 August 1934 Walthamstow London
Walthamstow 41 New Cross 65 (LC)

Walthamstow	New Cross
Dick Case 13	Ron Johnson 12
Jack Bibby 1	Joe Francis 6
Chun Moore 5+1	Stan Greatrex 18
Squib Burton 7	Nobby Key 5+1
Dusty Haigh 2+1	Tom Farndon 15
Eric Blain 12	George Newton 9+3
Wally Hull 1+1	

Thursday 6 September 1934 Walthamstow London
Walthamstow 25 Harringay 29 (NL)

Walthamstow	Harringay
Dick Case 8	Jack Parker 9
Wally Hull 3+2	George Wilks 1
Squib Burton 7	Norman Parker 8
Chun Moore 2+1	Cliff Parkinson 3+2
Dusty Haigh 3+1	Frank Arthur 5
Eric Blain 2	Phil Bishop 3+1

Monday 10 September 1934 Wimbledon London
Wimbledon 34 Walthamstow 19 (NL)

Wimbledon	Walthamstow
Claude Rye 9	Dick Case 5
Wally Little 5+2	Wally Hull 2
Gus Kuhn 6+1	Squib Burton 0
Syd Jackson 6	Chun Moore 3
Geoff Pymar 4+1	Dusty Haigh 5+1

Alf Sawford 1   Eric Blain 4+1
Bill Rogers 3   Clem Thomas 0

Thursday 13 September 1934 Walthamstow London
Walthamstow 23 New Cross 30 (NL)

Walthamstow   *New Cross*
Dick Case 8   Ron Johnson 8
Wally Hull 2+1   Roy Dook 2+1
Squib Burton 6   Stan Greatrex 7
Chun Moore 2   Nobby Key 2+1
Dusty Haigh 2+1   Tom Farndon 8
Eric Blain 3   George Newton 3+2

Tuesday 18 September 1934 West Ham London
West Ham 66 Walthamstow 37 (ACU)

West Ham   *Walthamstow*
Tiger Stevenson 0   Dick Case 14
Wal Morton 12   Wally Hull 4+1
Tommy Croombs 11+1   Squib Burton 3
Arthur Atkinson 9+2   Chun Moore 4
Bluey Wilkinson 15+3   Eric Blain 4
Jack Dixon 7+2   Dusty Haigh 5+1
Arthur Warwick 7+1   Jack Bibby 3
Stan Dell 5+1   Clem Thomas 0

Thursday 20 September 1934 Walthamstow London
Walthamstow 17 Belle Vue 36 (NL)

Walthamstow   *Belle Vue*
Dick Case 5   Bill Kitchen 9
Wally Hull 3+1   Frank Varey 3+1
Squib Burton 5   Max Grosskreutz 9
Dusty Haigh 0   Bob Harrison 4+1
Chun Moore 1   Frank Charles 5
Eric Blain 3   Joe Abbott 6+2

Saturday 22 September 1934 Belle Vue Manchester
Belle Vue 40 Walthamstow 14 (NL)

Belle Vue   *Walthamstow*
Frank Varey 7   Squib Burton 1
Bill Kitchen 7+2   Jack Bibby 2
Joe Abbott 6   Chun Moore 2+1
Oliver Langton 5+2   Wally Hull 4
Frank Charles 8+1   Dusty Haigh 1
Bob Harrison 7+2   Eric Blain 3
                       Clem Thomas 1

Thursday 27 September 1934 Walthamstow London
Walthamstow 21 West Ham 32 (NL)

Walthamstow   *West Ham*
Dick Case 6   Bluey Wilkinson 6
Wally Hull 2   Jack Dixon 5+1
Squib Burton 3   Arthur Atkinson 8
Dusty Haigh 4+1   Wal Morton 3+2
Jack Bibby 3   Tommy Croombs 5
Chun Moore 1+1   Stan Dell 5+1
Clem Thomas 2

Wednesday 3 October 1934 Walthamstow London
Walthamstow v Wembley 32 (NL) Postponed - rain

Wednesday 10 October 1934 Walthamstow London
Walthamstow 22 Wembley 32 (NL)

Walthamstow   *Wembley*
Dick Case 7+1   Ginger Lees 9
Wally Hull 2   Les Bowden 2+1
Squib Burton 2+2   Wally Kilmister 5
Dusty Haigh 6   Colin Watson 3
Chun Moore 2   Gordon Byers 7+1
Reg Stanley 3+1   Harry Whitfield 5 +1
                       Ken Kirkman 1+1

Walthamstow 1949

Monday 4 April 1949 Walthamstow London
Walthamstow 41 Southampton 41 (NL2)

Walthamstow   *Southampton*
Dick Shepherd 9+3   Bob Oakley 9
Wilf Jay 9   Tom Oakley 3+1
Bill Osborne 9   Roy Craighead 8
Ted Argall 2+1   Bill Griffiths 4+1
Charlie May 5   Cecil Bailey 8+1
Harry Edwards 4   Jimmy Squibb 8
Reg Reeves 3   Alf Kaines 1
Harold Bull 0   Geoff Woodger 0

Tuesday 5 April 1949 Southampton
Southampton 52 Walthamstow 29 (NL2)

Southampton   *Walthamstow*
Bob Oakley 12   Dick Shepherd 2+2
Tom Oakley 7+1   Wilf Jay 7
Roy Craighead 11   Bill Osborne 8
Bill Griffiths 4+2   Ted Argall 1+1
Cecil Bailey 10+1   Charlie May 3+1
Jimmy Squibb 4+1   Harry Edwards 2
Alf Kaines 3   Reg Reeves 4
Geoff Woodger 1   Harold Bull 2

Friday 8 April 1949 Cradley Heath
Cradley Heath 52 Walthamstow 32 (NL2)

Cradley Heath | *Walthamstow*
Les Beaumont 9 | Dick Shepherd 4
Eric Williams 6+1 | Wilf Jay 8
Geoff Godwin 9+1 | Bill Osborne 5
Ray Beaumont 0 | Ted Argall 1+1
Alan Hunt 12 | Charlie May 10
Bill Kemp 4+1 | Harry Edwards 0
Bill Clifton 4+1 | Reg Reeves 3
Roy Moreton 8+1 | Harold Bull 1

Monday 11 April 1949 Walthamstow London
Walthamstow 40½ Sheffield 43½ (NL2)

Walthamstow | *Sheffield*
Harry Edwards 2+1 | Jack Bibby 1+1
Wilf Jay 11 | Stan Williams 10
Bill Osborne 3½+2 | Len Williams 7+2
Dick Shepherd 5 | Tommy Bateman 8+1
Charlie May 11 | Bruce Semmens 9½
Ted Argall 0 | Tommy Allott 5+1
Reg Reeves 8+1 | Alf Parker 2
Harold Bull 0 | Brian Gorman 1

Saturday 16 April 1949 Norwich
Norwich 57 Walthamstow 25 (NL2)

Norwich | *Walthamstow*
Sid Littlewood 9+1 | Bill Osborne 3
Bert Spencer 2+1 | Dick Geary 3+1
Paddy Mills 12 | Wilf Jay 8+1
Ted Bravery 8+2 | Arch Windmill 1
Phil Clarke 12 | Charlie May 1
Fred Rogers 8+2 | Reg Reeves 5
Jack Freeman 4+2 | Ted Argall 2
Bob Leverenz 2 | Harry Edwards 2

Monday 18 April 1949 Walthamstow London
Walthamstow 48 Newcastle 36 (NL2)

Walthamstow | *Newcastle*
Bill Osborne 0 | Son Mitchell 3
Dick Geary 4+1 | Frank Hodgson 11
Wilf Jay 12 | Derek Close 8
Arch Windmill 4+1 | Herby King 1
Charlie May 11 | Ernie Brecknell 6+1
Reg Reeves 6+3 | Jack Hodgson 7+1
Ted Argall 4+1 | Don Lawson 0
Harry Edwards 7

Tuesday, 19 April 1949 Ashfield Glasgow
Ashfield 48 Walthamstow 36 (NL2)

Ashfield | *Walthamstow*
Ken Le Breton 12 | Bill Osbourne 6
Alec Grant 4+2 | Dick Geary 1
Keith Gurtner 9+1 | Wilf Jay 8
Merv Harding 8+1 | Arch Windmill 4+1
Gruff Garland 8+1 | Charlie May 10
Roll Stobbart 6 | Reg Reeves 4+1
Willie Wilson 0 | Ted Argall 1+1
Alf McIntosh 1+1 | Harry Edwards 2+1

Wednesday 20 April 1949 White City Glasgow
Glasgow 52 Walthamstow 32 (NL2)

Glasgow | *Walthamstow*
Buck Ryan 5+1 | Bill Osborne 3
Will Lowther 11 | Dick Geary 3+1
Joe Crowther 7+2 | Wilf Jay 11
Gordon McGregor 9+1 | Arch Windmill 1
Junior Bainbridge 7+1 | Charlie May 11
Norman Lindsay 8+2 | Reg Reeves 2
Nobby Downham 3+1 | Ted Argall 0
Billie Bates 2+1 | Harry Edwards 1

Saturday 23 April 1949 Coventry
Coventry 45 Walthamstow 39 (NL2)

Coventry | *Walthamstow*
Bob Fletcher 9 | Dick Geary 2
Jack Winstanley 4 | Bill Osborne 8
Bert Lacey 7 | Wilf Jay 12
Jack D. White 7+1 | Arch Windmill 3
Jack Gordon 10 | Charlie May 9
John Yates 5+1 | Reg Reeves 2+2
Ed Pye 3+2 | Ted Argall 1+1
Les Hewitt 0 | Harry Edwards 2

Monday 25 April 1949 Walthamstow London
Walthamstow 40 Norwich 43 (NL2)

Walthamstow | *Norwich*
Arch Windmill 9+1 | Ted Bravery 0
Wilf Jay 4+1 | Paddy Mills 12
Charlie May 10 | Bert Spencer 4+2
Bill Osborne 7+3 | Sid Littlewood 0
Dick Geary 0 | Fred Rogers 3
Reg Reeves 6 | Phil Clarke 11+1
Harry Edwards 2+1 | Jack Freeman 8
Ted Argall 2 | Bob Leverenz 5

Wednesday 27 April 1949 Fleetwood
Fleetwood 54 Walthamstow 30 (NL2)

Fleetwood	*Walthamstow*
Ernie Appleby 9+3	Arch Windmill 3+2
George Newton 12	Wilf Jay 6+1
Cyril Cooper 9+2	Charlie May 7
Norman Hargreaves 8+2	Reg Reeves 2
Wilf Plant 12	Dick Geary 5
Ron Hart 2	Bill Osborne 3
Don Potter 0	Harry Edwards 3+1
Frank Malouf 2	Ted Argall 1+1

Thursday 28 April 1949 Sheffield
Sheffield 56 Walthamstow 27 (NL2)

Sheffield	*Walthamstow*
Tommy Bateman 3	Arch Windmill 1+1
Stan Williams 11+1	Wilf Jay 8
Tommy Allott 7+1	Charlie May 7
Len Williams 11+1	Reg Reeves 4+2
Jack Bibby 6+1	Dick Geary 3
Bruce Semmens 12	Bill Osborne 2
Ralph Horne 5+1	Harry Edwards 2
Alf Parker 1	Ted Argall 0

Monday, 2 May 1949 Walthamstow London
Walthamstow 44 Ashfield 39 (NL2)

Walthamstow	*Ashfield*
Reg Reeves 5+1	Ken Le Breton 10+1
Wilf Jay 9	Alec Grant 7+2
Arch Windmill 9	Merv Harding 8+2
Bill Osborne 4	Keith Gurtner 8+1
Dick Geary 5	Gruff Garland 1
Charlie May 8+2	Rol Stobbart 3
Harry Edwards 4+3	Willie Wilson 1+1
Harold Bull D.N.R	Alf McIntosh 1

Saturday 7 May 1949 Hull

Hull 42 Walthamstow 42 (Ch)

Hull	*Walthamstow*
Norman Johnson 9+1	Reg Reeves 7
Mick Mitchell 5+1	Wilf Jay 9+1
Derek Glover 9	Arch Windmill 2
George Craig 1	Bill Osborne 6
Alf Webster 4	Dick Geary 9
Bob Baker 10	Charlie May 4
Jack Watts 3+1	Harry Edwards 4
Johnny Green 1	Harold Bull 1

Monday 9 May 1949 Walthamstow London
Walthamstow 45 Cradley Heath 39 (NL2)

Walthamstow	*Cradley Heath*
Reg Reeves 3+1	Les Beaumont 0
Wilf Jay 9	Gil Craven 3
Arch Windmill 3+2	Jack Arnfield 7+3
Bill Osborne 8	Roy Moreton 8
Dick Geary 1	Eric Williams 8
Charlie May 12	Alan Hunt 8+2
Harry Edwards 9	Geoff Godwin 5+1
Harold Bull DNR	Bill Clifton 0

Monday 16 May 1949 Walthamstow London
Best Pairs

Les Jenkins 14
Ken Adams 6
Total 20
Harry Edwards 9
Bill Osborne 8
Total 17
Dick Geary 3
Charlie May 14
Total 17
Alf Bottoms 14
Den Cosby 2
Total 16
Wilf Jay 6
Reg Reeves 8
Total 14
Bert Roger 8
Frank Lawrence 5
Total 13
Bert Lacey 5
Lionel Levy 0
Arch Windmill (res) 7
Total 12
Bruce Abernethy 7
Buster Brown 4
Total 11

Saturday 21 May 1949 Belle Vue Manchester
Walthamstow 42 Sheffield 30 (Ch)

Walthamstow	*Sheffield*
Wilf Jay 7+2	Bruce Semmens 7
Bill Osborne 4+1	Ralph Horne 4+1
Dick Geary 10+1	Len Williams 9
Harry Edwards 8+2	Jack Bibby 2+1
Charlie May 10+1	Tommy Bateman 6
Jim Boyd 3	Andy Menzies 2+1

Monday 23 May 1949 Walthamstow London
Walthamstow 42 Fleetwood 42 (NL2)

Walthamstow | *Fleetwood*
Reg Reeves 3+1 | Wilf Plant 12
Wilf Jay 6 | Frank Malouf 1
Jim Boyd 9 | George Newton 7
Bill Osborne 4+3 | Ernie Appleby 5+1
Arch Windmill 7 | Cyril Cooper 7
Charlie May 5 | N. Hargreaves 10+1
Dick Geary 5 | Larry Young 0
Harry Edwards 3+2 | Peter Lloyd 0

Friday 27 May 1949 Bristol
Bristol 60 Walthamstow 24 (NL2)

Bristol | *Walthamstow*
Fred Tuck 12 | Reg Reeves 2+1
Jack Mountford 9+3 | Wilf Jay 5
Billy Hole 12 | Jim Boyd 7
Mike Beddoe 7+2 | Bill Osborne 2
Roger Wise 9+2 | Arch Windmill 2
Eric Salmon 7+1 | Charlie May 3
Johnny Hole 1 | Dick Geary 2+1
Dick Bradley 3+1 | Harry Edwards 1+1

Saturday 28 May 1949 Rayleigh
Rayleigh 41 Walthamstow 42 (Ch)

Rayleigh | *Walthamstow*
Percy Brine 6 | Reg Reeves 2
Jim Gregory 7+1 | Wilf Jay 4
Ron Howes 5 | Jim Boyd 11
Charlie Mugford 5 | Bill Osborne 6+1
Jack Unstead 8+1 | Arch Windmill 10+2
Vic Gooden 4 | Dick Geary 8
Bob McFarlane 2+2 | Harold Bull 0
Wally Mawdsley 4+1 | Harry Edwards 1+1

Monday 30 May 1949 Walthamstow London
Walthamstow 63 Southampton 44 (NT)

Walthamstow | *Southampton*
Wilf Jay 11+1 | Bob Oakley 8
Reg Reeves 8+4 | Tom Oakley 10
Jim Boyd 10+2 | Jim Squibb 11
Bill Osborne 7+2 | Alf Kaines 1
Charlie May 16 | Roy Craighead 7+3
Arch Windmill 3+1 | Cecil Bailey 4
Dick Geary 5+1 | Geoff Woodger 2
Harry Edwards 3 | Bill Thatcher 1

Tuesday 31 May 1949 Southampton
Southampton 52 Walthamstow 56 (NT)

Southampton | *Walthamstow*
Bob Oakley 13+2 | Reg Reeves 2+1
Tom Oakley 8 | Wilf Jay 6+1
Jim Squibb 9+1 | Jim Boyd 18
Alf Kaines 5+2 | Bill Osborne 5
Roy Craighead 4+1 | Charlie May 14+1
Cecil Bailey 10+2 | Arch Windmill 2
Geoff Woodger 0 | Dick Geary 4
Bill Thatcher 3 | Harry Edwards 5+1

Monday 6 June 1949 Walthamstow London
Walthamstow 50 Newcastle 34 (NL2)

Walthamstow | *Newcastle*
Reg Reeves 5+1 | Herby King 1+1
Wilf Jay 3+1 | Jack Hodgson 7+1
Jim Boyd 10 | Benny King 9
Bill Osborne 7 | Derek Close 5+2
Dick Geary 6+3 | Son Mitchell 2
Charlie May 12 | Frank Hodgson 8
Arch Windmill 4 | Ernie Brecknell 1
Harry Edwards 3 | Don Lawson 1+1

Wednesday 8 June 1949 Newcastle
Newcastle 41 Walthamstow 43 (NL2)

Newcastle | *Walthamstow*
Son Mitchell 3 | Reg Reeves 7+1
Frank Hodgson 7+1 | Wilf Jay 6+1
Herby King 2 | Jim Boyd 10
Jack Hodgson 6+1 | Dick Geary 2+2
Benny King 5 | Arch Windmill 5+2
Derek Close 8+1 | Charlie May 11
Ernie Brecknell 7+1 | Bill Osborne 2
Don Lawson 3+1 | Harry Edwards 0

Monday 13 June 1949 Walthamstow London
World Championship Qualifying Round

Jim Boyd (res) 14^
Bob Baker 11
Bob Fletcher 11
Arthur Forrest 10
Will Lowther 10
Cyril Cooper 9
Derek Close 8
Harry Edwards (res) 8^
Bert Lacey 8
Tom Oakley 6
Paddy Mills 5

Cyril Page 5
Johnny White 5
Derek Glover 4
Clem Mitchell 4
Leif Samsing 2
Jack Bibby 0
George Craig (No.10) DNR
^ Scores did not count towards qualification for the next round

Saturday 18 June 1949 Edinburgh
Edinburgh 45 Walthamstow 39 (NL2)

Edinburgh	*Walthamstow*
Clem Mitchell 11	Reg Reeves 4+1
Eddie Lack 3+1	Wilf Jay 7
Dick Campbell 10	Jim Boyd 7+1
Danny Lee 2+1	Arch Windmill 1+1
Jack Young 11	Dick Geary 2+2
Dennis Parker 5+3	Charlie May 10
Don Cuppleditch 3	Bill Osborne 2
Bill Baird 0	Harry Edwards 6+1

Monday 20 June 1949 Walthamstow London
Walthamstow 64 Cradley Heath 39 (NT)

Walthamstow	*Cradley Heath*
Benny King 8+1	Eric Williams 3
Reg Reeves 2	Alan Hunt 8+1
Jim Boyd 14+1	Gil Craven 4
Bill Osborne 9	Jack Arnfield 6
Charlie May 17+1	Geoff Godwin 8
Arch Windmill 3	Roy Moreton 5
Dick Geary 6	Bill Clifton 4
Harry Edwards 5	Phil Malpass 1+1

Friday 24 June 1949 Cradley Heath
Cradley Heath 66 Walthamstow 41 (NT)

Cradley Heath	*Walthamstow*
Phil Malpass 8+3	Reg Reeves 4+1
Alan Hunt 7+3	Benny King 8
Gil Craven 9	Jim Boyd 7+1
Jack Arnfield 14	Bill Osborne 0
Eric Williams 14+1	Charlie May 17
Geoff Godwin 10+1	Arch Windmill 0
Bill Clifton 3+1	Dick Geary 5+1
Roy Moreton 1	Harry Edwards 0

Monday 27 June 1949 Walthamstow London
Walthamstow 58 Edinburgh 26 (NL2)

Walthamstow	*Edinburgh*
Benny King 11	Clem Mitchell 5
Dick Geary 8+3	Don Cuppleditch 4+1
Jim Boyd 10	Dick Campbell 8
Bill Osborne 5	Danny Lee 1
Reg Reeves 5+2	Jack Young 5
Charlie May 10	Dennis Parker 2
Arch Windmill 4+1	Tommy Lack 0
Harry Edwards 5+1	Bill Baird 1

Thursday 30 June 1949 Sheffield
Sheffield 48 Walthamstow 36 (NL2)

Sheffield	*Walthamstow*
Stan Williams 11+1	Benny King 4
Jack Chignell 6+1	Dick Geary 7+1
Len Williams 9	Jim Boyd 8
Jack Bibby 2	Bill Osborne 3+1
Tommy Bateman 6+1	Reg Reeves 3
Tommy Allott 12	Charlie May 7
Alf Parker 1	Arch Windmill 0
Guy Allott 1+1	Harry Edwards 4

Monday 4 July 1949 Walthamstow London
Walthamstow 62 Cradley Heath 44 (NT)

Walthamstow	*Cradley Heath*
Benny King 10+1	Phil Malpass 0
Dick Geary 2	Alan Hunt 6
Jim Boyd 15+1	Eric Williams 6
Bill Osborne 2	Gil Craven 12
Charlie May 7+1	Jack Arnfield 15
Reg Reeves 9+1	Roy Moreton 2
Harry Edwards 9+2	Les Tolley 1
Arch Windmill 8+2	Bill Clifton 2

Friday 8 July 1949 Cradley Heath
Cradley Heath 71 Walthamstow 37 (NT)

Cradley Heath	*Walthamstow*
Les Tolley 3	Dick Geary 3
Alan Hunt 17+1	Benny King 7+1
Jack Arnfield 17+1	Jim Boyd 4
Gil Craven 11+1	Harry Edwards 1
Eric Williams 7+2	Charlie May 9
Phil Malpass 9+3	Reg Reeves 2+1
Roy Moreton 7+1	Arch Windmill 6+2
Bill Clifton 0	Bill Osborne 5+2

Monday 11 July 1949 Walthamstow London
Walthamstow 67 Coventry 17 (NL2)

Walthamstow	*Coventry*
Dick Geary 10+1	Bob Fletcher 2
Benny King 7+2	Ed Pye 5
Jim Boyd 8+4	Lionel Levy 1
Harry Edwards 12	John Yates 3
Reg Reeves 9+3	Jack Gordon 4
Charlie May 11+1	Bert Lacey 0
Arch Windmill 4+2	Les Hewitt 1
Bill Osborne 6	John D. White 1

Tuesday 12th July 1949 Southampton
Southampton 42 Walthamstow 41 (NL2)

Southampton	*Walthamstow*
Bob Oakley 5+4	Dick Geary 2
Tom Oakley 9	Benny King 6
Jim Squibb 8+1	Jim Boyd 7
Roy Craighead 3	Harry Edwards 8
Cecil Bailey 9+1	Reg Reeves 4+2
Bill Rogers 3	Charlie May 10
Alf Kaines 5	Arch Windmill 1+1
Bill Thatcher 0	Bill Osborne 3

Monday 18 July 1949 Walthamstow London
Walthamstow 51 Southampton 32 (NL2)

Walthamstow	*Southampton*
Dick Geary 9	Tom Oakley 7
Benny King 4+1	Bob Oakley 4+1
Jim Boyd 12	Cecil Bailey 9
Harry Edwards 7+1	Alf Kaines 0
Reg Reeves 5+1	Jim Squibb 5
Charlie May 11	Roy Craighead 3+1
Arch Windmill 3+1	Bill Griffiths 4
Bill Osborne 0	Geoff Woodger 0

Friday 22 July 1949 Bristol
Bristol 51 Walthamstow 33 (NL2)

Bristol	*Walthamstow*
Mike Beddoe 6	Dick Geary 1
Billy Hole 7	Benny King 4
Eric Salmon 10+2	Jim Boyd 8
Roger Wise 11+1	Harry Edwards 7+1
Jack Mountford 10	Reg Reeves 3
Fred Tuck 0	Charlie May 9
Johnny Hole 4+2	Arch Windmill 1
Dick Bradley 3+1	Bill Osborne 0

Monday 25 July 1949 Walthamstow London
Walthamstow 55 Norwich Stars 28 (NDL2)

Walthamstow	*Norwich*
Dick Geary 7+1	Bob Leverenz 6
Benny King 8+2	Ted Bravery 0
Jim Boyd 12	Jack Freeman 4+1
Harry Edwards 4+1	Bert Spencer 3
Reg Reeves 9+2	Alec Hunter 2
Charlie May 10+1	Phil Clarke 9
Arch Windmill 4	Johnny Davies 2
Bill Osborne 1	Fred Rogers 2

Saturday 30 July 1949 Rayleigh
Walthamstow 58 Southampton 26 (Ch)

Walthamstow	*Southampton*
Dick Geary 6+3	Bob Oakley 7
Benny King 10	Tom Oakley 3
Jim Boyd 12	Cecil Bailey 2
Harry Edwards 8+2	Phil Bishop 4
Reg Reeves 7+1	Jim Squibb 4+1
Charlie May 8+1	Roy Craighead 5
Arch Windmill 5+1	Bill Griffiths 1
Bill Osborne 2+1	Alf Kaines 0

Monday 1 August 1949 Walthamstow London
Walthamstow 46 Bristol 37 (NL2)

Walthamstow	*Bristol*
Dick Geary 5+1	Dick Bradley 4+1
Benny King 7	Jack Mountford 10
Jim Boyd 8+1	Eric Salmon 8+1
Harry Edwards 7+1	Roger Wise 11+1
Reg Reeves 7	Billy Hole 4
Charlie May 7+1	Johnny Hole 0
Arch Windmill 3+2	Chris Boss 0
Bill Osborne 2+1	Graham Hole 0

Wednesday 3 August 1949 White City Glasgow
Glasgow 39 Walthamstow 45 (NL2)

Glasgow	*Walthamstow*
Will Lowther 8	Dick Geary 5+2
Bat Byrnes 4+1	Benny King 8+1
Joe Crowther 6	Jim Boyd 9
Norman Lindsay 2+1	Harry Edwards 3
Gordon McGregor 1+1	Reg Reeves 8+2
Junior Bainbridge 11	Charlie May 8+1
Buck Ryan 6+1	Arch Windmill 4+1
Ken McKinlay 1	Bill Osborne 0

Monday 8 August 1949 Walthamstow London
Walthamstow 55 Harringay 52 (LC)

Walthamstow	*Harringay*
Benny King 12	Jimmy Grant 9+1
Dick Geary 8+1	Lloyd Goffe 1
Jim Boyd 11+1	Danny Dunton 8
Harry Edwards 8	Geoff Pymar 16
Charlie May 6	Nobby Stock 3+1
Reg Reeves 3+1	Ray Duggan 9+2
Arch Windmill 4+1	Joe Bowkis 5
Bill Osborne 3	Sid Clark 1+1

Friday 12 August 1949 Walthamstow London
Harringay 60 Walthamstow 48 (LC)

Harringay	*Walthamstow*
Nobby Stock 10+2	Dick Geary 4
Ray Duggan 8	Benny King 8
Danny Dunton 8+2	Jim Boyd 10+3
Geoff Pymar 9+2	Harry Edwards 0
Jimmy Grant 4	Charlie May 13
Lloyd Goffe 15+1	Reg Reeves 5+1
Joe Bowkis 4+1	Arch Windmill 2+1
Sid Clark 2	Bill Osborne 6+1

Monday 15 August 1949 Walthamstow London
Walthamstow 54 Cradley Heath 30 (NLD2)

Walthamstow	*Cradley Heath*
Dick Geary 5+2	Phil Malpass 0
Benny King 7	Alan Hunt 11
Jim Boyd 8+1	Les Tolley 1
Harry Edwards 10+1	Eric Williams 8
Reg Reeves 8	Les Beaumont 2
Charlie May 8+1	Jack Arnfield 6
Arch Windmill 4+1	Bill Clifton 2
Bill Osborne 4+2	Jim Pain 0

Wednesday 17 August 1949 Fleetwood
Fleetwood 41 Walthamstow 43 (NL2)

Fleetwood	*Walthamstow*
Brian Wilson 1	Dick Geary 8+1
Norman Hargreaves 11+1	Benny King 4+2
George Newton 9	Jim Boyd 8+2
Stan Beardsall 5	Harry Edwards 8
Frank Malouf 2+1	Reg Reeves 5+1
Cyril Cooper 10	Charlie May 6
Fred Yates 2+1	Arch Windmill 3+1
Percy Day 1	Bill Osborne 1+1

Saturday 20 August 1949 Edinburgh
Edinburgh 61 Walthamstow 22 (NL2)

Edinburgh	*Walthamstow*
Eddie Lack 7+2	Dick Geary 2
Clem Mitchell 10	Benny King 4+1
Dick Campbell 11+1	Jim Boyd 5
Danny Lee 9+1	Harry Edwards 3
Don Cuppleditch 10+2	Reg Reeves 5
Jack Young 9+1	Charlie May 0
Harold Fairhurst 5+1	Bill Osborne 2
Bill Baird 0	Arch Windmill 1+1

Monday 22 August 1949 Walthamstow London
Walthamstow 48 Glasgow 34 (NL2)

Walthamstow	*Glasgow*
Dick Geary 4+1	Will Lowther 5
Benny King 10	Bat Byrnes 2+2
Jim Boyd 11+1	Joe Crowther 3
Harry Edwards 9+1	G. McGregor 2+1
Reg Reeves 2+2	Buck Ryan 1+1
Charlie May 8+1	Junior Bainbridge 11
Arch Windmill 2+1	Norman Lindsay 6
Bill Osborne 2	Alf McIntosh 4

Saturday 27 August 1949 Birmingham
Birmingham 49 Walthamstow 35 (Ch)

Birmingham	*Walthamstow*
Stan Dell 8+1	Dick Geary 4+1
Eric Williams 10+1	Benny King 3
Arthur Payne 11+1	Jim Boyd 7
Denis Hitchings 8+1	Harry Edwards 4
Buck Whitby 4	Reg Reeves 6+1
Dick Tolley 7+1	Charlie May 8+1
Fred Perkins 1	Arch Windmill 2+2
Bill Wilkins 0	Bill Osborne 1+1

Monday 29 August 1949 Walthamstow London
Walthamstow 53 Edinburgh 31 (NL2)

Walthamstow	*Edinburgh*
Dick Geary 3	Eddie Lack 6
Benny King 9	Clem Mitchell 0
Jim Boyd 10	Dick Campbell 10
Harry Edwards 7+4	Danny Lee 3
Reg Reeves 6+1	Don Cuppleditch 1
Charlie May 8+2	Jack Young 10
Arch Windmill 6	Harold Fairhurst 1+1
Bill Osborne 4+1	Bill Baird 0

Monday 5 September 1949 Walthamstow London
Walthamstow 52 Sheffield 32 (NL2)

Walthamstow	Sheffield
Dick Geary 4+1	Stan Williams 6
Benny King 12	Jack Chignell 1+1
Jim Boyd 4+2	Len Williams 9
Harry Edwards 11	Andy Menzies 1+1
Reg Reeves 7+1	Tommy Bateman 4+2
Charlie May 3	Tommy Allott 9
Arch Windmill 5+1	Jack Bibby 1
Bill Osborne 6	Alf Parker 1+1

Monday 12 September 1949 Walthamstow London
Walthamstow 49 Coventry 35 (NL2)

Walthamstow	Coventry
Dick Geary 1	Bob Fletcher 4+1
Benny King 11	Derrick Tailby 7
Jim Boyd 9+1	Les Hewitt 3
Harry Edwards 8+1	Roy Moreton 5+1
Reg Reeves 9	Les Wotton 6+2
Charlie May 0	Bert Lacey 4
Arch Windmill 8	John Yates 4
Bill Osborne 3+1	Lionel Levy 2

Monday 19 September 1949 Walthamstow London
Walthamstow 62 Fleetwood 21 (NL2)

Walthamstow	Fleetwood
Dick Geary 8	Frank Malouf 0
Benny King 10+2	Norman Hargreaves 8
Jim Boyd 11	George Newton 3
Reg Reeves 9+3	Don Potter 5
Arch Windmill 8+3	Brian Wilson 1
Harry Edwards 8	Wilf Plant 4+1
Bill Osborne 5+1	Ted Rawlinson 0
Harold Bull 3+2	Fred Yates 0

Thursday 22 September 1949 Plymouth
West of England 55 London 29 (Ch)

West of England	London
Don Hardy 9+1	Dick Geary 0
Norman Clay 6+2	Benny King 4
Eric Salmon 12	Jim Boyd 7
Johnny Hole 4+2	Harry Edwards 1
Hugh Geddes 11	Reg Reeves 4+1
Dick Bradley 6+1	Arch Windmill 10
Arthur Pilgrim 5+1	Harold Bull 1
Chris Boss 2+1	Bill Osborne 2+2

Note London = Walthamstow

Saturday 24 September 1949 Coventry
Coventry 36 Walthamstow 47 (NL2)

Coventry	Walthamstow
Bob Fletcher 6	Harry Edwards 6+2
Bert Lacey 7	Benny King 10
Les Wotton 2	Jim Boyd 12
Derek Tailby 9	Arch Windmill 5+1
Les Hewitt 0	Reg Reeves 8+1
Roy Moreton 3+1	Charlie May 2+1
Lionel Levy 3	Dick Geary 1+1
John Yates 6	Bill Osborne 3

Monday 26 September 1949 Walthamstow London
Walthamstow 56 Glasgow 27 (NDL2)

Walthamstow	Glasgow
Dick Geary 8+1	Alf McIntosh 3+1
Benny King 7+1	Gordon McGregor 10
Jim Boyd 10+1	Jack Hodgson 9
Harry Edwards 7+1	Buck Ryan 0
Reg Reeves 7+1	Junior Bainbridge 2
Charlie May 8+1	Norman Lindsay 3
Arch Windmill 5+1	Ivor Smith 0
Bill Osborne 4	Joe Ferguson 0

Tuesday 27 September 1949 Ashfield Glasgow
Ashfield 53 Walthamstow 31 (NL2)

Ashfield	Walthamstow
Eric Liddell 1	Harry Edwards 5
Keith Gurtner 3	Benny King 4+3
Merv Harding 11+1	Jim Boyd 6
Willie Wilson 8	Arch Windmill 5
Ken Le Breton 12	Reg Reeves 0
Alec Grant 3	Charlie May 6
Gruff Garland 6+2	Dick Geary 2
Norman Johnson 9+1	Bill Osborne 3

Saturday 1 October 1949 Newcastle
Newcastle 42 Walthamstow 42 (NL2)

Newcastle	Walthamstow
Ernie Brecknell 7	Harry Edwards 0
Derek Close 6+1	Benny King 8
Wilf Jay 11	Jim Boyd 11
Joe Arthur 5+1	Arch Windmill 1+1
Herby King 6	Reg Reeves 6+2
Will Lowther 3+1	Charlie May 3
Don Lawson 3+2	Dick Geary 11
Ken Allick 1	Bill Osborne 2

Monday 3 October 1949 Walthamstow London
Walthamstow 54 Ashfield 29 (NL2)

Walthamstow
Dick Geary 7+1
Benny King 6+1
Jim Boyd 8+2
Arch Windmill 8
Reg Reeves 9+1
Charlie May 11+1
Harold Bull 3+2
Bill Osborne 2+1

Ashfield
Norman Johnson 5
Alec Grant 2
Merv Harding 10
Willie Wilson 3+1
Ken Le Breton 9
Eric Liddell 0
Jim Reid 0
Larry Lazarus 0

Friday 7 October 1949 Cradley Heath
Cradley Heath 57 Walthamstow 27 (NL2)

Cradley Heath
Alan Hunt 9
Les Beaumont 6+1
Phil Malpass 7+2
Eric Williams 12
Les Tolley 8
Gil Craven 11+1
Bill Clifton 2+1
Geoff Godwin 2

Walthamstow
Harry Edwards 5
Benny King 4
Jim Boyd 7
Arch Windmill 2+1
Reg Reeves 3+2
Charlie May 4+1
Dick Geary 0
Bill Osborne 2

Saturday 8 October 1949 Norwich
Norwich 56 Walthamstow 28 (NL2)

Norwich
Sid Littlewood 10+1
Paddy Mills 7
Bob Leverenz 12
Jack Freeman 9+3
Ted Bravery 12
Phil Clarke 4+1
Johnny Davies 2+1
Bill Codling 0

Walthamstow
Harry Edwards 5
Benny King 2+1
Jim Boyd 5
Arch Windmill 0
Reg Reeves 4+1
Charlie May 6
Dick Geary 3+1
Bill Osborne 3+1

Monday 10 October 1949 Walthamstow London
Walthamstow 35 Bristol 49 (NL2)

Walthamstow
Dick Geary 1
Benny King 4
Jim Boyd 5+3
Harry Edwards 9
Reg Reeves 7
Charlie May 5+1
Arch Windmill 3+1
Bill Osborne 1+1

Bristol
Johnny Hole 7+1
Billy Hole 6+2
Dick Bradley 1
Roger Wise 12
Fred Tuck 7
Jack Mountford 7+1
Mike Beddoe 6+1
Chris Boss 3

Saturday 15 October 1949 Rayleigh
Rayleigh 46 Walthamstow 38 (Ch)

Rayleigh
Jack Unstead 1
Les McGillivray 12
Vic Gooden 6+1
Ron Howes 6
Pat Clarke 8+2
Jim Gregory 9+2
Wally Mawdsley 4
Doug Ible 0

Walthamstow
Harry Edwards 1
Benny King 5
Jim Boyd 9
Arch Windmill 2
Reg Reeves 8+1
Charlie May 4
Dick Geary 4+1
Bill Osborne 5+3

Monday 17 October 1949 Walthamstow London
Walthamstow 43 Belle Vue 40 (Ch)

Walthamstow
Harry Edwards 4+3
Benny King 9
Jim Boyd 8+1
Arch Windmill 5
Reg Reeves 7
Charlie May 0
Dick Geary 2
Bill Osborne 8+1

Belle Vue
Ron Mason 3
Jack Parker 9
Ken Sharples 5
George Smith 0
Bruce Semmens 5
Louis Lawson 8+1
Charles Cullum 7
Bob Harrison 3

Friday 21 October 1949 Leicester
Leicester 46 Walthamstow 38 (Ch)

Leicester
Harwood Pike 6
Cyril Page 9+2
Ron Wilson 1+1
Johnny Carpenter 11
Jack Baxter 3+2
Vic Pitcher 10
Ernie Palmer 2
Jack Winstanley 4

Walthamstow
Harry Edwards 9+1
Benny King 4+1
Jim Boyd 12
Arch Windmill 2
Reg Reeves 1
Charlie May 4+1
Dick Geary 1
Bill Osborne 5

Thursday 27 October 1949 Oxford
Oxford, Bristol & Cradley 41 Walthamstow 43 (Ch)

Oxford, Bristol & Cradley
Roger Wise 2+2
Jack Mountford 10
Alan Hunt 11
Gil Craven 7+3
Bert Croucher 3+1
Dennis Gray 5
Alf Viccary 2
Bill Kemp 1+1

Walthamstow
Harry Edwards 10
Benny King 0
Jim Boyd 10+1
Arch Windmill 4
Reg Reeves 8+1
Charlie May 6+1
Dick Geary 1
Bill Osborne 4+1

Walthamstow 1950

Saturday 1 April 1950 Hanley Stoke
Hanley 28 Walthamstow 56 (Ch)

Hanley	*Walthamstow*
Ken Adams 8	Harry Edwards 12
Ray Harris 1	Benny King 7+3
Les Jenkins 3	Jim Boyd 10
Bill Harris 4	Dick Geary 2+2
Gil Blake 3+1	Reg Reeves 5+2
Frank Evans 3	Charlie May 12
Stan Bradbury 2+1	Dick Shepherd 4+1
John Fitzpatrick 4+1	Arch Windmill 4+1

Monday 3 April 1950 Walthamstow London
Walthamstow 57 Norwich 27 (SS)

Walthamstow	*Norwich*
Harry Edwards 10+1	Fred Rogers 3
Benny King 9+2	Paddy Mills 9
Jim Boyd 11	Phil Clarke 6
Dick Geary 1	Ted Bravery 3+1
Reg Reeves 5+2	Jack Freeman 2
Charlie May 11+1	Alec Hunter 3
Dick Shepherd 6+1	Bill Codling 1+1
Arch Windmill 4	Johnny Davies 0

Saturday 8 April 1950 Norwich
Norwich 38 Walthamstow 46 (SS)

Norwich	*Walthamstow*
Sid Littlewood 3	Harry Edwards 11
Paddy Mills 9	Benny King 6+4
Phil Clarke 8+1	Jim Boyd 11
Alec Hunter 4	Dick Shepherd 4+1
Ted Bravery 8	Reg Reeves 3
Jack Freeman 2	Charlie May 8
Fred Rogers 1+1	Dick Geary 0
Bill Codling 3+1	Arch Windmill 3+2

Monday 10 April 1950 Walthamstow London
Walthamstow 49 Southampton 35 (SS)

Walthamstow	*Southampton*
Harry Edwards 4+1	Bob Oakley 11
Benny King 11	Tom Oakley 1+1
Jim Boyd 8	Roy Craighead 6+1
Dick Shepherd 5+2	Jim Squibb 5+1
Reg Reeves 9	Les Wotton 10
Charlie May 6+2	Steve Langton 1
Dick Geary 3+1	Buck Whitby 1
Arch Windmill 3+2	Bill Griffiths 0

Monday 17 April 1950 Walthamstow London
Walthamstow 56 Yarmouth 28 (SS)

Walthamstow	*Yarmouth*
Harry Edwards 7+2	Bill Carruthers 10
Benny King 9+1	Johnny White 3+2
Jim Boyd 12	Reg Morgan 6
Dick Shepherd 6+1	Bert Rawlinson 4+1
Reg Reeves 12	Wally Higgs 3
Charlie May 4+2	Fred Brand 2
Dick Geary 4+1	George Flower 0
Arch Windmill 2	Stan Page 0

Monday 24 April 1950 Walthamstow London
Walthamstow 51 Plymouth 33 (SS)

Walthamstow	*Plymouth*
Harry Edwards 6+1	Peter Robinson 10
Benny King 11	Cecil Bailey 4+1
Jim Boyd 12	Pete Lansdale 3
Dick Shepherd 4+1	George Wall 4
Reg Reeves 9	Len Read 9
Charlie May 1	Alan Smith 3+2
Dick Geary 2+1	Johnny Bradford 0
Arch Windmill 6+3	Bill Thatcher 0

Tuesday 25 April 1950 Southampton
Southampton 37 Walthamstow 47 (SS)

Southampton	*Walthamstow*
Bob Oakley 11	Harry Edwards 9+1
Tom Oakley 2	Benny King 7+2
Roy Craighead 9	Jim Boyd 8+1
Jim Squibb 4	Dick Shepherd 2
Les Wotton 6	Reg Reeves 6
Steve Langton 2	Charlie May 9
Phil Bishop 3	Dick Geary 1+1
Bill Griffiths 0	Arch Windmill 5+2

Thursday 27 April 1950 Plymouth
Plymouth 58 Walthamstow 26 (SS)

Plymouth	*Walthamstow*
Pete Lansdale 10+1	Harry Edwards 5
George Wall 4+1	Benny King 1+1
Peter Robinson 12	Jim Boyd 7+1
Cecil Bailey 6+1	Dick Shepherd 2
Len Read 12	Reg Reeves 3+1
Alan Smith 9+3	Charlie May 1
Johnny Bradford 4+1	Dick Geary 4
Bill Thatcher 1	Arch Windmill 3

Monday 1 May 1950 Walthamstow London
Walthamstow 32 Bristol 52 (Ch)

Walthamstow | *Bristol*
Harry Edwards 0 | Jack Mountford 7
Benny King 8 | Fred Tuck 8
Jim Boyd 6 | Billy Hole 12
Dick Shepherd 3+1 | Roger Wise 3
Reg Reeves 5+2 | Dick Bradley 12
Charlie May 5+1 | Chris Boss 3
Dick Geary 1 | Johnny Hole 3
Arch Windmill 4 | Mike Beddoe 4+2

Monday 8 May 1950 Walthamstow London
Walthamstow 41 Coventry 42 (SS)

Walthamstow | *Coventry*
Harry Edwards 4+2 | Bob Fletcher 9
Benny King 12 | Cyril Cooper 0
Jim Boyd 7 | Stan Williams 10+1
Arch Windmill 4 | Les Hewitt 8+2
Reg Reeves 7 | Johnnie Reason 6
Charlie May 2+1 | Lionel Levy 1+1
Dick Geary 4 | Derek Tailby 4+2
Dick Shepherd 1+1 | Roy Moreton 4+1

Tuesday 9 May 1950 Yarmouth
Yarmouth 48 Walthamstow 35 (SS)

Yarmouth | *Walthamstow*
Bert Rawlinson 4+3 | Harry Edwards DNR
Billy Bales 7 | Benny King 5
Bill Carruthers 12 | Jim Boyd 10
Johnny White 4+1 | Arch Windmill 0
Tip Mills 0 | Reg Reeves 5
Reg Morgan 8½+1½ | Charlie May 6+1
Wally Higgs 8+2 | Dick Shepherd 4
Fred Brand 4½+½ | Dick Geary 5+2

Saturday 13 May 1950 Cradley Heath
Cradley Heath 49 Walthamstow 35 (SS)

Cradley Heath | *Walthamstow*
Jack Arnfield 0 | Harry Edwards 5+2
Phil Malpass 10+1 | Benny King 5
Gil Craven 3 | Jim Boyd 7
Les Tolley 9+1 | George Newton 3
Bill Clifton 6+3 | Reg Reeves 7+1
Alan Hunt 11 | Charlie May 2+1
Jim Pain 3+1 | Arch Windmill 6
Harry Bastable 7+1 | Harold Bull 0

Monday 15 May 1950 Walthamstow London
Walthamstow 60 Cradley Heath 24 (SS)

Walthamstow | *Cradley Heath*
Harry Edwards 7 | Bill Clifton 1
Benny King 7+1 | Alan Hunt 8
Jim Boyd 11+1 | Les Tolley 3+1
George Newton 9+1 | Gil Craven 4
Reg Reeves 9+1 | Phil Malpass 5+1
Charlie May 10+1 | Harry Bastable 2
Arch Windmill 3+1 | Jim Pain 0
Bert Edwards 4+2 | Frank Young 1

Saturday 20 May 1950 Coventry
Coventry 57 Walthamstow 27 (SS)

Coventry | *Walthamstow*
Bob Fletcher 8 | Harry Edwards 0
Derek Tailby 3+2 | Benny King 6
Les Hewitt 12 | Jim Boyd 8
Stan Williams 7+3 | George Newton 2+1
Johnnie Reason 9+1 | Reg Reeves 6+1
Lionel Levy 11+1 | Charlie May 2
Cyril Cooper 6 | Arch Windmill 3
Roy Moreton 1 | Bert Edwards 0

Monday 22 May 1950 Walthamstow London
Walthamstow 45 Birmingham 38 (Ch)

Walthamstow | *Birmingham*
Harry Edwards 4+3 | Graham Warren 12
Benny King 8+1 | Arthur Payne 6+2
Jim Boyd 9 | Doug McLachlan 4
George Newton 5+1 | Wilf Willstead 3
Reg Reeves 7+1 | Geoff Bennett 11
Charlie May 9+1 | Ron Mountford 0
Arch Windmill 3+1 | Fred Perkins 1+1
Bert Edwards 0 | Jim Tolley 1+1

Monday 29 May 1950 Walthamstow London
Walthamstow 66 Yarmouth 42 (NT)

Walthamstow | *Yarmouth*
Benny King 17+1 | Johnny White 7
Harry Edwards 7+2 | Bill Carruthers 0
Jim Boyd 15+2 | Fred Brand 5+1
George Newton 0 | Reg Morgan 12
Charlie May 10 | Tip Mills 3
Reg Reeves 10+1 | Wally Higgs 8+1
Arch Windmill 7+1 | Stan Page 4+1
Bert Edwards 0 | Bert Rawlinson 3

Tuesday 30 May 1950 Yarmouth
Yarmouth 57 Walthamstow 50 (NT)

Yarmouth | *Walthamstow*
Johnny White 7 | Benny King 11+1
Bill Carruthers 15 | Harry Edwards 3+1
Tip Mills 9 | Jim Boyd 12+1
Wally Higgs 4+2 | George Newton 6+1
Fred Brand 9+1 | Charlie May 4
Reg Morgan 5+1 | Reg Reeves 11+1
Stan Page 5+1 | Arch Windmill 1
Bert Rawlinson 3 | Bert Edwards 2

Monday 5 June 1950 Walthamstow London
Walthamstow 51 Sheffield 33 (NL2)

Walthamstow | *Sheffield*
Harry Edwards 4+1 | Charlie New 7+2
Benny King 12 | Len Williams 4
Jim Boyd 12 | Jack Chignell 1+1
Charlie May 5+1 | Peter Orpwood 6
Reg Reeves 11+1 | Bill Dalton 9
George Newton 4 | Guy Allott 3+1
Arch Windmill 2 | Bert Lacey 1
Bert Edwards 1 | Jack Winstanley 2

Saturday 10 June 1950 Hanley Stoke
Hanley 42 Walthamstow 41 (Ch)

Hanley | *Walthamstow*
Ken Adams 10+1 | Harry Edwards 5+2
Les Jenkins 1+1 | Benny King 6+1
Lindsay Mitchell 7 | Jim Boyd 7
Gil Blake 6+2 | Charlie May 1+1
Brian Pritchett 4 | Reg Reeves 10
Bill Harris 8 | George Newton 5+1
Stan Bradbury 3 | Arch Windmill 4
Ray Harris 3+2 | Bert Edwards 3

Monday 12 June 1950 Walthamstow London
Walthamstow 46 Southern Stars 35 (Ch)

Walthamstow | *Southern Stars*
Harry Edwards 3+2 | Peter Robinson 7
Benny King 9 | Reg Morgan 3+2
Jim Boyd 11 | Bill Carruthers 3
Charlie May 3 | Johnnie Reason 10
Reg Reeves 8+1 | Bob Fletcher 1+1
George Newton 7 | Len Read 7
Arch Windmill 4+1 | Joe Bowkis 0
Bert Edwards 1+1 | Harold Bull 4+1

Monday 19 June 1950 Walthamstow London
Walthamstow 67 Southampton 41 (NT)

Walthamstow | *Southampton*
Benny King 6 | Bob Oakley 10+1
Harry Edwards 3 | Buck Whitby 2+1
Jim Boyd 16+2 | Jim Squibb 8
George Newton 5+1 | Steve Langton 6+1
Charlie May 16+2 | Les Wotton 6+1
Reg Reeves 13+1 | Roy Craighead 4+2
Arch Windmill 6 | Bill Griffiths 5
Bert Edwards 2+1 | Phil Bishop 0

Tuesday 20 June 1950 Southampton
Southampton 59 Walthamstow 49 (NT)

Southampton | *Walthamstow*
Bob Oakley 8+1 | Benny King 6
Tom Oakley 11 | Harry Edwards 3
Jim Squibb 10+2 | Jim Boyd 7
Steve Langton 7 | George Newton 6+1
Les Wotton 7 | Charlie May 6+2
Roy Craighead 9+2 | Reg Reeves 16
Bill Griffiths 2+1 | Arch Windmill 4
Buck Whitby 5 | Bert Edwards 1

Wednesday 21 June 1950 Aldershot
Walthamstow 45 Southampton 39 (Ch)

Walthamstow | *Southampton*
Harry Edwards 11 | Bob Oakley 12
Benny King 5+1 | Buck Whitby 0
Jim Boyd 10 | Jim Squibb 7+1
Charlie May 6+3 | Steve Langton 4
Reg Reeves 1 | Les Wotton 11
George Newton 5+1 | Roy Craighead 4+2
Arch Windmill 4+3 | Bill Griffiths 1
Bert Edwards 3 | Phil Bishop 0

Friday 23 June 1950 Sheffield
Sheffield 34 Walthamstow 49 (NL2)

Sheffield | *Walthamstow*
Jack Gordon 1 | Harry Edwards 9
Len Williams 12 | Benny King 1+1
Bert Lacey 0 | Jim Boyd 8+1
Peter Orpwood 6 | Charlie May 8+1
Bill Dalton 3+1 | Reg Reeves 9+2
Guy Allott 8 | George Newton 7
Jack Winstanley 3 | Arch Windmill 5+1
Johnny Green 1+1 | Bert Edwards 2+1

Saturday 24 June 1950 Newcastle
Newcastle 10 Walthamstow 8 (NL2)
Abandoned after three heats

Newcastle
Son Mitchell 1
Frank Hodgson 3
Will Lowther 2
Wilf Jay 1+1
Herby King 1+1
Derek Close 2
Tommy Bateman DNR
Don Lawson DNR

Walthamstow
Harry Edwards 0
Benny King 2
Jim Boyd 3
Charlie May 0
Reg Reeves 3
George Newton 0
Arch Windmill DNR
Bert Edwards DNR

Monday 26 June 1950 Walthamstow London
Walthamstow 66 Ashfield 41 (NT)

Walthamstow
Benny King 10+1
Harry Edwards 3+1
Jim Boyd 15+1
George Newton 0
Charlie May 11+2
Reg Reeves 13+1
Arch Windmill 8+3
Bert Edwards 6

Ashfield
Ken Le Breton 16
Bob Lovell 1
Merv Harding 11+2
Willie Wilson 5+1
Keith Gurtner 4+1
Eric Liddell 0
N Johnson 2+1
Bill Baird 2

Monday 3 July 1950 Walthamstow London
Walthamstow 40 Plymouth 43 (NL2)

Walthamstow
Harry Edwards 2+1
Benny King 10
Jim Boyd 9
Charlie May 3+2
Reg Reeves 9+1
George Newton 2
Arch Windmill 5
Bert Edwards 0

Plymouth
Peter Robinson 11
Cecil Bailey 2
Len Read 7
Johnny Bradford 3+3
Pete Lansdale 12
George Wall 3+1
Geoff Woodger 0
Bill Thatcher 5

Tuesday, 4 July 1950 Ashfield Glasgow
Ashfield 67 Walthamstow 41 (NT)

Ashfield
Ken Le Breton 17+1
Bob Lovell 4+1
Merv Harding 16+2
Willie Wilson 9
Keith Gurtner 8+1
Bruce Semmens 11+1
Eric Liddell 1
Bill Baird 1

Walthamstow
Benny King 3
Harry Edwards 9+1
Jim Boyd 8+1
George Newton 4
Charlie May 3+1
Reg Reeves 3+1
Arch Windmill 7+1
Bert Edwards 4+2

Monday 10 July 1950 Walthamstow London
Walthamstow 52 Edinburgh 32 (NL2)

Walthamstow
Charlie May 6+2
Benny King 11
Jim Boyd 8+2
Arch Windmill 9
Reg Reeves 10+1
Harry Edwards 6+2
Bert Edwards 2+1
Bruce Gardiner 0

Edinburgh
Eddie Lack 3
Jack Young 11
Tommy Allott 6
Don Cuppleditch 0
Harold Booth 2
Dick Campbell 2+1
Danny Lee 5+1
Harold Fairhurst 3+1

Wednesday 12 July 1950 Fleetwood
Fleetwood 40 Walthamstow 44 (NL2)

Fleetwood
Dick Geary 5
Norman Hargreaves 6
Bill Reynolds 6+2
Don Potter 10
Wilf Plant 4+1
Alf Parker 3
Geoff Culshaw 1
Graham Williams 5

Walthamstow
Harry Edwards 3+2
Benny King 8
Jim Boyd 9
Charlie May 2
Reg Reeves 7+3
George Newton 11
Arch Windmill 4
Jimmy Grant 0

Sunday 16 July 1950 Shelbourne Dublin
Shelbourne 54 Walthamstow 30 (Ch)

Shelbourne
Ronnie Moore 12
Jim Gregory 7+2
Dennis Gray 11
Dick Harris 5+2
Ernie Roccio 12
Reg Trott 4+1
Les Moore 2
Barry Pickering 1

Walthamstow
Harry Edwards 3+1
Benny King 3+1
Jim Boyd 9
Charlie May 3+1
Reg Reeves 5
Arch Windmill 5+1
Jimmy Grant 2
Bruce Gardiner 0

Monday 17 July 1950 Walthamstow London
Walthamstow 54 Fleetwood 30 (NL2)

Walthamstow
Harry Edwards 5+2
Benny King 10
Jim Boyd 9
Arch Windmill 9+2
Reg Reeves 8+2
George Newton 6
Charlie May 4
Jimmy Grant 3

Fleetwood
Dick Geary 5
N Hargreaves 4
Wilf Plant 6
Alf Parker 3+1
Bill Reynolds 0
Don Potter 10
Graham Williams 0
Geoff Culshaw 2+1

Monday 24 July 1950 Walthamstow London
Walthamstow 59 Cradley Heath 25 (NL2)

Walthamstow	Cradley Heath
Harry Edwards 8+3	Brian Shepherd 0
Benny King 10	Alan Hunt 11
Jim Boyd 12	Eric Boothroyd 0
Arch Windmill 7+2	Phil Malpass 4+1
Reg Reeves 9+2	Les Tolley 2
George Newton 8+2	Gil Craven 1
Jimmy Grant 3+2	Bill Clifton 5
Charlie May 2+1	Frank Young 2

Monday 31 July 1950 Walthamstow London
World Championship Qualifying Round

Jim Boyd 15
Tommy Miller 11
Jimmy Grant (res) 11
Gordon McGregor 10
Pat Clarke 10
Dennis Gray 10
Fred Pawson 10
Bob Baker 9
Fred Brand 8
Eric Salmon 5
Tom Oakley 5
Ray Moore 5
Howdy Byford 3
Les Wotton 3
Willie Wilson 2
Len Williams 1
Bert Edwards (res) 1
Ticker James 0

Tuesday 1 August 1950 West Ham London
West Ham 66 Walthamstow 42 (LC)

West Ham	Walthamstow
Wally Green 9+1	Benny King 2
Aub Lawson 17+1	George Newton 3+1
Lloyd Goffe 4+1	Jim Boyd 9
Eric Chitty 9+2	Reg Reeves 11
Malcolm Craven 16	Harry Edwards 2
Fred Curtis 7+1	Jimmy Grant 3+2
Howdy Byford 1	Charlie May 9
Reg Fearman 3	Arch Windmill 3+1

Monday 7 August 1950 Walthamstow London
Walthamstow 62 West Ham 46 (LC)

Walthamstow	West Ham
Benny King 10+1	Wally Green 18
Harry Edwards 3+1	Aub Lawson 9+1
Jim Boyd 11+1	Lloyd Goffe 0
George Newton 12+1	Eric Chitty 4
Reg Reeves 8+3	Malcolm Craven 6+1
Arch Windmill 10+1	Fred Curtis 2+1
Jimmy Grant 6+2	Howdy Byford 5+1
Charlie May 2	Reg Fearman 2

Wednesday 9 August 1950 Glasgow
Glasgow 43 Walthamstow 41 (NL2)

Glasgow	Walthamstow
Tommy Miller 12	Harry Edwards 4+2
Peter Dykes 0	Benny King 0
Norman Lindsay 1	Jim Boyd 8+2
Jack Hodgson 10+1	Arch Windmill 4+1
Frank Hodgson 10	Reg Reeves 2
Gordon McGregor 2	George Newton 8
Alf McIntosh 1+1	Jimmy Grant 6
Ken McKinlay 7+1	Charlie May 9+1

Saturday 12 August 1950 Edinburgh
Edinburgh 48 Walthamstow 36 (NL2)

Edinburgh	Walthamstow
Danny Lee 0	Harry Edwards 7
Jack Young 12	Benny King 1+1
Harold Fairhurst 6+3	Jim Boyd 5+2
Don Cuppleditch 11	Arch Windmill 0
Eddie Lack 7+1	Reg Reeves 5+2
Dick Campbell 11+1	George Newton 6
Harold Booth 0	Jimmy Grant 2+2
Bob Mark 1	Charlie May 10

Monday 14 August 1950 Walthamstow London
Walthamstow 53 Glasgow 31 (NL2)

Walthamstow	Glasgow
Harry Edwards 5+2	Jack Hodgson 7+1
Benny King 12	Tommy Miller 6+1
Jim Boyd 12	Gordon McGregor 3
Arch Windmill 4	Peter Dykes 4
Reg Reeves 10	Norman Lindsay 5
George Newton 1	Frank Hodgson 6
Jimmy Grant 4+1	Ken McKinlay 0
Charlie May 5+2	Alf McIntosh 0

Monday 21 August 1950 Walthamstow London
Walthamstow 61 Newcastle 23 (NL2)

Walthamstow	Newcastle
Harry Edwards 9+1	Will Lowther 3
Jimmy Grant 11+1	Wilf Jay 5+1

Walthamstow		Yarmouth	
Benny King	12	Son Mitchell	4
Charlie May	5+3	Don Lawson	0
George Newton	6+1	Herby King	2+1
Reg Reeves	11+1	Derek Close	7
Arch Windmill	4+1	Ernie Brecknell	2
Bert Edwards	3+1	Don Wilkinson	0

Monday 28 August 1950 Walthamstow London
Walthamstow 46 Yarmouth 38 (NL2)

Walthamstow		Yarmouth	
Harry Edwards	3+1	Reg Morgan	9+1
Jimmy Grant	11	Fred Brand	4
Benny King	12	Tip Mills	5+1
Charlie May	3+1	Wally Higgs	1
Reg Reeves	10+1	Bill Carruthers	8+1
George Newton	2	Johnny White	4+2
Arch Windmill	5	Stan Page	2+2
Bert Edwards	0	Bill Maddern	5

Monday 4 September 1950 Walthamstow London
Walthamstow 47 Halifax 34 (NL2)

Walthamstow		Halifax	
Harry Edwards	9+1	Vic Emms	7
Jimmy Grant	7+2	Al Allison	1
Benny King	6+1	Arthur Forrest	12
Charlie May	4+1	Jack Dawson	2
Reg Reeves	9+1	Jack Hughes	10
George Newton	2+2	Bill Crosland	1+1
Arch Windmill	5+1	Ray Johnson	0
Jim Boyd	5	Alec Burrow	1

Wednesday 6 September 1950 Aldershot
Aldershot 39 Walthamstow 45 (Ch)

Aldershot		Walthamstow	
Ivor Powell	2	Harry Edwards	3
Trevor Redmond	8+1	Jim Boyd	8+1
Doug Papworth	8+1	Benny King	6+2
Doug Ible	5	Jimmy Grant	8+2
Basil Harris	10+1	Reg Reeves	0
Joe Rodwell	5+1	George Newton	6
Bill Grimes	1	Arch Windmill	9+1
Pat Flanagan	0	Charlie May	5+1

Saturday 9 September 1950 Hanley Soke
Hanley 49 Walthamstow 35 (NL2)

Hanley		Walthamstow	
Ken Adams	10+1	Harry Edwards	0
Les Jenkins	6	Jim Boyd	7+1
Lindsay Mitchell	12	Benny King	4+1
Gil Blake	2	Jimmy Grant	3+1
Brian Pritchett	8+1	Reg Reeves	11
Bill Harris	5+1	George Newton	1
John Fitzpatrick	1+1	Arch Windmill	8
Ray Harris	5+2	Charlie May	1

Monday 11 September 1950 Walthamstow London
Walthamstow 52 Norwich 32 (NL2)

Walthamstow		Norwich	
Harry Edwards	5+3	Paddy Mills	2+1
Jim Boyd	12	Jack Freeman	7
Benny King	7+1	Phil Clarke	5+1
Jimmy Grant	11+1	Alec Hunter	7
Reg Reeves	7+1	Bob Leverenz	6
George Newton	0	Fred Rogers	5+1
Arch Windmill	8	Ted Bravery	0
Bert Edwards	2+1	Johnny Davies	0

Tuesday 12 September 1950 Ashfield Glasgow
Ashfield 56 Walthamstow 28 (NL2)

Ashfield		Walthamstow	
Keith Gurtner	6	Harry Edwards	3+1
Ken Le Breton	8	Jim Boyd	6
Willie Wilson	10+1	Benny King	1
Merv Harding	6+1	Jimmy Grant	7
Bob Lovell	8+1	Reg Reeves	7
Bruce Semmens	10+1	George Newton	3
Larry Lazarus	4+1	Arch Windmill	0
Ed Noakes	4+2	Bert Edwards	1

Saturday 16 September 1950 Norwich
Norwich 66 Walthamstow 17 (NL2)

Norwich		Walthamstow	
Jack Freeman	8+4	Harry Edwards	5
Paddy Mills	12	Jim Boyd	1
Phil Clarke	12	Benny King	3
Alec Hunter	8+ 2	Jimmy Grant	3
Bob Leverenz	11+1	Reg Reeves	3
Fred Rogers	9+ 3	George Newton	0
Ted Bravery	4	Arch Windmill	0
Sid Littlewood	2+1	Charlie May	2+1

Monday 18[h] September 1950 Walthamstow London
Walthamstow 49 Hanley 34 (NL2)

Walthamstow		Hanley	
Harry Edwards	5+1	Ken Adams	9
Jim Boyd	10+1	Les Jenkins	2
Benny King	11	Lindsay Mitchell	8
Jimmy Grant	2+1	Gil Blake	6+3

Reg Reeves 5+1
Arch Windmill 12
George Newton 4
Bert Edwards 0

Bill Harris 2
Brian Pritchett 5
John Fitzpatrick 1
Bill Bridgett 1+1

Reg Reeves 5+2
Jimmy Grant 11
Peter Robinson 1+1

Bob Leverenz 14
Alec Hunter 2+1
Keith Gurtner DNR

Tuesday 19 September 1950   Southampton
Southampton 46 Walthamstow 38 (NL2)

Southampton
Steve Langton 4
Jim Squibb 8
Tom Oakley 7
Cecil Bailey 5
Harold McNaughton 5
Roy Craighead 10
Buck Whitby 7+1
Bill Holden 0

Walthamstow
George Newton 2
Jim Boyd 8+1
Benny King 0
Jimmy Grant 5
Reg Reeves 9+1
Harry Edwards 6+1
Arch Windmill 5
Charlie May 3+2

Tuesday 26 September 1950 Yarmouth
Yarmouth 31 Walthamstow 51 (NL2)

Yarmouth
Bill Maddern 2
Tip Mills 1
Bert Rawlinson 3
Billy Bales 8
Fred Brand 6+1
Reg Morgan 4
Stan Page 4
Johnny White 3+1

Walthamstow
George Newton 6
Jim Boyd 5
Benny King 8+1
Jimmy Grant 9+1
Reg Reeves 6+3
Harry Edwards 12
Arch Windmill 3+1
Charlie May 2

Friday 22 September 1950 Plymouth
Plymouth 44 Walthamstow 40 (NL2)

Plymouth
Pete Lansdale 12
Dennis Hayles 2
Peter Robinson 9
George Wall 6
Len Read 12
Alan Smith 3+1
Broncho Slade 0
Wally Mawdsley 0

Walthamstow
George Newton 5+2
Jim Boyd 9
Benny King 5+1
Jimmy Grant 6+2
Reg Reeves 0
Harry Edwards 6+2
Arch Windmill 6+1
Charlie May 3+1

Saturday 30 September 1950 Rayleigh
Rayleigh 44 Walthamstow 60 (Ch)

Rayleigh
Frank Bettis 10
Jack Unstead 4+3
Ron Howes 7
Vic Gooden 5
Gerald Jackson 7+2
Les McGillivray 7
Oz Osborne 2
Tom O'Connor 2

Walthamstow
George Newton 12
Jim Boyd 1
Benny King 5
Jimmy Grant 14+2
Reg Reeves 6+1
Harry Edwards 11
Arch Windmill 9
Bert Edwards 2

Saturday 23 September 1950 Swindon
Swindon 33 Walthamstow 51 (Ch)

Swindon
Alex Gray 7
Frank Evans 3+1
Ron Clark 4+1
Bob Jones 2+1
Reg Lambourne 4+1
Hugh Geddes 9
George Craig 2
Danny Malone 2

Walthamstow
Harry Edwards 7+2
Jim Boyd 9
Benny King 0
Jimmy Grant 11
Reg Reeves 8+1
George Newton 10
Arch Windmill 3+2
Charlie May 3

Tuesday 2 October 1950 Walthamstow London
Walthamstow 54 Ashfield 29 (NL2)

Walthamstow
Harry Edwards 5+3
Jim Boyd 9+1
Benny King 10+1
Jimmy Grant 3
Reg Reeves 6+2
Arch Windmill 12
George Newton 5
Charlie May 4

Ashfield
Ken Le Breton 6
Keith Gurtner 4
Willie Wilson 5
Merv Harding 6
Bob Lovell 4
Bruce Semmens DNR
Ed Noakes 1+1
Larry Lazarus 3

Monday 25 September 1950 Walthamstow London
Britain 42 Overseas 65 (International)

Britain
Jim Boyd 11
Vic Emms 2
Benny King 11
Phil Clarke 0
Stan Williams 1+1

Overseas
Jack Young 18
Dick Campbell 6+1
Ken Le Breton 17+1
Les Hewitt 4
Merv Harding 4+2

Saturday 7 October 1950 Coventry
Coventry 53 Walthamstow 30 (NL2)

Coventry
Bob Fletcher 5
Cyril Cooper 8+1
Les Hewitt 12
Derrick Tailby 8+2
Stan Williams 9+2
Johnnie Reason 7+1

Walthamstow
George Newton 1+1
Jim Boyd 3
Benny King 4
Jimmy Grant 6+1
Reg Reeves 3
Harry Edwards 6

Lionel Levy 4+1
Peter Brough 0

Arch Windmill 3
Charlie May 4+1

Monday 9 October 1950 Walthamstow London
Walthamstow 46 Coventry 37 (NL2)

Walthamstow
Harry Edwards 6
Jim Boyd 4+1
Benny King 12
Jimmy Grant 6+1
Reg Reeves 3+2
Arch Windmill 9
George Newton 4+3
Charlie May 2

Coventry
Bob Fletcher 6+3
Cyril Cooper 10
Les Hewitt 6+1
Derrick Tailby 8+1
Stan Williams 5
Johnnie Reason 0
Lionel Levy 0
Peter Brough 2

Wednesday 11 October 1950 Halifax
Halifax 55 Walthamstow 29 (NL2)

Halifax
Vic Emms 12
Alec Burrow 4+1
Bill Crosland 9+3
Jack Hughes 12
Al Allison 12
Jack Dawson 4+1
Ray Johnson 2
Jack Wright 0

Walthamstow
George Newton 5
Jim Boyd 4+1
Benny King 3+1
Jimmy Grant 2+1
Reg Reeves 6+1
Harry Edwards 5
Arch Windmill 2
Bert Edwards 2

Monday 16 October 1950 Walthamstow London
Walthamstow 49 Southampton 34 (NL2)

Walthamstow
Harry Edwards 5
Jim Boyd 7+1
Benny King 12
Jimmy Grant 8+3
Reg Reeves 2+1
Arch Windmill 9
George Newton 2+1
Charlie May 4

Southampton
Steve Langton 7+1
Jim Squibb 8+1
Tom Oakley 8
Les Wotton 3+1
Harold McNaughton 4
Cecil Bailey 3
Buck Whitby 1
Bill Holden 0

Friday 20 October 1950 Leicester
Leicester 51 Walthamstow 33 (Ch)

Leicester
Cyril Page 6
Harwood Pike 6+2
Joe Bowkis 1+1
Lionel Benson 9+2
Johnny Carpenter 9+2

Walthamstow
George Newton 3
Jim Boyd 3
Benny King 7+1
Jimmy Grant 0
Reg Reeves 2+2

Ron Wilson 7+1
Mick Mitchell 1
Les Beaumont 12

Harry Edwards 10
Arch Windmill 3
Charlie May 5

Saturday 21 October 1950 Cradley Heath
Cradley Heath 56 Walthamstow 28 (NL2)

Cradley Heath
Phil Malpass 7+3
Alan Hunt 12
Eric Boothroyd 6+2
Brian Shepherd 8+1
Gil Craven 8
Les Tolley 5+1
Laurie Schofield 7+1
Bill Clifton 3

Walthamstow
George Newton 3
Jim Boyd DNR
Benny King 5+1
Bert Edwards 3
Reg Reeves 1+1
Harry Edwards 6
Arch Windmill 9
Charlie May 1

Monday 23 October 1950 Walthamstow London
Third Division Riders Championship

Pat Clarke 15 (1st)
Trevor Redmond 13 (2nd)
Ken Middleditch 11 (3rd)
Norman Street 9
Gerald Jackson 9
Dick Tolley 8
Reg Duval 8
Basil Harris 7
Harwood Pike 6
Alex Gray 6
Cyril Quick 6
Jack Unstead 6
Lionel Watling 5
Ray Ellis 3
Don Hardy 3
Hugh Geddes 3
Arthur Pilgrim (Res) 1
Brian Wilson (Res) DNR

Monday 23 October 1950 Newcastle
Newcastle 51 Walthamstow 33 (NL2)

Newcastle
Wilf Jay 8
Will Lowther 6+1
Son Mitchell 4+1
Herby King 12
Ernie Brecknell 6+1
Derek Close 12
Don Lawson 1
Ray Maughan 2

Walthamstow
George Newton 3
Arch Windmill 2
Benny King 3
Jimmy Grant 9
Reg Reeves 4+1
Harry Edwards 8
Charlie May 1
Bert Edwards 3+1

Walthamstow 1951

Monday 26 March 1951 Walthamstow London
Walthamstow 51 Southampton 33 (SS)

Walthamstow	Southampton
Jim Boyd 8+1	Jim Squibb 5
Reg Reeves 7+2	Les Wotton 6
Jimmy Grant 3+2	Roy Craighead 4+1
Harry Edwards 9	Charlie May 7
Benny King 8+2	Tom Oakley 5
Pete Lansdale 9	H McNaughton 5+1
Arch Windmill 5	Bill Holden 1
Bert Edwards 2	Bert Croucher 0

Tuesday 30 March 1951 Southampton
Southampton 34 Walthamstow 50 (SS)

Southampton	Walthamstow
Jim Squibb 5+1	Jim Boyd 10
Les Wotton 1	Reg Reeves 5+2
Roy Craighead 10	Jimmy Grant 4
Charlie May 1	Harry Edwards 11
Tom Oakley 6	Benny King 8+1
Harold McNaughton 5	Pete Lansdale 9+2
Bill Holden 6	Arch Windmill 2+1
Bert Croucher 0	Bert Edwards 1+1

Monday 2 April 1951 Walthamstow London
Walthamstow 55 Norwich 29 (SS)

Walthamstow	Norwich
Jim Boyd 12	Bob Leverenz 9
Reg Reeves 5	Fred Rogers 0
Jimmy Grant 5	Phil Clarke 7
Harry Edwards 12	Johnny Davies 4+2
Benny King 10+1	Paddy Mills 0
Pete Lansdale 7+2	Jack Freeman 7
Arch Windmill 3+1	Bill Codling 1+1
Bert Edwards 1	Trevor Davies 1

Saturday 7 April 1951 Norwich
Norwich 56 Walthamstow 28 (SS)

Norwich	Walthamstow
Bob Leverenz 11+1	Jim Boyd 4+1
Fred Rogers 8+2	Reg Reeves 9
Phil Clarke 8+3	Jimmy Grant 3+1
Johnny Davies 11	Harry Edwards 6
Paddy Mills 3+1	Benny King 3
Jack Freeman 9	Pete Lansdale 1
Trevor Davies 5+1	Arch Windmill 1+1
Bill Codling 1	Sid Clark 1+1

Monday 9 April 1951 Walthamstow London
Walthamstow 50 Yarmouth 34 (SS)

Walthamstow	Yarmouth
Jim Boyd 6+1	Reg Morgan 5
Reg Reeves 9+2	Fred Brand 6+1
Jimmy Grant 5	Johnny White 1
Harry Edwards 8+1	Tip Mills 8+1
Benny King 6+1	Bob Baker 8
Pete Lansdale 8+1	Stan Page 4+1
Arch Windmill 4	George Flower 0
Sid Clark 4+1	Vic Ridgeon 2

Tuesday 10 April 1951 Yarmouth
Yarmouth 28 Walthamstow 56 (SS)

Yarmouth	Walthamstow
Johnny White 3	Jim Boyd 7+3
Reg Morgan 6	Reg Reeves 12
Tip Mills 6	Jimmy Grant 6+2
Fred Brand 2	Harry Edwards 11
Bob Baker 8	Benny King 12
Stan Page 2+2	Pete Lansdale 2
George Flower 0	Arch Windmill 4
Vic Ridgeon 1	Sid Clark 2+1

Saturday 14 April 1951 Aldershot
Aldershot 37 Walthamstow 70 (Ch)

Aldershot	Walthamstow
Basil Harris 8	Benny King 11
Ivor Powell 3+1	Pete Lansdale 12+1
Trevor Redmond 15	Jim Boyd 12+1
Bert Edwards 4	Arch Windmill 10+2
Geoff Mardon 2	Harry Edwards 10
Bob Harrison 1+1	Jimmy Grant 5+2
Pat Flanagan 4	Reg Reeves 8
Bill Grimes 0	Sid Clark 2

Monday 16 April 1951 Walthamstow London
Walthamstow 39 Oxford 45 (SS)

Walthamstow	Oxford
Jim Boyd 5+2	Frank Boyle 5
Reg Reeves 8+1	Pat Clarke 8+1
Jimmy Grant 6	Bob McFarlane 4+1
Harry Edwards 8	Harry Sunders 11
Benny King 5	Ernie Rawlins 6
Pete Lansdale 0	Bill Osborne 8
Arch Windmill 6	Bill Kemp 2+1
Sid Clark 1	Cyril Quick 1+1

Wednesday 18 April 1951 Walthamstow London
New Cross 45 Walthamstow 38 (Ch)

New Cross	Walthamstow
Eric French 10	Jim Boyd 2
Don Gray 1	Reg Reeves 6
Bill Longley 10	Jimmy Grant 5+2
Bert Roger 5+3	Harry Edwards 7
Cyril Roger 6	Benny King 6+2
Frank Lawrence 7	Trevor Redmond 11
Ray Moore 4	Arch Windmill 1
Eric Minall 2+1	Sid Clark 0

Monday 23 April 1951 Walthamstow London
Walthamstow 51 Coventry 32 (SS)

Walthamstow	Coventry
Jim Boyd 7+1	Bob Fletcher 4
Reg Reeves 8	Cyril Cooper 2
Jimmy Grant 7+2	Les Hewitt 9
Harry Edwards 11	Derrick Tailby 1
Benny King 9+1	Stan Williams 5+1
Arch Windmill 7+2	Wilf Plant 6+1
Sid Clark 1+1	Jack Wright 5+1
Alby Smith 1	John Yates 0

Saturday 28 April 1951 Coventry
Coventry 40 Walthamstow 43 (SS)

Coventry	Walthamstow
Derrick Tailby 7+2	Jim Boyd 3+2
Cyril Cooper 9	Reg Reeves 9+1
Les Hewitt 5+1	Jimmy Grant 6+1
Stan Williams 3	Harry Edwards 7+1
Jack Wright 1+1	Benny King 6
Wilf Plant 5	Pete Lansdale 7+1
John Yates 3	Arch Windmill 5
Peter Brough 7	Sid Clark 0

Monday 30 April 1951 Walthamstow London
Walthamstow 77 Southampton 31 (NT)

Walthamstow	Southampton
Benny King 15+1	Bill Holden 1
Harry Edwards 7+1	Jim Squibb 4+1
Jim Boyd 18	Harold McNaughton 3
Pete Lansdale 12+1	Tom Oakley 4
Reg Reeves 10+3	Charlie May 11
Jimmy Grant 7+4	Roy Craighead 4
Arch Windmill 6	Les Wotton 1+1
Sid Clark 2+1	Bert Croucher 3

Thursday 3 May 1951 Oxford
Oxford 49 Walthamstow 35 (SS)

Oxford	Walthamstow
Frank Boyle 1+1	Jim Boyd 9+1
Pat Clarke 9+1	Reg Reeves 2
Bill Kemp 7+1	Jimmy Grant 5
Harry Saunders 6+2	Harry Edwards 2+1
Ernie Rawlins 9+1	Benny King 7+1
Bill Osborne 9	Pete Lansdale 9
Bob McFarlane 4	Arch Windmill 0
Eric Irons 4+2	Sid Clark 1

Tuesday 4 May 1951 Southampton
Southampton 60 Walthamstow 48 (NT)

Southampton	Walthamstow
Jim Squibb 10+2	Benny King 10
Bill Holden 1	Pete Lansdale 13
Harold McNaughton 7+1	Harry Edwards 6+1
Tom Oakley 13	Jim Boyd 4+1
Charlie May 11+2	Reg Reeves 7
Roy Craighead 12+2	Jimmy Grant 2+1
Les Wotton 3	Arch Windmill 3
Bert Croucher 3	Sid Clark 3

Monday 7 May 1951 Walthamstow London
Walthamstow 45 Wembley 39 (Ch)

Walthamstow	Wembley
Jim Boyd 8	Bob Oakley 12
Reg Reeves 5+2	Bruce Abernethy 7+2
Jimmy Grant 4	George Wilks 4
Harry Edwards 4+1	Eric Williams 4
Benny King 10+1	Freddie Williams 6
Pete Lansdale 8+2	Bill Kitchen 2
Arch Windmill 3+1	Jimmy Gooch 3
Sid Clark 3	Bob Wells 1

Thursday 12 May 1951 Hanley Stoke
Hanley 59 Walthamstow 49 (NT)

Stoke	Walthamstow
Lindsay Mitchell 13	Benny King 9
Ken Adams 13+4	Pete Lansdale 8+1
Les Jenkins 9+2	Harry Edwards 7
John Fitzpatrick 8+1	Jim Boyd 7
Brian Pritchett 1	Reg Reeves 7
Gil Blake 5	Jimmy Grant 4
Bill Bridgett 2	Arch Windmill 4
Ray Harris 8+1	Sid Clark 3

Monday 14 May 1951 Walthamstow London
Walthamstow 81 Hanley 26 (NT)

Walthamstow
Benny King 13+2
Harry Edwards 13+2
Jim Boyd 9+1
Pete Lansdale 12+1
Reg Reeves 13+2
Jimmy Grant 9+3
Arch Windmill 6
Sid Clark 6+1

Hanley
Brian Pritchett 4+1
Ken Adams 5+1
Les Jenkins 8
John Fitzpatrick 0
Lindsay Mitchell 4
Gil Blake 0
Ray Harris 4
Bill Bridgett 1

Wednesday 16 May 1951 White City Glasgow
Glasgow 49 Walthamstow 35 (NL2)

Glasgow
Jack Hodgson 5+1
Junior Bainbridge 12
Ken McKinlay 6+1
Tommy Miller 12
Norman Lindsay 4
Frank Hodgson 8
Alf McIntosh 2+1
Jim Blyth 0

Walthamstow
Jim Boyd 7
Reg Reeves 2+2
Jimmy Grant 3
Harry Edwards 10
Benny King 6
Peter Lansdale 5+1
Arch Windmill 1
Sid Clark 1+1

Monday 21 May 1951 Walthamstow London
Walthamstow 57 Halifax 27 (NLD2)

Walthamstow
Jim Boyd 4+1
Reg Reeves 9+2
Jimmy Grant 6+3
Harry Edwards 9+1
Benny King 10+1
Pete Lansdale 8+1
Arch Windmill 8+1
Sid Clark 3+1

Halifax
Al Allison 0
Vic Emms 5
Arthur Forrest 12
Ray Johnson 2
Jack Hughes 5
Bill Crosland 2
Jack Dawson 1
Dyson Harper 0

Wednesday 23 May 1951 Chapelizod Dublin
Dublin Eagles 44 Walthamstow 40 (Ch)

Dublin
Derrick Edwardes 0
Freddie Williams 11
Eric Williams 11+1
Oliver Hart 6
Ron Mountford 12
Ivor Davies 3+1
David Couse 0
Danny O'Neill 1

Walthamstow
Jim Boyd 5
Reg Reeves 6+2
Benny King 5+1
Pete Lansdale 5
Jimmy Grant 4+3
Harry Edwards 9
Arch Windmill 4
Alby Smith 2+2

Monday 28 May 1951 Walthamstow London
Walthamstow 56 Yarmouth 28 (NLD2)

Walthamstow
Jim Boyd 12
Reg Reeves 7+3
Jimmy Grant 9+1
Harry Edwards 4+2
Benny King 7+2
Pete Lansdale 11
Arch Windmill 5+1
Sid Clark 1

Yarmouth
Bob Baker 10
Stan Page 0
Fred Brand 9
Tip Mills 2
Reg Morgan 2
Cyril Quick 4
Sid Hipperson 0
Johnny White 1+1

Tuesday 29 May 1951 Yarmouth
Yarmouth 57 Walthamstow 51 (NT)

Yarmouth
Sid Hipperson 9+2
Bob Baker 10+2
Tip Mills 2+1
Fred Brand 18
Reg Morgan 3
Cyril Quick 9+1
Stan Page 4+1
Johnny White 2+1

Walthamstow
Benny King 8
Pete Lansdale 4
Harry Edwards 3+1
Jim Boyd 8+1
Reg Reeves 9
Jimmy Grant 11+1
Arch Windmill 5+1
Sid Clark 3

Monday 4 June 1951 Walthamstow London
Walthamstow 56 Southampton 28 (NL2)

Walthamstow
Jim Boyd 9+1
Reg Reeves 6+1
Jimmy Grant 9+1
Harry Edwards 6+2
Benny King 12
Pete Lansdale 8+2
Arch Windmill 4
Sid Clark 2+1

Southampton
Les Wotton 1+1
Jim Squibb 7+1
Charlie May 6
Tom Oakley 4
Harold McNaughton 4
Roy Craighead 5+1
Bill Holden 1
Bert Croucher 0

Friday 8 June 1951 Motherwell
Motherwell 47 Walthamstow 37 (NL2)

Motherwell
Noel Watson 9+1
Gordon McGregor 10
Joe Crowther 5+1
Keith Gurtner 6
Bill Dalton 4+2
Will Lowther 7
Stan Bradbury 4+2
Bluey Scott 2

Walthamstow
Jim Boyd 5+1
Reg Reeves 7+2
Jimmy Grant 3
Harry Edwards 11
Benny King 0
Pete Lansdale 8
Sid Clark 1
Arch Windmill 2

Saturday 9 June 1951 Edinburgh
Edinburgh 48 Walthamstow 36 (NL2)

Edinburgh	*Walthamstow*
Jack Young 12	Jim Boyd 5
Eddie Lack 1	Reg Reeves 4+2
Don Cuppleditch 11+1	Jimmy Grant 5+1
Harold Fairhurst 9+1	Harry Edwards 6
Bob Mark 3+1	Benny King 0
Dick Campbell 11	Pete Lansdale 9
Jimmy Cox 0	Sid Clark 5+2
Jackie Campbell 1	Arch Windmill 2+2

Monday 11 June 1951 Walthamstow London
Walthamstow 73 Yarmouth 35 (NT)

Walthamstow	*Yarmouth*
Benny King 16+2	Cyril Quick 2+1
Harry Edwards 10	Bob Baker 9+1
Jim Boyd 18	Fred Brand 11
Pete Lansdale 6+1	Reg Morgan 2
Reg Reeves 4+1	Stan Page 4+1
Jimmy Grant 8+3	Sid Hipperson 3
Arch Windmill 9+1	Johnny White 2
Sid Clark 2	Vic Ridgeon 2

Saturday 16 June 1951 Coventry
Coventry 44 Walthamstow 40 (NL2)

Coventry	*Walthamstow*
Johnny Reason 10	Jim Boyd 5+1
Stan Williams 9+1	Reg Reeves 0
Derrick Tailby 4	Jimmy Grant 3+2
Les Hewitt 5	Harry Edwards 9
Wilf Plant 2	Benny King 4+1
Charlie New 7+1	Pete Lansdale 9
John Yates 2+1	Arch Windmill 9+1
Peter Brough 5	Sid Clark 1

Monday 18 June 1951 Walthamstow
Walthamstow 67 Fleetwood 16 (NL2)

Walthamstow	*Fleetwood*
Jim Boyd 10+2	Wilf Jay 3
Reg Reeves 8+2	N Hargreaves 3
Jimmy Grant 12	Russ Pursehouse 0
Harry Edwards 6+2	Don Potter 3
Benny King 12	Jeff Crawford 0
Pete Lansale 9+3	Alf Parker 4
Arch Windmill 6	Angus McGuire 0
Alby Smith 4+2	Ray Harker 3

Sunday 24 June 1951 Shelbourne Dublin
Shelbourne 43 Walthamstow 39 (Ch)

Shelbourne	*Walthamstow*
Nick Nicolaides 6	Jimmy Grant 7+1
Manuel Trujillo 9+2	Harry Edwards 5
Royal Carroll 8+1	Jim Boyd 11
Lloyd Campbell 2	Reg Reeves 4+1
Johnny Gibson 3+2	Benny King 2+2
Don Hawley 10	Pete Lansdale 5
Johnnie Roccio 5	Arch Windmill 5+2
	Alby Smith 0

Monday 25 June 1951 Walthamstow London
Walthamstow 50 Motherwell 34 (NL2)

Walthamstow	*Motherwell*
Jim Boyd 8	Bill Dalton 2
Reg Reeves 2	Gordon McGregor 5
Jimmy Grant 6+2	Noel Watson 5
Harry Edwards 10	Will Lowther 6+2
Benny King 10+1	Joe Crowther 0
Pete Lansdale 7+3	Keith Gurtner 12
Arch Windmill 6+2	Stan Bradbury 3
Alby Smith 1	Danny Lee 1

Saturday 30 June 1951 Norwich
Norwich 60 Walthamstow 24 (NL2)

Norwich	*Walthamstow*
Phil Clarke 10+1	Jimmy Grant 2
Alec Hunter 8+2	Harry Edwards 3
Paddy Mills 8+2	Jim Boyd 1+1
Jack Freeman 12	Reg Reeves 5
Fred Pawson 8+2	Benny King 3
Fred Rogers 12	Pete Lansdale 7
Bill Codling 2+1	Arch Windmill 1+1
Trevor Davies 0	Alby Smith 2

Monday 2 July 1951 Walthamstow London
Walthamstow 74 Halifax 34 (NT)

Walthamstow	*Halifax*
Arch Windmill 9+3	Arthur Forrest 11+1
Harry Edwards 10+2	Al Allison 0
Jim Boyd 12+1	Jack Hughes 8
Pete Lansdale 9+1	Vic Emms 9
Benny King 16+1	Bill Crosland 3
Jimmy Grant 8+3	Dyson Harper 0
Reg Reeves 5+1	Ray Johnson 2
Alby Smith 5+1	Jack Dawson 1

Wednesday 4 July 1951 Halifax
Halifax 71 Walthamstow 37 (NT)

Halifax / *Walthamstow*
Jack Hughes 10+1 / Benny King 4
Vic Emms 16+2 / Pete Lansdale 12
Arthur Forrest 16+2 / Harry Edwards 4
Al Allison 14 / Jim Boyd 0
Bill Crosland 6 / Jimmy Grant 2+1
Dyson Harper 1+1 / Reg Reeves 7+1
Ray Johnson 5+2 / Arch Windmill 0
Jack Dawson 3+1 / Sid Clark 8+1

Monday 9 July 1951 Walthamstow London
Walthamstow 59 Leicester 25 (NLD2)

Walthamstow / *Leicester*
Jim Boyd 10 / Joe Bowkis 5
Arch Windmill 8 / Len Williams 1
Jimmy Grant 5+3 / Lionel Benson 10
Harry Edwards 11 / Les Beaumont 3
Benny King 7+2 / Harwood Pike 5
Pete Lansdale 11+1 / Cyril Page 1
Reg Reeves 4+2 / Jock Grierson 0
Sid Clark 3+1 / Vic Pitcher 0

Monday 16 July 1951 Walthamstow London
World Championship Qualifying Round

Jim Boyd 14
Benny King 13
Jack Mountford 13
Ron Mountford 13
Chris Boss 10
Harry Edwards 9
Reg Reeves 9
Cliff Watson 9
Norman Lindsay 7
Lindsay Mitchell 5
Don Potter 5
Harold Fairhurst 4
Norman Hargreaves 4
Bob Lovell 2
Arthur Pilgrim 2
Hugh Geddes 0

Monday 23 July 1951 Walthamstow London
Walthamstow 53 West Ham 55 (LC)

Walthamstow / *West Ham*
Arch Windmill 8+1 / Wally Green 16+1
Harry Edwards 4+1 / Eric Chitty 2+2
Jim Boyd 13 / Arthur Atkinson 5
Pete Lansdale 7+2 / Aub Lawson 16+1
Benny King 11+2 / Malcolm Craven 8+1
Jimmy Grant 3 / Howdy Byford 3+1
Reg Reeves 5 / Fred Curtis 3
Sid Clark 2+1 / Johnny Guilfoyle 2

Tuesday 24 July 1951 Walthamstow London
West Ham 78 Walthamstow 29 (LC)

West Ham / *Walthamstow*
Wally Green 12+1 / Benny King 4
Eric Chitty 14+2 / Pete Lansdale 5
Arthur Atkinson 4+1 / Harry Edwards 9
Aub Lawson 18 / Jim Boyd 6+1
Malcolm Craven 12 / Jimmy Grant 2
Howdy Byford 9+3 / Reg Reeves 0
Johnny Guilfoyle 3+2 / Sid Clark 3
Fred Curtis 6 / Arch Windmill 0

Saturday 28 July 1951 Norwich
Norwich 83 Walthamstow 25 (NT)

Norwich / *Walthamstow*
Bob Leverenz 16+2 / Benny King 7+1
Fred Pawson 10+2 / Harry Edwards 5
Phil Clarke 17+1 / Reg Reeves 0
Alec Hunter 9+3 / Jim Boyd 1
Paddy Mills 11+1 / Pete Lansdale 6
Jack Freeman 10+4 / Jimmy Grant 3+1
Fred Rogers 6 / Sid Clark 1
Bill Codling 4+2 / Alby Smith 2

Monday 30 July 1951 Walthamstow London
Walthamstow 50 Norwich 58 (NT)

Walthamstow / *Norwich*
Arch Windmill 7 / Bob Leverenz 18
Harry Edwards 5+2 / Fred Pawson 6+1
Jim Boyd 12+2 / Phil Clarke 9
Peter Lansdale 4 / Alec Hunter 6+3
Benny King 12 / Paddy Mills 2+1
Jimmy Grant 2 / Jack Freeman 7
Reg Reeves 6+1 / Fred Rogers 10+1
Sid Clark 2+1 / Bill Codling 0

Friday 3 August 1951 Leicester
Leicester 48 Walthamstow 36 (NL2)

Leicester / *Walthamstow*
Joe Bowkis 7+2 / Harry Edwards 6
Len Williams 8+1 / Jimmy Grant 4+1
Lionel Benson 7 / Sid Clark 0
Les Beaumont 5+1 / Benny King 9

Harwood Pike 8
Cyril Page 2
Jock Grierson 9
Vic Pitcher 2+1

Jim Boyd 10
Pete Lansdale 3+1
Alby Smith 3+1
Arch Windmill 1

Saturday 4 August 1951 Hanley Stoke
Hanley 34 Walthamstow 49 (NL2)

Hanley
Ken Adams 9+1
Brian Pritchett 5+1
Les Jenkins 4
Bill Harris 5
Lindsay Mitchell 6
Ray Harris 1+1
John Fitzpatrick 3+2
Bill Bridgett 1+1

Walthamstow
Jim Boyd 12
Arch Windmill 4+2
Jimmy Grant 0
Harry Edwards 10
Benny King 8
Pete Lansdale 8+1
Reg Reeves 2+1
Alby Smith 5+1

Monday 6 August 1951 Walthamstow London
Walthamstow v Oxford (NL2) Postponed - rain

Monday 13 August 1951 Walthamstow London
Walthamstow 54 Newcastle 29 (NL2)

Walthamstow
Jim Boyd 11
Arch Windmill 6+2
Reg Reeves 9+1
Harry Edwards 7+2
Benny King 9
Pete Lansdale 4+1
Jimmy Grant 5+1
Sid Clark 3+2

Newcastle
Wal Morton 0
Don Wilkinson 6
Son Mitchell 6
Peter Orpwood 3
Johnny Green 1
Derek Close 12
Jack Chignell 1
Mike Tams 0

Monday 20 August 1951 Liverpool
Liverpool 49 Walthamstow 35 (NL2)

Liverpool
Bill Griffiths 8
Len Read 5+1
Harry Welch 8+1
Reg Duval 7
George Newton 6+2
Peter Robinson 11
Buck Whitby 1
Alf Webster 3+2

Walthamstow
Benny King 6+1
Pete Lansdale 10
Reg Reeves 2
Harry Edwards 9
Jimmy Grant 5
Jim Boyd 2
Alby Smith 1
Arch Windmill 0

Wednesday 22 August 1951 Fleetwood
Fleetwood 49 Walthamstow 35 (NL2)

Fleetwood
Wilf Jay 11
Alf Parker 8+3

Walthamstow
Jim Boyd 6+1
Jimmy Grant 5+1

Don Potter 6
Jeff Crawford 3
Norman Hargreaves 11+1
Ray Harker 6+1
Ron Hart 4+1
Ray Moore 0

Reg Reeves 6
Harry Edwards 6
Benny King 4
Pete Lansdale 3+1
Alby Smith 0
Arch Windmill 5+2

Friday 24 August 1951 Newcastle
Newcastle 50 Walthamstow 34 (NL2)

Newcastle
Peter Orpwood 5+1
Son Mitchell 12
Wal Morton 4+1
Don Wilkinson 10
Jack Chignell 7
Derek Close 10+2
Roy Dook 0
Mike Tams 2+2

Walthamstow
Jim Boyd 6
Arch Windmill 2+1
Reg Reeves 1
Harry Edwards 7
Benny King 7+1
Pete Lansdale 6
Jimmy Grant 4
Alby Smith 1

Monday 27 August 1951 Walthamstow London
Walthamstow 58 Oxford 25 (NL2)

Walthamstow
Jim Boyd 11+1
Arch Windmill 7+2
Reg Reeves 7+2
Harry Edwards 12
Benny King 6+1
Pete Lansdale 11+1
Jimmy Grant 3+1
Alby Smith 1

Oxford
Harry Saunders 2
Herby King 3
Ernie Rawlins 3
Bill Osborne 3+1
Bob McFarlane 2
Bill Kemp 3
Eric Irons 4
Roger Wise 5

Friday 31 August 1951 Wolverhampton
Wolverhampton 26 Walthamstow 58 (Ch)

Wolverhampton
Jack Cunningham 2
Dick Harris 2
Geoff Mardon 9
Roy Moreton 2
Maury Dunn 2+1
Gerald Jackson 4
Ronnie Genz 2
Cyril Maidment 3+1

Walthamstow
Jim Boyd 8+3
Benny King 11
Jimmy Grant 8+2
Harry Edwards 8
Pete Lansdale 11+1
Arch Windmill 8+2
Reg Reeves 4+2
Sid Clark 0

Monday 3 September 1951 Walthamstow London
Walthamstow 48 Coventry 36 (NL2)

Walthamstow
Jim Boyd 3
Arch Windmill 6+2
Reg Reeves 11

Coventry
Bob Fletcher 6
Stan Williams 2
Les Hewitt 5

Harry Edwards 5+1
Benny King 4+2
Pete Lansdale 10
Jimmy Grant 8+1
Sid Clark 1+1

Derrick Tailby 5+1
Johnny Reason 4+2
Charlie New 9
Peter Brough 3
Jack Wright 2

Tuesday 4 September 1951 Yarmouth
Yarmouth 46 Walthamstow 38 (NL2)

Yarmouth
Cyril Quick 6+1
Bob Baker 12
Fred Brand 12
Tip Mills 3+1
Stan Page 4+2
Vic Ridgeon 6
Alby Thomas 3+1
Johnny White 0

Walthamstow
Jim Boyd 10
Benny King 5+2
Jimmy Grant 6
Harry Edwards 5
Pete Lansdale 10
Reg Reeves 0
Arch Windmill 1
Sid Clark 1+1

Friday 7 September 1951 Cradley Heath
Cradley Heath 32 Walthamstow 52 (NL2)

Cradley Heath
Dick Tolley 4+1
Gil Craven 6
Phil Malpass 9
Dennis Hitchings 0
Harry Bastable 2
Guy Allott 2
Laurie Schofield 6
Bill Clifton 3+1

Walthamstow
Jim Boyd 6
Benny King 7+2
Jimmy Grant 6+3
Harry Edwards 11
Pete Lansdale 10+2
Arch Windmill 9
Reg Reeves 3+1
Sid Clark 0

Monday 10 September 1951 Walthamstow London
Walthamstow 63 Cradley Heath 21 (NL2)

Walthamstow
Jim Boyd 12
Arch Windmill 5+1
Reg Reeves 9+2
Harry Edwards 10+2
Benny King 9+2
Pete Lansdale 10+1
Jimmy Grant 5+1
Sid Clark 3+2

Cradley Heath
Dick Tolley 1
Gil Craven 8
Phil Malpass 7
Dennis Hitchings 0
Harry Bastable 4
Guy Allott 0
Bill Clifton 1
Les Tolley 0

Monday 10 September 1951 Walthamstow London
Walthamstow 52 Ashfield 31 (NL2)

Walthamstow
Jim Boyd 6
Arch Windmill 6+1
Reg Reeves 10
Harry Edwards 5+2

Ashfield
Bruce Semmens 7
Cyril Cooper 0
Merv Harding 8
Ron Phillips 2

Benny King 8+2
Pete Lansdale 12
Jimmy Grant 5
Sid Clark 0

Willie Wilson 10
Jackie Gates 1
Ron Johnson 1+1
Larry Lazarus 2

Tuesday 11 September 1951 Ashfield Glasgow
Ashfield 47 Walthamstow 37 (NL2)

Ashfield
Bruce Semmens 9
Cyril Cooper 0
Merv Harding 12
Ron Phillips 5+1
Willie Wilson 10+2
Jackie Gates 8
Ron Johnson 0
Larry Lazarus 3

Walthamstow
Pete Lansdale 10
Jimmy Grant 4+1
Jim Boyd 8
Harry Edwards 2+2
Benny King 3+1
Syd Clark 1
Reg Reeves 6+1
Arch Windmill 3+1

Monday 17 September 1951 Walthamstow London
Walthamstow 61 Hanley 23 (NL2)

Walthamstow
Jim Boyd 11
Arch Windmill 6+3
Reg Reeves 10+2
Harry Edwards 10
Benny King 12
Pete Lansdale 6+1
Jimmy Grant 3+1
Sid Clark 3+1

Hanley
Ken Adams 7
Les Jenkins 2
John Fitzpatrick 3
Brian Pritchett 1
Lindsay Mitchell 4
Gil Blake 1+1
Ray Harris 2
Bill Harris 3

Wednesday 19 September 1951 Halifax
Halifax 43 Walthamstow 41 (NL2)

Halifax
Jack Dawson 2
Arthur Forrest 8
Vic Emms 11
Bill Crosland 3
Jack Hughes 6+1
Al Allison 9
Dyson Harper 4+1
George Stringer 0

Walthamstow
Pete Lansdale 10
Jimmy Grant 4+1
Reg Reeves 7+3
Harry Edwards 10
Benny King 1
Jim Boyd 5+1
Arch Windmill 0
Sid Clark 4

Monday 24 September 1951 Walthamstow London
Walthamstow 49 Glasgow 35 (NL2)

Walthamstow
Jim Boyd 11
Arch Windmill 0
Reg Reeves 9
Harry Edwards 5+2
Benny King 10+1

Glasgow
Tommy Miller 11
Alf McIntosh 2
Junior Bainbridge 11
Jack Hodgson 1+1
Ken McKinlay 1

Peter Lansdale 7+2
Jimmy Grant 6+1
Sid Clark 1+1

Frank Hodgson 5
Norman Lindsay 4+1
Jim Blyth 0

Monday 24 September 1951 Walthamstow London
Walthamstow 54 Liverpool 29 (NL2)

Walthamstow
Jim Boyd 11
Arch Windmill 1+1
Reg Reeves 10+2
Harry Edwards 9
Benny King 10+1
Pete Lansdale 8+1
Jimmy Grant 4+2
Sid Clark 1

Liverpool
Bill Griffiths 3+1
Len Read 4
Harry Welch 6
Reg Duval 4+2
George Newton 2+1
Buck Whitby 2
Alf Webster 7
Peter Craven 1

Thursday 27 September 1951 Oxford
Oxford 33 Walthamstow 47 (NLD2)

Oxford
Harry Saunders 0
Frank Boyle 4
Ernie Rawlins 5
Bill Osborne 6
Bill Kemp 6
Bob McFarlane 2+1
Roger Wise 7+1
Eric Irons 3+1

Walthamstow
Reg Reeves 7
Pete Lansdale 7+2
Jim Boyd 7+1
Harry Edwards 7+1
Benny King 11
Jimmy Grant 5+2
Arch Windmill 3
Alby Smith 0

Monday 1 October 1951 Walthamstow London
Walthamstow 39 Norwich 45 (NL2)

Walthamstow
Jim Boyd 7
Jimmy Grant 2+1
Reg Reeves 8
Harry Edwards 3
Benny King 7
Pete Lansdale 11+1
Arch Windmill 1
Alby Smith 0

Norwich
Bob Leverenz 10
Fred Rogers 2+1
Phil Clarke 9
Fred Pawson 7
Alec Hunter 9
Paddy Mills 0
Jack Freeman 3+1
Bill Codling 5+1

Monday 8 October 1951 Walthamstow London
Walthamstow 51 Edinburgh 33 (NLD2)

Walthamstow
Jim Boyd 6+2
Jimmy Grant 8
Reg Reeves 11
Harry Edwards 6+3
Benny King 10+1
Pete Lansdale 5+2
Sid Clark 5+1
Alby Smith 0

Edinburgh
Harold Fairhurst 3+1
Jack Young 12
Bob Mark 1+1
Dick Campbell 6
Eddie Lack 5
Don Cuppleditch 1+1
Jimmy Cox 1+1
Johnny Green 4

Appendix 2: League tables

National League 1934

	M	W	D	L	F	A	Pts
Belle Vue	32	27	0	5	1040	650	54
Wembley	32	26	0	6	980	731	52
New Cross	32	21	0	11	935½	762½	42
West Ham	32	16	1	15	865	841	33
Wimbledon	32	16	0	16	840	863	32
Harringay	32	14	1	17	867½	837½	29
Birmingham Hall Green	32	9	0	23	757	949	18
Plymouth	32	8	2	22	668	1007	18
Walthamstow	32	5	0	27	694	1006	10

National League Second Division 1949

	M	W	D	L	F	A	Pts
Bristol	44	34	1	9	2290½	1393½	69
Sheffield	44	29	1	14	2015½	1667½	59
Norwich	44	27	0	17	2031	1649	54
Cradley Heath	44	25	0	19	1908½	1772½	50
Edinburgh	44	24	0	20	1804	1878	48
Walthamstow	44	21	3	20	1841½	1833½	45
Southampton	44	21	3	20	1741½	1924½	45
Glasgow White City	44	20	0	24	1757½	1924½	40
Fleetwood	44	18	1	25	1765	1916	37
Newcastle	44	17	1	26	1735	1949	35
Glasgow Ashfield	44	12	1	31	1645	2034	25
Coventry	44	10	1	33	1540	2134	21

National League Second Division 1950

	M	W	D	L	F	A	Pts
Norwich	28	18	1	9	1310½	1038½	37
Glasgow White City	28	18	0	10	1272	1074	36
Cradley Heath	28	18	0	10	1258½	1090½	36
Coventry	28	16	0	12	1273	1072	32
Walthamstow	28	16	0	12	1212	1127	32
Halifax	28	16	0	12	1212	1134	32
Southampton	28	14	1	13	1215½	1133½	29
Edinburgh	28	14	1	13	1176	1166	29
Plymouth	28	13	0	15	1170	1177	26
Sheffield	28	13	0	15	1158	1193	26
Glasgow Ashfield	28	12	0	16	1141	1205	24
Yarmouth	28	12	0	16	1059	1287	24
Newcastle	28	10	0	18	1072½	1274½	20
Hanley (Stoke)	28	10	0	18	1046	1295	20
Fleetwood	28	8	1	19	1020	1329	17

Southern Shield 1950

	M	W	D	L	F	A	Pts
Cradley Heath	12	8	0	4	528½	477½	16
Coventry	12	8	0	4	519½	486½	16
Walthamstow	12	7	0	5	530	476	14
Plymouth	12	6	0	6	520	487	12
Norwich	12	5	0	7	499½	503½	10
Southampton	12	4	0	8	479	527	8
Yarmouth	12	4	0	8	442½	561½	8

National League Second Division 1951

	M	W	D	L	F	A	Pts
Norwich	30	24	0	6	1526	990	48
Leicester	30	19	0	11	1350	1169	38
Edinburgh	30	18	0	12	1333	1179	36
Coventry	30	16	3	11	1311	1199	35
Walthamstow	30	17	0	13	1394	1116	34
Halifax	30	17	0	13	1300	1219	34
Motherwell	30	16	1	13	1277	1237	33
Glasgow Ashfield	30	16	0	14	1287	1228	32
Stoke	30	15	0	15	1242	1268	30
Glasgow White City	30	14	0	16	1303	1215	28
Yarmouth	30	13	1	16	1158	1355	27
Oxford	30	12	2	16	1183	1330	26
Liverpool	30	12	1	17	1211	1300	25
Fleetwood	30	9	2	19	1049	1453	20
Cradley Heath	30	9	0	21	1139	1372	18
Newcastle	30	7	1	22	1039	1472	15

Southern Shield 1951

	M	W	D	L	F	A	Pts
Oxford	10	8	0	2	466	372	16
Norwich	10	7	1	2	510	328	15
Walthamstow	10	7	0	3	458	380	14
Southampton	10	4	1	6	410	428	9
Yarmouth	10	2	0	6	334	505	4
Coventry	10	1	0	9	334	499	2

Appendix 3: Riders' statistics

M = Matches, R = Rides, P = Points, B = Bonus Points, T = Total Points, CMA = Calculated Match Average (CMA is the calculated match average, used for comparison purposes to show the scoring of each rider assuming they had taken four rides per meeting. It is arrived at by dividing the total number of points scored by the number of rides taken and multiplying the result by four).

1934

National League

	M	R	P	B	T	CMA
Dick Case	9	26	56	1	57	8.77
Squib Burton	10	28	37	2	39	5.57
Reg Stanley	1	3	3	1	1	5.33
Dusty Haigh	10	29	31	4	35	4.83
Wally Hull	7	20	18	4	22	4.40
Eric Blain	8	23	23	1	24	4.17
Clem Thomas	5	8	7	0	7	3.50
Chun Moore	10	28	20	4	24	3.43
Jack Bibby	5	13	9	2	11	3.38

ACU Cup

	M	R	P	B	T	CMA
Dick Case	1	6	14	0	14	9.33
Chun Moore	1	3	4	0	4	5.33
Dusty Haigh	1	6	5	1	6	4.00
Jack Bibby	1	3	3	0	3	4.00
Wally Hull	1	6	4	1	5	3.33
Eric Blain	1	6	4	0	4	2.67
Squib Burton	1	5	3	0	3	2.40
Clem Thomas	1	1	0	0	0	0.00

London Cup

	M	R	P	B	T	CMA
Dick Case	2	12	24	0	24	8.00
Eric Blain	2	12	18	3	21	7.00
Clem Thomas	1	4	3	3	6	6.00
Squib Burton	2	12	14	0	14	4.67
Chun Moore	2	12	12	1	13	4.33
Wally Hull	2	4	2	2	4	4.00
Dusty Haigh	2	12	5	2	7	2.33
Jack Bibby	1	4	1	0	1	1.00

1949

National League Second Division

	M	R	P	B	T	CMA
Jim Boyd	30	120	255	19	274	9.13
Wilf Jay	19	76	148	6	154	8.11
Charlie May	43	165	317	16	333	8.07
Benny King	25	100	171	17	188	7.52
Dick Shepherd	4	15	21	4	25	6.67
Harry Edwards	43	147	213	26	239	6.50
Reg Reeves	44	169	226	44	270	6.39
Arch Windmill	40	122	147	32	179	5.87
Harold Bull	6	9	9	4	13	5.78
Bill Osborne	44	128	153½	19	172½	5.39
Dick Geary	40	148	166	29	195	5.27
Ted Argall	12	34	15	7	22	2.59

National Trophy

	M	R	P	B	T	CMA
Charlie May	6	33	80	3	83	10.06
Jim Boyd	6	34	68	5	73	8.59
Wilf Jay	2	11	17	2	19	6.91
Benny King	4	23	33	3	36	6.26
Reg Reeves	6	27	27	8	35	5.57
Arch Windmill	6	20	22	5	27	5.40
Harry Edwards	6	20	23	3	26	5.20
Bill Osborne	6	25	28	4	32	5.12
Dick Geary	6	23	25	2	27	4.70

London Cup

	M	R	P	B	T	CMA
Jim Boyd	2	12	21	4	25	8.33
Charlie May	2	10	19	0	19	7.60
Benny King	2	11	20	0	20	7.27
Bill Osborne	2	7	9	1	10	5.71
Harry Edwards	2	6	8	0	8	5.33
Arch Windmill	2	6	6	2	8	5.33
Dick Geary	2	10	12	1	13	5.20
Reg Reeves	2	9	9	2	11	4.89

1950

National League Second Division

	M	R	P	B	T	CMA
Jim Boyd	24	93	182	14	196	8.43
Reg Reeves	28	108	183	31	214	7.93
Benny King	28	103	193	10	203	7.88

	M	R	P	B	T	CMA
Arch Windmill	28	87	151	10	161	7.40
Jimmy Grant	23	83	127	20	147	7.08
Harry Edwards	28	111	157	29	186	6.70
Charlie May	24	73	93	20	113	6.19
George Newton	27	97	107	12	119	4.91
Bert Edwards	12	27	19	5	24	3.56
Bruce Gardiner	1	2	0	0	0	0.00

Southern Shield

	M	R	P	B	T	CMA
Jim Boyd	12	48	112	3	115	9.58
Benny King	12	48	89	11	100	8.33
Reg Reeves	12	47	81	6	87	7.40
Charlie May	12	40	62	9	71	7.10
Harry Edwards	11	44	68	10	78	7.09
Arch Windmill	12	33	42	10	52	6.30
Bert Edwards	2	4	4	2	6	6.00
George Newton	3	12	14	2	16	5.33
Dick Geary	9	23	24	6	30	5.22
Dick Shepherd	9	33	34	7	41	4.97

National Trophy

	M	R	P	B	T	CMA
Reg Reeves	6	31	66	5	71	9.16
Jim Boyd	6	35	73	7	80	9.14
Arch Windmill	6	20	33	5	38	7.60
Charlie May	6	31	50	7	57	7.35
Benny King	6	33	53	3	56	6.79
Bert Edwards	6	12	15	3	18	6.00
Harry Edwards	6	30	28	5	33	4.40
George Newton	6	24	21	3	24	4.00

London Cup

	M	R	P	B	T	CMA
Reg Reeves	2	11	19	3	22	8.00
Jim Boyd	2	12	20	1	21	7.00
Jimmy Grant	2	7	9	4	13	7.43
Charlie May	2	6	11	0	11	7.33
George Newton	2	10	15	2	17	6.80
Arch Windmill	2	9	13	2	15	6.67
Benny King	2	9	12	1	13	5.78
Harry Edwards	2	8	5	1	6	3.00

1951

National League Second Division

	M	R	P	B	T	CMA
Pete Lansdale	30	120	244	27	271	9.03
Jim Boyd	30	116	228	12	240	8.28
Harry Edwards	30	118	224	20	244	8.27
Benny King	30	117	206	23	229	7.83
Reg Reeves	29	106	176	30	206	7.77
Jimmy Grant	30	105	146	30	176	6.70
Arch Windmill	29	85	114	26	140	6.59
Sid Clark	20	48	39	14	53	4.42
Alby Smith	12	26	18	4	22	3.38

Southern Shield

	M	R	P	B	T	CMA
Harry Edwards	10	40	85	3	88	8.80
Jim Boyd	10	40	72	12	84	8.40
Benny King	10	39	74	7	81	8.31
Reg Reeves	10	40	74	8	82	8.20
Pete Lansdale	9	32	52	6	58	7.25
Arch Windmill	10	24	37	5	42	7.00
Jimmy Grant	10	39	50	8	58	5.95
Sid Clark	7	16	10	4	14	3.50
Alby Smith	1	2	1	0	0	2.00

National Trophy

	M	R	P	B	T	CMA
Arch Windmill	9	26	49	5	54	8.31
Benny King	10	59	110	8	118	8.00
Reg Reeves	10	41	68	9	77	7.51
Jim Boyd	10	52	89	6	95	7.31
Pete Lansdale	10	52	86	5	91	7.00
Harry Edwards	10	49	70	9	79	6.45
Jimmy Grant	10	49	56	17	73	5.96
Alby Smith	2	6	7	1	8	5.33
Sid Clark	9	26	30	4	34	5.23

London Cup

	M	R	P	B	T	CMA
Jim Boyd	2	12	19	1	20	6.67
Benny King	2	11	15	2	17	6.18
Pete Lansdale	2	10	12	2	14	5.60
Arch Windmill	2	7	8	1	9	5.14
Harry Edwards	2	11	13	1	14	5.09
Sid Clark	2	5	5	1	6	4.80
Reg Reeves	2	6	5	0	5	3.33
Jimmy Grant	2	10	5	0	5	2.00

Appendix 4: Walthamstow statistical highlights (official matches)

Most appearances:	Reg Reeves	151
	Harry Edwards	150
	Arch Windmill	146
Most races:	Reg Reeves	595
	Harry Edwards	584
	Jim Boyd	574
Most race points:	Jim Boyd	1139
	Benny King	975
	Harry Edwards	894
Most bonus points:	Reg Reeves	146
	Harry Edwards	107
	Arch Windmill	103
Highest total number of points:	Jim Boyd	1223
	Benny King	1065
	Reg Reeves	1020
Highest overall calculated match average:	Dick Case	8.64
	Jim Boyd	8.54
	Wilf Jay	7.95

Harry Edwards and Reg Reeves
- Both joined Walthamstow from the Rye House training school
- Both made their Walthamstow debut on 4 April 1949
- Both appeared for Walthamstow in the final meeting on 8 October 1951
- Reg Reeves was ever-present during the 1949 to 1951 seasons; Harry Edwards missed only one meeting.

Appendix 5: Walthamstow track records

Four Laps Flying Start
16 August 1934	Dick Case	70.48
16 August 1934	Joe Abbott	70.03
30 August 1934	Dick Case	67.35
20 September 1934	Max Grosskreutz	66.89

Four Laps Clutch Start
16 August 1934	Gus Kuhn	72.01
30 August 1934	Ron Johnson	68.52
20 September 1934	Bill Kitchen	68.42
10 October 1934	Ginger Lees	67.26
4 April 1949	Bob Oakley	66.2
25 April 1959	Paddy Mills	65.8
23 May 1949	George Newton	65.4
6 June 1949	Jim Boyd	65.4=
6 June 1949	Charlie May	65.4=
13 June 1949	Bob Baker	65.4=
13 June 1949	Jim Boyd	65.2
20 June 1949	Benny King	64.8
27 June 1949	Charlie May	64.0
18 July 1949	Eric French	63.8
25 July 1949	Bob Leverenz	63.6
17 October 1949	Jack Parker	63.6=
22 May 1950	Graham Warren	62.6
12 June 1950	Jim Boyd	62.6=
19 June 1950	Benny King	62.6=
26 June 1950	Ken Le Breton	62.6=
3 July 1950	Graham Warren	62.6=
3 July 1950	Graham Warren	62.4
10 July 1950	Jack Young	61.4
25 September 1950	Ken Le Breton	60.6
18 June 1951	Bob Oakley	60.6=
1 October 1951	Bob Leverenz	60.2

The track length in 1934 was 305 yards per lap. In 1949 the length was reduced to 282 yards per lap.

Fastest times during compulsory use of the narrower rear tyre in 1950
3 April 1950	Jim Boyd	64.6
3 April 1950	Charlie May	64.6=
17 April 1950	Bill Carruthers	64.2
17 April 1950	Jim Boyd	64.2=
17 April 1950	Jim Boyd	64.0
17 April 1950	Jim Boyd	64.0=
24 April 1950	Benny King	64.0=
24 April 1950	Peter Robinson	63.4

Appendix 6: Walthamstow riders in World Championship and other meetings

World Championship

1949

10 meetings were staged in the First Round of the World Championship and 96 riders qualified to take part in six Second Round meetings, from which 48 went forward to the Third Round, where they were joined by 32 riders from Division One. The top two scorers from each of five Third Round meetings progressed to the Championship Round, where they were joined by 32 seeded star riders. Each rider took part in three of the eight meetings staged on First Division tracks, with the top 16 scorers qualifying for the final at Wembley, which was won by Tommy Price of England, from Jack Parker and Louis Lawson.

Walthamstow riders record in the 1949 championship:

Dick Geary
Halifax	First Round	18 May 1949	2	1	2	0	1	6
Edinburgh	Second Round	11 Jun 1949	1	1	2	2	2	8
Southampton	Third Round	5 Jul 1949	0	1	0	0		1

Wilf Jay
Halifax	First Round	18 May 1949	3	0	F	1	2	6
Edinburgh	Second Round	11 Jun 1949	2	3	3	0	2	10
Glasgow White City	Third Round	6 Jul 1949	1	0	1	1	1	4

Charlie May
Leicester	First Round	20 May 1949	3	3	3	3	3	15 (winner)
Cradley Heath	Second Round	10 Jun 1949	E	3	2	3		8
Glasgow White City	Third Round	6 Jul 1949	X	3	3	E	3	9

Bill Osborne
Plymouth	First Round	19 May 1949	0	1	2	X	2	5

Reg Reeves
Hanley	First Round	21 May 1949	1	1	0	1	1	4

Arch Windmill
Rayleigh	First Round	21 May 1949	3	3	3	3	0	12
Norwich	Second Round	11 Jun 1949	1	0	0	0	1	2

Jim Boyd
Walthamstow (reserve)	Second Round	13 Jun 1949	2	3	3	3	3	14 (winner)

Harry Edwards
Walthamstow (reserve)	Second Round	13 Jun 1949	2	3	3		8

Boyd and Edwards scored enough points to qualify but they were ineligible as they were in the meeting at Walthamstow as reserve substitutes. Jay had transferred to Newcastle by the time the third round meetings were staged.

1950

The format for the qualifying rounds in 1950 was the same as for the previous season. Freddie Williams of Wales won the title with Wally Green and Graham Warren taking the other rostrum places.

Walthamstow riders record in the 1950 championship:

Jim Boyd
Edinburgh	Second Round	8 Jul 1950	3	3	2	0	2	10
Walthamstow	Third Round	31 Jul 1950	3	3	3	3	3	15 (winner)

Jim Boyd did not ride in the Championship Round due to injury.

Harry Edwards
St Austell	First Round	13 Jun 1950	0	2	1	1	1	5

Benny King
Fleetwood	Second Round	5 Jul 1950	1	1	0	1	1	4

Charlie May
Glasgow White City	Second Round	5 Jul 1950	3	3	E	1	2	9
Yarmouth	Third Round	25 Jul 1950	3	2	1	3	2	11

George Newton
Coventry	Second Round	11 Jun 1950	3	2	F	3	F	8
Newcastle	Third Round	31 Jul 1950	3	X	0			3

Reg Reeves
Leicester	First Round	16 Jun 1950	3	2	3	2	3	13
Sheffield	Second Round	6 Jul 1950	0	0	2	1	1	4

Dick Shepherd
St Austell	First Round	13 Jun 1950	1	3	3	1	0	8
Fleetwood	Second Round	5 Jul 1950	2	0	0	0	0	2

Arch Windmill
Swindon	First Round	17 Jun 1950	2	3	3	2	1	11
Halifax	Second Round	7 Jul 1950	0	0	0	1		1

Jimmy Grant
Walthamstow (reserve)	Third Round	13 Jun 1949	1	2	2	3	3	11

1951

80 riders took part in one meeting each in the First Round, with 18 progressing to the Second Round when 17 qualifying meetings were staged. Each of the 136 competitors were scheduled to ride in two meetings and the top 51 scorers went through to the Championship Round. 21 seeded First Division riders joined the competition for the Championship Round, when nine meetings were staged and each

rider was drawn to ride in two of them. The top 16 scorers proceeded to the final, which was won by Second Division rider Jack Young of Edinburgh and Australia. Split Waterman was runner-up, with Jack Biggs third.

Walthamstow riders record in the 1951 championship:

Jim Boyd
Leicester	Second Round	13 Jul 195	1	0	1	0	0	0	1
Walthamstow	Second Round	16 Jul 1951	3	2	3	3	3		14 (winner)

Harry Edwards
Walthamstow	Second Round	16 Jul 1951	2	2	3	2	0	9
Coventry	Second Round	21 Jul 1951	2	0	3	3	2	10
West Ham	Championship Round	14 Aug 1951	3	2	0	0	0	5
Birmingham	Championship Round	18 Aug 1951	1	0	0	0	0	1

Jimmy Grant
Aldershot	First Round	2 Jun 1951	2	2	2	0	2	8

Benny King
Fleetwood	Second Round	11 Jul 1951	1	0	0	0	1	2
Walthamstow	Second Round	16 Jul 1951	2	3	2	3	3	13

Pete Lansdale
Aldershot	First Round	2 Jun 1951	3	3	1	3	3	13
Ashfield	Second Round	10 Jul 1951	1	2	0	2	2	7
Fleetwood	Second Round	11 Jul 1951	1	1	2	2	2	8

Reg Reeves
Glasgow White City	Second Round	11 Jul 1951	2	2	0			4
Walthamstow	Second Round	16 Jul 1951	3	3	1	1	1	9

Other Meetings

1934

Eric Blain
Belle Vue: **North** v South	18 Aug 1934	0	0	0

Dick Case
Harringay: Home v **Abroad**	11 Aug 1934	2	3	3				8
Wimbledon: Cearns Trophy	20 Aug 1934	0	0	0	2	3		5
West Ham: England v **Australia**	21 Aug 1934	1	1	1	2	1	2	8
Wembley: Star Championship Final	23 Aug 1934	Semi-finalist						
Wimbledon: **London** v Manchester	3 Sep 1934	1'	2	2'				5+2
Harringay: London v **Australia**	22 Sep 1934	F	2	2	1	3	3	11
Belle Vue: England v **Australasia**	29 Sep 1934	1	3	3	3	3	3	16

Dusty Haigh
Belle Vue: **North** v South	18 Aug 1934	2	0	1	0	3
Wembley: Star Championship Final	23 Aug 1934	Semi-finalist				
Wimbledon: **North** v South	27 Aug 1934	1	1			2
Belle Vue: **England** v Australasia	29 Sep 1934	2				2

Harringay v **The Rest**	13 Oct 1934	1	0	2			3
Wembley v **English Tour Team**	18 Oct 1934	2	2	2			6

1949

Jim Boyd

Plymouth: Best Pairs with Benny King	7 Jul 1949	3	0	3	0	3	9
Southampton: Best Pairs with Charlie May	16 Aug 1949	3	3	1	3	3	13 (winners)
Plymouth v **London**	22 Sep 1949	1	1	2	3		7

Harold Bull

Rye House: Whitsun Trophy	5 Jun 1949	2	3	3			8
Rye House: Rainham v **The Rest**	12 Jun 1949	0	0	2	3		5
Rye House: **Red & Blue** v White & Yellow	26 Jun 1949	1	0	0			1
Rye House: **Red & Blue** v White & Yellow	10 Jul 1949	3	3	3	3		12
Rye House: Hertford Cup	24 Jul 1949	F	2	3	3		8
Plymouth v **London**	22 Sep 1949	0	1				1
St Austell: The Lions v **Kangaroos**	19 Oct 1949	0	1	0	0		1

Harry Edwards

Plymouth v **London**	22 Sep 1949	0	1	0	0	1

Dick Geary

Plymouth v **London**	22 Sep 1949	0	0	E	0	0

Wilf Jay

Southampton: North v **South**	10 May 1949	0	0	1	1	2

Benny King

Plymouth: Best Pairs with Jim Boyd	7 Jul 1949	2	2	2	1	2	9
Plymouth v **London**	22 Sep 1949	1	1	2	0		4

Charlie May

Southampton: Best Pairs with Jim Boyd	16 Aug 1949	1	2	3	2	2	10 (winners)

Bill Osborne

Southampton: Charles Knott Trophy	20 Mar 1949	0	0	1	0	1	2
Plymouth v **London**	22 Sep 1949	1'	1'				2+2

Reg Reeves

Plymouth v **London**	22 Sep 1949	1	0	1'	2	4+1

Arch Windmill

Plymouth v **London**	22 Sep 1949	3	3	2	2	10

1950

Jim Boyd

Plymouth: West of England Trophy	30 Mar 1950	0	3	2	1	3	9
Coventry: Best Pairs with Benny King	17 Jun 1950	1	2	3	1	3	10
Yarmouth: The East Coast Trophy	27 Jun 1950	1	2	2	2		7
Stoke: Best Pairs with Reg Reeves	1 Jul 1950	3	2	2	1	3	11
Norwich: **Eric Chitty's Select** v New Cross	5 Aug 1950	0	1	0	2		3

Wembley v **Second Division Stars**	14 Sep 1950	0	2				2

Bert Edwards
Rayleigh: Rayleigh Trophy	7 Oct 1950	3	2	0	3	3	11

Harry Edwards
Plymouth: West of England Trophy	30 Mar 1950	1	2	3	3	2	11
Plymouth Devils v **Team Captains**	8 Jun 1950	2	0	1	0		3
Rayleigh: Best Pairs with Reg Reeves	8 Jul 1950	3	1	3	E	3	10
Wolverhampton v Sheffield	13 Oct 1950	3	2	2	3		10

Dick Geary
Southampton: Charlie Knott Trophy	28 Mar 1950	1	0	2	1	0	5

Jimmy Grant
Coventry: **Brandon Select v** Goffe Select	19 Aug 1950	3	2	0	1		6
Wolverhampton v Sheffield	13 Oct 1950	3	2				5

Benny King
Coventry: Best Pairs with Jim Boyd	17 Jun 1950	0	0	0	0	0	0
Yarmouth: The East Coast Trophy	27 Jun 1950	3	0	1	2		6
Rayleigh: Best Pairs with Arch Windmill	8 Jul 1950	0	3	2	2	3	10

Charlie May
Southampton: Charles Knott Trophy	28 Mar 1950	2	3	3	2	2	12
Southampton: Supporters Trophy	13 Jun 1950	0	0	1	2	3	6
Southampton v **Southern Stars**	27 Jun 1950	1'	0	3	2		6+1
Coventry: **Brandon Select v** Goffe Select	19 Aug 1950	2	0	2	4		

George Newton
Leicester: **Trailers** v Forwards	14 Jul 1950	1	3	0	3	2	9

Reg Reeves Coventry: Best Pairs with S. Williams	17 Jun 1950	F	3	1	2	1	9
Stoke: Best Pairs with Jim Boyd	1 Jul 1950	1	F	0	0	0	1
Rayleigh: Best Pairs with Harry Edwards	8 Jul 1950	1	3	0	2	2	8

Arch Windmill
Rayleigh: Best Pairs with Benny King	8 Jul 1950	1	2	1	1	1	6

1951

Jim Boyd
Southampton: Charlie Knott Trophy	23 Mar 1951	2	1	2	1	1	7

Sid Clark
Ipswich v Rayleigh	24 May 1951	3	3	2	3	11
Ipswich v Exeter	31 May 1951	3	3	3	1	10
Ipswich v Poole	14 Jun 1951	3	3	3	3	12
Ipswich v Aldershot	21 Jun 1951	3	3	2		8
Ipswich v American Touring Team	28 Jun 1951	E	3	3	3	9
Ipswich v St Austell	5 Jul 1951	3	3	1	1'	8+1
Ipswich v Rayleigh	12 Jul 1951	3	F	3	2'	8+1
Ipswich v Swindon	26 Jul 1951	2'	3	3	1	9+1

Ipswich v Yarmouth	2 Aug 1951	1	3	2	2'			8+1
Ipswich v Exeter	9 Aug 1951	1	3	1	3			8
Ipswich: **Eastern Counties** v Norwich	16 Aug 1951	3	3	3	3			12

Harry Edwards

Southampton: Charlie Knott Trophy	23 Mar 1951	3	3	3	3	3		15 (winner)
New Cross: Gold Star Trophy	2 May 1951	1	0	0	1	0		2
Leicester: **Britain** v Overseas	25 May 1951	1'						1+1
Glasgow White City: Scotland v **England**	13 Jun 1951	1	1'	1'	0	1'	1	5+3
Norwich: Brand's Team v **Close's Team**	1 Sep 1951	3	0	2				5

Bruce Gardiner

Rye House: Viccary's Team v **Barratt's Team**	2 Jul 1950	1'	1	2	2			6+1
Rye House: Reds v Blues v **Whites** v Yellows	30 Jul 1950	0	3	1				4
Rye House: Holiday Cup	6 Aug 1950	0						0

Jimmy Grant

Plymouth: Devon v **1st & 2nd Division Stars**	23 Mar 1951	2	0	2	2			6
Ipswich v Exeter	9 Aug 1951	1'	2	1				2+1

Benny King

Southampton: Charlie Knott Trophy	23 Mar 1951	0	0	1	1	1		3
Norwich: Brand's Team v **Close's Team**	1 Sep 1951	0	2	1	1			4

Pete Lansdale

Southampton: Charles Knott Trophy	23 Mar 1951	3	2	3	2	0		10
New Cross v **Rest of London**	4 Apr 1951	0	1	1	0			2
Southampton v **Ex Saints**	19 Jun 1951	0	2	3	3			8
Southampton: Festival of Sport	21 Jul 1951							
Cradley Heath: **England** v Scotland	18 Sep 1951	2	0	3	1	1	2	9

Reg Reeves

Plymouth: Devon v **1st & 2nd Division Stars**	23 Mar 1951	2	3	2	3			10
Norwich: Brand's Team v **Close's Team**	1 Sep 1951	1	0	0	0			1

Arch Windmill

Plymouth: Devon v **1st & 2nd Division Stars**	23 Mar 1951	0	2'	2'	3			7+2

Tigers at White City
– Glasgow Speedway 1928 to 1968

By Jim Henry

This is a fascinating new book about the team that have been at the centre of Scottish speedway since the sport's early days.

Glasgow's White City Stadium was one of British speedway's key venues from when the sport started in 1928 until 1968, when the Glasgow Tigers moved as the Stadium faced potential demolition.

This book covers the full history of the Glasgow Tigers – and briefly Lions – at White City. It recalls some of the legendary riders who rode for the Tigers before and after the Second World War, including Billy Galloway, Will Lowther, Junior Bainbridge, Tommy Miller and Ken McKinlay. In more recent times, Jim McMillan and Charlie Monk were the Tigers' big stars in the period covered by this book.

As well as a detailed account of each season, there are also profiles of all the post-war Glasgow Tigers riders up to 1968 and statistical records.

Well-illustrated, the book includes forewords by **Jim McMillan** and **Bert Harkins**, who was a childhood Tigers fan.

The author, **Jim Henry**, is a life-long speedway fan, and has written widely on the sport.

It can be ordered from London League Publications Ltd (www.llpshop.co.uk), from Amazon, AbeBooks and EBay. It can be ordered from any bookshop. There is also an electronic version available on Amazon Kindle.

Published in February 2023 @ £16.95.
Book details: 306-page paperback illustrated with over 70 photos.
ISBN: 9781909885318

Where Eagles Dared – Speedway in Motherwell by Jim Henry
Speedway came to Motherwell in 1950. The first season saw a makeshift team provide a variety of meetings to introduce the sport to the town. The positive response saw the Lanarkshire Eagles enter the National League Division Two in 1951. As speedway declined nationally in the early 1950s, the Eagles' fellow Scottish teams closed down – Glasgow Ashfield for league racing after 1952 and both the Glasgow Tigers and Edinburgh Monarchs in 1954. The Eagles were willing to race in 1955, but the English teams refused to travel north for only one meeting in Scotland, effectively forcing the team out of business.
A short resurgence in 1958 did not last and 1972 saw a flicker of bike action on the site of the demolished stadium. This book gives a fascinating insight into speedway in Motherwell, when the Eagles dared in Scotland's black county. **Published in 2021 @ £13.95**

My Crazy Speedway World by Bert Harkins
"Here we are folks, after many months of being stuck to my computer keyboard, I finally finished my autobiography having bashed out every word, dot and comma along the way. It covers my early days growing up in Glasgow, to cycle speedway, road racing, speedway and life after I had hung up my white boots and tartan leathers. This is the story of a wandering Speedway Scotsman and I hope that you enjoy it." **Bert Harkins**
Published in February 2018. Now available @ £16.95

For both books: order direct from the publishers: London League Publications Ltd post free in the UK. Visit www.llpshop.co.uk for credit card orders or write to (cheques payable to London League Publications Ltd): PO Box 65784, London NW2 9NS. Also available on Amazon, AbeBooks, EBay and as an E-Book on Amazon for Kindle. Or order from any bookshop.

Other speedway books from London League Publications Ltd

Life on the Edge – Split Waterman by Trevor Davies
Authorised biography of one of speedway's most famous riders. Covers his full speedway career and much more. Published in April 2021 @ £14.95

Freddie Williams – Double World Speedway Champion
By Peter Lush
The full story of the first British double World Champion. Also includes his brothers Eric and Ian, both international speedway stars, and the other sporting members of the Williams family. Published in March 2019 @ £13.95

Dave Jessup – A Speedway Journey by Peter Lush
Authorised biography of one of the top British speedway riders from the 1970s and 1980s. Also covers his time as England team manager and playing golf for the England Amateur Senior team. Published in October 2020 @ £14.95.

When the Lions Roared – the story of the famous Wembley Speedway team by Peter Lush & John Chaplin
The story of the Wembley Lions from 1929 to 1971. Includes full statistics and rider profiles. Published in October 2016 @ £14.95

Warzone Speedway by Trevor Davies.
Last few copies of a speedway classic. Covers the riders who rode in speedway meetings in Europe while in the Army during and after the Second World War. £13.95

For all books: order direct from the publishers: London League Publications Ltd post free in the UK. Visit www.llpshop.co.uk for credit card orders or write to (cheques payable to London League Publications Ltd): PO Box 65784, London NW2 9NS. Also available on Amazon, AbeBooks, EBay and as an E-Book on Amazon for Kindle. Or order from any bookshop.